Legalines

ADMINISTRATIVE LAW

Adaptable to Ninth Edition of Gellhorn Casebook

By Paul S. Dempsey
Professor of Law

THE **barbri** GROUP

HARCOURT BRACE LEGAL AND PROFESSIONAL PUBLICATIONS, INC.
EDITORIAL OFFICES: 176 W. Adams, Suite 2100, Chicago, IL 60603

Legalines

REGIONAL OFFICES: New York, Chicago, Los Angeles, Washington, D.C.
Distributed by: **Harcourt Brace & Company** 6277 Sea Harbor Drive, Orlando, FL 32887 (800)787-8717

SERIES EDITOR
Deirdre E. Whelan, J.D.
Attorney at Law

PRODUCTION COORDINATOR
Sanetta Hister

FIRST PRINTING—1997

SHORT SUMMARY OF CONTENTS

TABLE OF CONTENTS AND SHORT REVIEW OUTLINE

I. INTRODUCTION TO ADMINISTRATIVE LAW

A. INTRODUCTION

1. **Introductory Case--Dalton v. Specter,** 511 U.S. 462 (1994).

   a. **Facts.** The Defense Base Closure and Realignment Act of 1990 ("Act") established three rounds of base closures across the nation. The Secretary of Defense (D) submits his recommendations for closure to Congress and to the Defense Base Closure and Realignment Commission (D). The Commission in turn submits report to the President, who has two weeks to approve the recommendations. In 1991, the Commission recommended 82 closures, including the Philadelphia Naval Shipyard, which President Bush also approved. Shipyard employees and their unions, and certain states and state officials (Ps) sought to enjoin this closure because the procedure adhered to by Ds was procedurally flawed.

   b. **Issue.** Because the Act does not limit the President's discretion regarding recommendations of administrative actors, is judicial review available when the President has relied on procedurally-flawed recommendations?

   c. **Held.** No. Judicial review not available. Judgment reversed in part and affirmed in part.

      1) The actions of Ds are not reviewable, as their recommendations are not "final agency actions" under the Administrative Procedure Act ("APA").

      2) Once the President approves the recommendations, the decision falls within unreviewable executive discretion. Here, this discretion is derived from statutory language, giving the President power to approve or disapprove for whatever reason he wishes. Also, the President is not an "agency" under the APA and is thus not reviewable under the Act.

B. NATURE AND BACKGROUND OF THE SUBJECT

1. **Nature of Administrative Law.** Administrative law is basically ***procedural*** law. Each administrative agency is responsible for a particular body of substantive law, but certain procedural principles apply to all agencies. In this outline, the term "administrative law" refers to the body of requirements resting upon administrative agencies that affect private interests by making rules, adjudicating cases, investigating, threatening, prosecuting, publicizing, and advising.

2. **Outline Approach.** This outline will consider the following aspects of administrative law:

   a. The *position of the agency* in government.

   b. The *administrative process—i.e.,* the complex of government activity which includes the formulation of rules (other than by the legislature) and the investigation and adjudication of cases (other than by the courts).

    1)   Consideration will be given to the statutory and constitutional requirements for *rulemaking*.

    2)   Also considered will be the statutory and constitutional requirements for *adjudication*.

  c.   *Judicial review* of agency decisions.

3.   **State Law.** Although the principles discussed herein frequently apply to state and local agencies, this outline focuses primarily on federal agencies and the federal Constitution, statutes, and court decisions.

4.   **Statutes.** Much of administrative law is statutory in nature. The statute creating a particular agency usually sets out the substantive law (as well as organization and procedures) for the agency; the federal Administrative Procedure Act of 1946 ("APA") governs the procedural aspects in most areas of administrative law. There also exists a Model State Administrative Procedure Act.

5.   **Analytical Approach.** Regarding any agency action, the student should ask the following questions:

  a.   **Delegation.** Is the particular legislative or judicial authority which the agency seeks to exercise one that can be and has, in fact, been delegated to it by the legislature?

  b.   **Hearings.** Has the agency provided the necessary hearing?

    1)   Is there a constitutional or statutory right to a *trial-type* hearing in the matter? If so, has the agency complied with the minimum requirements for such a hearing?

    2)   Does the relevant statute require a *legislative-type* hearing? Has one been provided?

    3)   Has the agency violated any *constitutional or statutory rules* in its actions?

    4)   Is *judicial review* available?

    5)   If judicial review is available, what is the *scope of review*?

    6)   Finally, consider the applicability of the APA and/or constitutional doctrines to *each* of the potential issues suggested above.

C.   VARIETIES OF ADMINISTRATIVE AGENCIES

There is a wide variety of federal, state, and local administrative agencies, carrying on a multitude of responsibilities. Some 15 million bureaucrats are employed by the government. Agencies create legally binding obligations upon individuals and businesses through case-by-case adjudication, through the promulgation of rules and regulations, and through less formal means. The collective volume of these obligations exceeds that produced by the legislative or judicial branches.

1. **Administrative Functions.**

   a. **Regulation of private conduct.** Usually, economic regulation of price, entry, or business practices is targeted at commercial enterprises.

   b. **Government exactions.** Administrative agencies collect taxes and conscript soldiers for the military.

   c. **Disbursement of benefits.** Agencies distribute subsidies to large sectors of the nation, including farmers, welfare recipients, and the elderly.

   d. **Direct provision of goods or services.** Some enterprises in our largely capitalist economy are government-owned or government-operated, such as the postal service, Amtrak, several large public utilities, and enterprises constructing highways and dams. Such proprietary activities also include the running of prisons, public housing, and mental hospitals.

2. **Administrative Tools.** Most agencies possess a wide variety of coercive means to implement the obligations they impose. Often, actual sanctions may be imposed only through the use of the courts. But many less severe coercive mechanisms may be utilized by agencies without judicial enforcement, such as license denial, restrictions, revocation, or withholding economic benefits. Another significant weapon in the arsenal of coercive devices is investigation and the dissemination of adverse information.

3. **Structure and Organization.** There is a wide variety of organizational structures for administrative agencies. Most have large staffs and highly specialized responsibilities. Federal administrative agencies are defined by the APA, 5 U.S.C. section 551, by what they are not—agencies do not consist of the legislature, the courts, or the governments of the states or the District of Columbia. But they employ more people, dispense more money, and regulate more activities than the other three combined.

   a. **Executive Branch agencies.** In the Executive Branch of the federal government, most agencies are pyramidal in structure, with a single individual at the apex of the pyramid, appointed by and serving at the discretion of the President. Examples include the Department of Transportation, the Department of Commerce, and the Department of the Interior.

   b. **Independent regulatory agencies.** Several federal agencies have been created outside the Executive Branch, under the powers conferred to Congress under Article I, section 8 of the Constitution to regulate interstate and foreign commerce. These agencies are headed by collegial bodies rather than a single individual. The appointees hold fixed terms and cannot be removed without cause prior to the expiration of such terms. Usually, no more than a simple majority of the members of the agency may be members of a single political party. Examples include the Interstate Commerce Commission ("ICC"), the Federal Trade Commission ("FTC"), and the Securities and Exchange Commission ("SEC"). Recently, Congress has established several "independent" agencies, but housed them in the

Executive Branch, such as the Federal Energy Regulatory Commission ("FERC") of the Department of Energy.

c. **Multi-member and single-head agencies.** Administrative agencies generally fall into two structural categories.

   1) **Agencies headed by a single individual who serves at the discretion of the President.** Most administrative agencies of the Executive Branch (*e.g.*, Departments of Labor and Agriculture) are headed by a single individual who may be removed from office without cause.

   2) **Agencies headed by a multi-member commission.** Most independent regulatory commissions (*e.g.*, ICC, SEC, FTC) are comprised of several individuals (usually an odd number), no more than a simple majority of whom may be members of a single political party. Once appointed to their staggered, multi-year terms, they ordinarily may not be removed by the President without cause (*e.g.*, "inefficiency, neglect of duty, or malfeasance in office").

d. **Regulatory and nonregulatory agencies.**

   1) **Regulatory agencies.** Regulatory agencies are usually vested with comprehensive jurisdiction to regulate a wide spectrum of economic activities of specific industries.

      a) **Interstate Commerce Commission.** The ICC was the first independent regulatory commission created by Congress. It was established in 1887.

      b) **The Big Seven.** Since then, several major agencies have been established by Congress, utilizing the ICC as a model. The FTC was created in 1914. Five major regulatory agencies were established during the administration of Franklin Roosevelt (*i.e.*, the Federal Power Commission ("FPC"), FCC, SEC, National Labor Relations Board ("NLRB"), and Civil Aeronautics Board ("CAB")). Collectively, the Big Seven regulates the major industries of the United States economy: communications, transportation, and energy. The responsibilities of the FPC were transferred to the nascent FERC in 1977. The jurisdiction of the CAB was transferred to the United States Department of Transportation in 1985. The ICC was sunset in 1995. Its remaining functions were transferred to the Surface Transportation Board of the United States Department of Transportation.

      c) **State administrative agencies.** Each state usually has comparable intrastate jurisdiction over the major industries vested in a single administrative agency, frequently named the state Public Utilities Commission. Many are modeled after the first such federal agency, the ICC.

      d) **Regulatory powers.** Economic regulation can be divided into three categories.

(1) **Licensing.** Most regulatory agencies regulate entry into the affected industry by issuing certificates of "public convenience and necessity" to successful applicants.

(2) **Ratemaking.** Many such agencies establish both maximum and minimum rates to be charged the consumers of such products or services.

(3) **Business practices.** Many agencies have been given comprehensive jurisdiction over a multitude of corporate practices of the regulated industries, including purchases, mergers, consolidations, interlocking directorates, stock issuances, and various antitrust activities.

e) **Regulatory power widely held.** Although almost all independent regulatory agencies hold regulatory powers, several Executive Branch agencies do as well (*e.g.,* Department of Agriculture).

f) **Social regulation.** More recent in origin than economic regulation are those agencies dedicated to the regulation of nonmarket behavior by business enterprises (*e.g.,* Environmental Protection Agency ("EPA"), Occupational Safety and Health Administration ("OSHA")). Health, environmental, and safety regulation attempts to force business to internalize the costs of public interest protection rather than perpetuating the "tragedy of the commons."

2) **Nonregulatory agencies.** These agencies typically dispense monies (*e.g.,* government insurance and pensions) to promote social and economic welfare. Benefactors fall into three categories.

a) **Employee protection.** Employee protection includes workers' compensation and other economic schemes designed to protect the individual from the hazards of the employment.

b) **Social insurance.** Social security and unemployment compensation constitute social insurance.

c) **Welfare and veterans assistance.**

e. **Characteristics of administrative agencies.**

1) **Size.** Most federal administrative agencies employ several hundred to several thousand people.

2) **Specialization.** Typically, an agency focuses on a particular industry or specialized problem and is expected to develop expertise therein.

3) **Responsibility for results.** Congress usually identifies objectives it expects the administrative agency to satisfy.

4) **Variety of duties.** Agencies frequently engage in adjudication, rule-making, and the performance of quasi-executive administrative functions.

5) **Heavy workload.** Most agencies have a congested docket comprised of scores of proceedings, some of which may be of considerable complexity.

f. **Appointment and composition.**

1) **Appointment.** All officers of the United States must be appointed by the President with the advice and consent of the Senate. Congress may vest the appointment of inferior officers in the President alone, the courts, or the heads of departments. [U.S. Const. art. II, §2; *see* Buckley v. Valeo, *infra*]

2) **The Civil Service System.** In 1883, Congress established the Civil Service System to reduce abuses of the "spoils system" of political patronage appointments. Under it, appointment is ostensibly determined by merit, and removal is severely circumscribed. Almost 85% of federal employees fall under its umbrella. Excessive job security has been criticized as breeding lethargy among low-level and mid-level government workers.

4. **Procedures.** Many (but not all) agencies have been given both quasi-judicial and quasi-legislative authority. The former includes the power to decide controversies between parties. The latter involves the power to promulgate rules and regulations which, like statutes, have the force and effect of law. Agency rules have the force and effect of law as long as they are constitutional, were promulgated in a procedurally proper manner, and do not stray beyond the authority conferred by the legislature (*i.e.,* they are not ultra vires).

a. **Formal.** Many agency adjudications must use trial-type procedures, in which live witnesses are subject to attorney examination and cross-examination.

b. **Hybrid.** Between the alternatives of formal and informal procedures lies a gray area in which a variety of procedural mechanisms exist, combining various elements of the judicial trial-type and legislative informal models.

c. **Informal.** Informal procedures are frequently used in rulemaking. They essentially include the publication of notice followed by the opportunity to submit written comments in response.

II. THE CONSTITUTIONAL FRAMEWORK FOR ADMINISTRATION

A. SEPARATION OF POWERS

The United States Constitution divides power among the three branches of government.

1. **Legislative Powers.** Legislative powers are vested in Congress. These include the power to promulgate all "necessary and proper" laws for executing Constitutional powers.

2. **Executive Power.** The executive power is vested in the President.

3. **Judicial Power.** The judicial power is vested in the courts.

B. ADMINISTRATIVE AGENCIES

Notice that nowhere does the Constitution explicitly provide for the "headless fourth branch of government," as many refer to the vast bureaucracy. Nonetheless, as the needs of the Republic have proliferated, government has grown, as well as the need for delegation of power to governmental administrators. Most administrative agencies possess quasi-legislative authority to promulgate rules, quasi-judicial power to adjudicate disputes, and quasi-executive powers to administer various programs.

1. **Delegation Doctrine and Separation of Powers--Mistretta v. United States,** 488 U.S. 361 (1989).

    Mistretta v. United States

    a. **Facts.** The United States Sentencing Commission was created by Congress in 1984. Prior to its establishment, Congress gave wide latitude regarding penalty assessment to the judiciary. According to Congress, this system led to "serious disparities in sentencing practice." The Commission established a new system providing mandatory sentencing guidelines, narrowing the latitude of the judiciary, and abolishing parole by the Executive Branch. It was left to the Commission to set sentencing guidelines. The members of the Commission were appointed by the President and approved by the Senate. Removal was allowed for "good cause." Mistretta (D) was convicted under the guidelines, and charged that the Commission was unconstitutional because it violated separation of powers, and Congress delegated too much power to the Commission.

    b. **Issue.** Was the Commission unconstitutional because it violated separation of powers and Congress gave it too much authority?

    c. **Held.** No. The Commission was not unconstitutional.

        1) The nondelegation doctrine does not prevent Congress from obtaining the assistance of its coordinate branches. In order to delegate, Congress must do so with specificity, so that the coordinate branch understands the scope of its authority. In this case, Congress's delegation of authority to the Sentencing Com-

mission is sufficiently specific and detailed, as it established specific goals, set up a "specific tool" (sentencing guidelines) to meet these goals, and enunciated factors that the Commission had to consider in setting the guidelines.

2) In *Youngstown Sheet & Tube Co. v. Sawyer*, 343 U.S. 579 (1952), Justice Jackson wrote that the Constitution "enjoins upon its branches separateness but interdependence, autonomy but reciprocity." Just because the Commission was placed under the judicial branch, it does not violate separation of powers so long as it does not undermine the Judicial Branch or has powers belonging to another branch. Here, the act does not vest legislative powers in the judiciary, and the president's removal power does not encroach on "judicial independence."

C. CONSTITUTIONAL LIMITS ON AGENCY POWER

Administrative agency jurisdiction is limited by the perimeters of statutes pursuant to which the legislature conferred the agency with its authority. If the agency strays beyond the authority so conferred, it acts ultra vires and, hence, unlawfully.

1. Delegation of Authority to Make Rules of Conduct.

Industrial Union Department, AFL-CIO v. American Petroleum Institute

a. **Illustration--Industrial Union Department, AFL-CIO v. American Petroleum Institute,** 448 U.S. 607 (1980).

1) **Facts.** The Secretary of Labor (D) adopted regulations limiting occupational exposure to benzene to one part per million ("ppm"). D took the position that whenever a toxic material was determined to be a carcinogen, no safe exposure level could be determined, and that the lowest technologically feasible level that would not impair the viability of the regulated industry would be set. A lower court ruling invalidated the regulations. D appeals.

2) **Issue.** Did D appropriately find that benzene poses a significant health risk to the environment and that the one ppm standard is "reasonably necessary or appropriate to provide safe or healthful employment and places of employment" within the meaning of the Occupational Safety and Health Act?

3) **Held.** No. Judgment affirmed.

a) Most of D's explanation for the new standards justifies a 10 ppm standard, but is largely silent as to a one ppm standard. At no point did D explain how its rule satisfied the statutory requirement of the Act rule quoted above. D failed to sustain its burden of proof, on the basis of substantial evidence, that the more stringent environmental standard is mandated by the Act. While it need not establish the threshold requirement with "anything approaching scientific certainty" and must be given "some leeway where its findings must be made on the frontiers of scientific knowledge," D must nevertheless support its conclusion with the "best available evidence." By relying on a special policy for carcinogens, imposing a burden on the industry to identify a safe level of exposure, D exceeded its authority.

    b)   Because D failed to satisfy this threshold burden, we need not address the issue of whether the Act embraces a cost-benefit analysis requirement.

4) **Concurrence** (Powell, J.). The Act requires D to engage in a cost-benefit analysis before imposing substantial new costs on an industry, because a standard-setting process that ignored economic considerations would result in a serious misallocation of resources and a lower effective level of safety than could be achieved under standards set with reference to the comparative benefits available at a lower cost.

5) **Concurrence** (Rehnquist, J.). Although a majority of the Court invalidated the benzene rules on other grounds, I believe that the delegation was unlawful.

    a)   John Locke argued that the legislature's power is to make laws, not to establish legislatures. Hence, Congress may not vest lawmaking power in other bodies.

    b)   Many modern decisions have allowed delegation on grounds that the subject addressed is technical and large, and Congress is ill-equipped to handle its evolving problems. In such situations, it is sufficient that Congress merely expresses general policy and standards, allowing the agency to "fill in the blanks."

    c)   The appropriate inquiry is whether standards governing delegation are ascertainable from the statute, its context, or its legislative history and, if not, whether the delegation should nonetheless be allowed because of the inherent necessities of the situation (*i.e.,* because it is "unreasonable or impracticable to compel Congress to prescribe detailed rules").

    d)   Three essential purposes of the delegation doctrine are that it: (i) insures that significant policy decisions are made by the legislature, the branch most responsive to the democratic will; (ii) assures that the agency receiving new jurisdiction will have an "intelligible principle" to guide its exercise; and (iii) allows courts reviewing agency action to test it against ascertainable standards.

    e)   Congress's delegation to OSHA to decide the occupational exposure issue was unconstitutional, failing all the above tests.

6) **Dissent** (Marshall, Brennan, White, Blackmun, JJ.). The delegation doctrine is dead, at least in the absence of "overbroad, unauthorized, and arbitrary application of criminal sanctions in an area of [constitutionally] protected freedoms."

7) **Comment.** In a subsequent decision, Chief Justice Burger joined Justice Rehnquist in arguing that OSHA was an unlawful delegation.

b. **Traditional model.** The traditional model of judicial review provided four means for striking down agency decisions: (i) nondelegation, that the legislature had conferred excessively broad powers to the agency; (ii) review of fact; (iii) review of law; and (iv) compliance with proper procedure.

c. **Pre-1935 Supreme Court cases.** Prior to 1935, the United States Supreme Court upheld a number of delegations of legislative power under a variety of theories.

    1) **Conditional conferral.** The Court upheld a statute that authorized the President to impose import restrictions if France or Great Britain violated the neutral commerce of the United States. [*See* The Brig Aurora, 11 U.S. (7 Cranch) 382 (1813)]

    2) **Named contingency.** A statute allowing the President to impose a retaliatory tariff on imports from countries that imposed duties on United States products was upheld in *Field v. Clark*, 143 U.S. 649 (1892), on the ground that the President was merely ascertaining a fact upon which the tariffs were contingent.

    3) **Fill in the details.** The statutory authority of the Secretary of Agriculture to "make provision for the protection against destruction and depredations upon the public forests" was upheld on the ground that it merely gave him the responsibility to "fill up the details." [*See* United States v. Grimaud, 220 U.S. 506 (1911)]

    4) **Intelligible principle.** A statute giving the President the power to revise tariffs to equalize the cost of production of products in the United States and abroad was upheld as establishing an intelligible principle. [*See* J.W. Hampton, Jr. & Co. v. United States, 276 U.S. 394 (1928)]

d. **1935:** *Panama Refining* **and** *Schechter Poultry*.

Panama Refining Co. v. Ryan

    1) **Oil transportation--Panama Refining Co. v. Ryan,** 293 U.S. 388 (1935).

        a) **Facts.** The National Industrial Recovery Act ("NIRA") section 9(c) enabled the President to prohibit the transportation of petroleum and petroleum products in an amount exceeding that authorized to be produced by any state. Violation resulted in fine and/or imprisonment. Panama Refining Company (P), a Texas oil refiner, sued federal officials (Ds) to restrain enforcement of regulations promulgated by the Secretary of the Interior pursuant to this section. P argued that the NIRA constituted an unconstitutional delegation of legislative power to the President.

        b) **Issue.** Is section 9(c) an unconstitutional delegation to the President?

        c) **Held.** Yes.

            (1) We find no place in the statute where Congress had established standards to govern the President's action, or where the President was obligated to make specific findings prior to acting. No conditions precedent to the President's action were specified in

the statute. The states were left with the determination of whether production should be permitted.

(2) Under the NIRA, the President held unlimited authority to implement the prohibition, and disobedience of his determination would be punishable by fine or imprisonment. The absence of standards governing his exercise of power, if upheld, could allow the legislature to delegate the power to regulate virtually any commercial activity to the President.

d) **Dissent** (Cardozo, J.). I agree that the legislation must specify reasonably clear standards to govern the President's discretion, but I find such standards in the NIRA. The President's means of implementing the statute's specific policies are limited to prohibiting the transportation of specified commodities, and then only if the affected state had limited production thereof. The policy of Congress, express or implied, is sufficient to make the delegation valid.

2) **Unlimited authority--A.L.A. Schechter Poultry Corp. v. United States,** 295 U.S. 495 (1935).

A.L.A. Schechter Poultry Corp. v. United States

a) **Facts.** The NIRA delegated to the President authority to approve "codes of fair competition" upon application by a trade or industrial group, provided that (i) the group imposes no inequitable restriction on membership, and (ii) the code is not designed to promote monopolies or suppress competition, and will serve to effectuate the policies of NIRA section 1. A.L.A. Schechter Poultry Corporation (D) was convicted of violating the "Live Poultry Code" promulgated under the NIRA.

b) **Issue.** Was the "Live Poultry Code" approved by the President pursuant to an unconstitutional delegation of legislative power?

c) **Held.** Yes. Judgment reversed.

(1) In assessing whether the delegation is unconstitutional, we must ask whether there were any adequate definitions in the NIRA of the subjects to which the exercise of authority is to be addressed. We find no limitation on the things that could be subject to "codes of fair competition," and no statutory standards identifying the conduct such codes were to proscribe.

(2) Moreover, no procedural safeguards were identified for promulgation of the codes. Hence, the presidential promulgation of these codes could be distinguished from similar authority held by the FTC, for that agency offered parties before it procedural protection.

d) **Concurrence** (Cardozo, J.). Unlike the delegation in *Panama Refining*, the delegation here was "unconfined and vagrant" and "delegation run riot." The authority delegated was not confined to any specified acts or standards. The legislature seemed to create a "roving commission to inquire into evils and upon discovery correct them."

3) General rule of *Panama Refining* and *Schechter Poultry*. A delegation of legislative authority that is found to be wholly without standards specifying conditions pursuant to which it is to be exercised is unconstitutional.

e. Post-*Schechter* delegation—price controls. Only in *Panama Refining* and *Schechter Poultry* has the Supreme Court concluded that delegations have been unconstitutional. Nevertheless, the nondelegation doctrine has never been overruled. Moreover, *Schechter Poultry* addressed perhaps the most liberal delegation in United States history. Hence, it marks a line beyond which the legislature may not go in delegating authority. However, many post-1935 cases on the issue of delegation appear to embrace the philosophy expressed by Justice Cardozo in his dissent in *Panama Refining*.

1) Price controls. *Yakus v. United States*, 321 U.S. 414 (1944), upheld the constitutionality of the Emergency Price Control Act of 1942 ("EPC"). Under the EPC, the price administrator was given jurisdiction to establish maximum prices on commodities when the prices rose or threatened to rise to a level inconsistent with the purpose of the Act. EPC section 1 provided that its purposes were to stabilize prices, prohibit their abnormal increase, eliminate profiteering, and so on. Chief Justice Stone concluded that the standards expressed in the EPC, coupled with the statement of considerations required to be made by the administrator, were "sufficiently definite and precise to enable Congress, the Courts, and the public to ascertain whether the Administrator, in fixing the designated prices, had conformed to those standards." Hence, the statute was upheld as a lawful delegation. Justice Roberts filed a vigorous dissent in which he argued that the EPC "set no limits upon the discretion or judgment of the Administrator."

2) War contracts. *Lichter v. United States*, 334 U.S. 742 (1948), upheld the constitutionality of the Renegotiation Act of 1942, which delegated to administrative officers the power to recover "excessive profits" on the renegotiation of war contracts. The Court held that it was not necessary that the legislature "supply administrative officials with a specific formula for their guidance in a field where flexibility and the adoption of the congressional policy to infinitely variable conditions constitute the essence of the program."

3) Wartime delegations. Both *Yakus* and *Lichter* were wartime delegations.

4) Foreign affairs. Decisions of the Supreme Court have suggested that the traditional limitations on congressional delegation may not apply in the area of foreign affairs.

5) No standards. Indeed, delegations have been upheld even though Congress provided *no* standards at all. In *Arizona v. California*, 373 U.S. 546 (1963), the Court sustained a delegation to the Secretary of Interior to apportion Colorado River water in time of shortage, even though there were no standards as to how this was to be done. (Three dissents questioned the constitutionality of such delegation.)

f. Economic stabilization. In the 1970s, Congress again enacted several vague statutes giving the President broad economic powers—this time in response to inflation rather than depression. Although the *Schechter Poultry* and *Panama*

Refining cases posed potential problems for these statutes, the post-1930s cases (upholding broad delegations) suggested that Congress essentially had a free hand.

1) **The *Amalgamated Meat Cutters* case.** Although the Court in *Amalgamated Meat Cutters & Butcher Workmen v. Connally*, 337 F. Supp. 737 (D. D.C. 1971), did not consider the anti-inflation statutes, it upheld the Economic Stabilization Act of 1970. This Act authorized the President to stabilize wages and prices at levels not less than those on May 15, 1970, with such adjustments as might be necessary to prevent "gross inequities." The Court held that the statute—under which the President had imposed a wage-price freeze—sufficiently "marked out" the field in which the President was to act by setting a base date and providing for adjustment of inequities.

g. **Narrowing--Kent v. Dulles,** 357 U.S. 116 (1958).

Kent v. Dulles

1) **Facts.** The Secretary of State (D) denied two applications for passports filed by individuals (Ps) who refused to sign an affidavit required by D's regulations stating that Ps neither were Communists nor embraced "adherence to the Communist Party line."

2) **Issue.** Are D's regulations consistent with legislative delegations of authority to regulate issuance of passports?

3) **Held.** No.

a) The right to travel is a liberty interest for which there may be no deprivation without due process under the Fifth Amendment to the Constitution.

b) The long-standing practice of D was to refuse issuance of a passport only on one of two grounds: (i) the applicant's citizenship and allegiance to the United States, or (ii) his participation in illegal conduct. These were the only two criteria for disapproval when the Passport Act of 1926 was promulgated. While more restrictive regulations have been imposed during wartime, these are inapposite during peacetime.

c) If an important liberty interest such as the freedom to travel is to be constrained, it must be done under the authority of Congress. Where such activities are sought to be infringed upon by an administrative agency, we will construe narrowly all delegated powers that curtail or dilute them. Congress did not delegate the power exercised here.

h. **Delegation and standards: coda.** The modern trend is for courts to uphold virtually all delegations of legislative authority, except perhaps in areas affecting individual liberty. Nevertheless, the delegation doctrine stands for the notion that, in a democratic society, standards of conduct ought to be prescribed by our elected representatives, rather than by administrative agencies. It remains as a potential check against the conferral of boundless discretion to administrative agencies.

i. **Definition of "controlled substances"--Touby v. United States,** 500 U.S. 160 (1991).

1) **Facts.** Under the Controlled Substances Act, the Attorney General ("AG") is authorized, upon following a specific procedure, to add new drugs to the schedules of "controlled substances," which are prohibited by the Act. Under the procedure, the AG must request a scientific and medical evaluation from the Secretary of Health and Human Services ("HHS"). The AG must then examine eight factors with respect to the substance's potential for abuse, pharmacological effect, etc. He then must comply with the notice and hearing provisions of the APA, allowing comment by the public. This procedure typically takes six to 12 months. Because of this time lag, drug traffickers were able to formulate "designer drugs" which were slightly different than the potentially banned drugs so that the schedules would not apply. In response to this problem, Congress amended the Act to provide for an expedited procedure, temporarily including a drug on a schedule when it was "necessary to avoid an imminent hazard to the public safety." The AG need only consider three of the eight factors, provide a 30-day notice of the proposed change in the Federal Register, give notice to the HHS Secretary, and temporarily suspend judicial review. The AG further delegated the temporary scheduling power to the Drug Enforcement Agency ("DEA"). The Touby's were indicted for manufacture of the drug "euphoria" under the amendment. They argued that the amendment unconstitutionally delegates legislative power to the AG.

2) **Issues.**

a) Does the expedited procedure under the Act unconstitutionally delegate legislative power to the AG?

b) Did the AG improperly delegate his temporary scheduling power to the DEA?

3) **Held.** a) No. b) No. Judgment affirmed.

a) The nondelegation doctrine does not prevent Congress from seeking assistance, within proper limits, from its coordinate branches, as long as it establishes an "intelligible principle" under which the body must conform. There are constraints on the AG's actions, including a necessity of imminent harm, examination of three factors (*i.e.,* the drug's history and pattern of abuse, scope of abuse, and risk to the public), as well as the notice requirements.

b) Allowing the AG to schedule and prosecute does not violate separation of powers, as separation of powers is not concerned with how power is distributed within a single branch.

c) Petitioners' argument that the amendment is unconstitutional because it temporarily suspends judicial review is not applicable, as there is a judicial review provision for permanently scheduled drugs, meaning that such review is merely suspended.

d) There was no improper delegation of powers to the DEA, as the Act specifically allows such delegation.

j. **Direct judicial control of administrative discretion.**

1) **Limiting agency discretion through "creative" statutory construction.** Sometimes courts will constrict an agency's jurisdiction by narrowly construing the ambit of its statutory authority.

2) **Delegation in the states.**

> **a)** **Introduction.** State courts differ among themselves and with federal courts on the constitutional significance of standards in delegation; hence, the resulting case law is quite inconsistent. Reasons for differences among the states are: (i) the typical paucity of the legislative history of state laws make resort to it less promising, haphazard, and unreliable when attempted; (ii) while federal delegation is recognized to be almost wholly statutory, counsel and judges in state courts tend to approach a public law case from a common law background of practice, with common law rather than statutory law methods of briefing and arguments; (iii) there may exist a different degree of institutional respect and deference toward the Legislative Branch and its products (the state courts are far less reluctant to hold that a legislature has misconstrued and exceeded its powers than federal courts are to hold that Congress has done so); and (iv) similarly, state courts may have a different—and more realistic—view of the professional capacity and impartiality of many agencies to whom power is delegated in the state as compared with federal agencies.

> **b)** **Analytical approach to judicial reaction to the delegation question.** The student should consider: (i) the kind of substantive power to be delegated, *e.g.*, manage government property, employ civil servants, and enter into contracts; (ii) the statutory language to be used in directing the agency in the exercise of the delegated substantive power—general vs. specific directions; (iii) the identity, character, selection process, and tenure of the delegatee; (iv) the nature of the processes to be utilized in exercising the delegated substantive power—rulemaking, investigating, inspecting, testing, examining, requiring reports, jawboning, prosecuting, adjudicating, etc.; (v) procedural safeguards to be required—publication of, and conformance to, administrative standards, notice, hearing, statement of reasons, etc.; (vi) ongoing legislative controls, such as legislative veto, oversight committee, annual appropriations, etc.; (vii) presidential or gubernatorial authority to direct or coordinate the exercise of delegated powers; (viii) participation by interested members of the public concerning what issues are considered and what proceedings are used (and whether public funds are used); (ix) the availability and scope of judicial review; and (x) the proper balance between procedural (regularity) costs and substantive benefits.

> **c)** **Publication of administrative rules.** Both federal and state courts have struck down administrative law acts which authorized agencies to adopt rules and regulations with a concomitant responsibility to publish such administrative rules. Where federal or state statutes require the filing or publication of administrative rules adopted by administrative agencies, compliance with a filing and publication

requirement has been regarded by some of the state courts as an absolute precondition of a regulation having legal effect.

Boreali v. Axelrod

d) **Smoking in public places--Boreali v. Axelrod,** 517 N.E.2d 1350 (N.Y. Ct. App. 1987).

    (1) **Facts.** In 1975, New York passed a Public Health Law restricting smoking to designated areas in certain public spaces (*e.g.,* libraries, museums, theaters). In 1987, the New York Public Health Council ("PHC"), which was authorized by the Public Health Law to "deal with any matters affecting the . . . public health," added to the smoking restrictions. Prohibitions were placed in schools, hospitals, food markets, banks, and taxis; furthermore, restaurants with capacities greater than 50 people had to provide nonsmoking areas, and employers had to provide smoke-free work areas and common areas.

    (2) **Issues.**

        (a) Can the New York State legislature delegate these powers to prohibit smoking in certain areas to the agency?

        (b) Did the PHC exceed its mandate by engaging in legislative activities?

    (3) **Held.** (a) No. (b) Yes. Affirmed lower court holding that the PHC exceeded its mandate by engaging in legislation.

    The Legislative Branch may not delegate its legislative powers to an Executive Branch agency. The PHC overstepped its mandate because:

        (a) The law has several waivers, which gives the PHC the power to balance the promotion of health with its social costs, "acting solely on [its] own ideas of sound public policy." This is a legislative function.

        (b) The PHC created its own set of rules without legislative guidance.

        (c) The PHC acted in an area in which the legislature had tried and failed to legislate effectively. It is up to elected representatives in the legislature to solve these types of problems, not agencies; they may not delegate their failures.

        (d) There was no technical competence in the health field involved in the development of the regulations.

Allen v. California Board of Barber Examiners

e) **Administrative agency consisting of industry members--Allen v. California Board of Barber Examiners,** 25 Cal. App. 3d 1014 (1972).

    (1) **Facts.** An apprentice barber, a journeyman barber, and owners of a barber shop (Ps) sued the California Board of Barber Examiners (D), seeking a writ of mandate directed to the Board commanding it to vacate and set aside its orders revoking Ps' certificates. The California Barbers Act authorized D to establish minimum price schedules for barbering services for any city or county. These sections directed that in establishing a minimum price schedule, D shall consider all conditions affecting the practice of barbering in that county and city, the relation of those conditions to the public health and safety, and the necessary costs incurred in that city or county in maintaining a barbershop in a clean, healthful, and sanitary condition. D could also modify the previously established minimum price schedule if, after investigation, D determined that the minimum prices so established are insufficient to properly provide healthful services to the public and to maintain the sanitary barber shop, or if any minimum price set creates an undue hardship on barbershop owners and operators. D revoked Ps' certificates for furnishing barbering services at prices below those prescribed in the minimum price schedule established by D for San Diego County. The trial court found the minimum price schedules invalid and issued a preemptory writ of mandate. D appeals.

(2) **Issue.** Where the legislature purports to confer power to regulate the business of one's competitors, must the courts insist upon stringent standards to contain and guide the exercise of the delegated power?

(3) **Held.** Yes. Judgment affirmed.

    (a) When the power which the legislature purports to confer is the power to regulate the business of one's competitors, a real danger of abuse arises, and the court accordingly insists upon stringent standards to contain and guide the exercise of the delegated power.

    (b) The State Board of Barber Examiners consists of five members, including one public member and four barbers who have engaged in the practice of barbering in the State of California for at least five years immediately prior to their appointment. Of the five, "one member shall be a journeyman barber and one member shall be a barber employing one or more journeymen barbers." The legislation attempts to delegate powers to an administrative board made up of interested members of the industry, a majority of which can initiate regulatory action by the board in that industry. The power that the legislation purports to confer is the power to regulate the business of one's competitors. A journeyman barber whose compensation is no doubt affected by the price of barbering services is as personally interested in the price of such services as an "owner."

2. **Delegation of Enforcement Authority--Industrial Union Department, AFL-CIO v. American Petroleum Institute,** *see supra*.

3. **Delegation of Authority to Resolve Disputes.**

Industrial Union Department, AFL-CIO v. American Petroleum Institute

a. **Agency adjudication of common law--Commodity Futures Trading Commission v. Schor,** 478 U.S. 833 (1986).

1) **Facts.** Respondent Schor filed a reparation complaint with the Commodity Futures Trading Commission ("CFTC") against petitioner Conti Commodity Service Ltd. ("Conti") for alleged violations of the Commodity Exchange Act ("CEA"). Conti then counterclaimed in the CFTC proceedings. The CFTC ruled in Conti's favor in both the counterclaim and Schor's original claim. The United States Court of Appeals for the District of Columbia upheld the decision regarding Schor's claim, and on remand reinstated its decision holding that the CEA authorized the CFTC to "adjudicate only counterclaims arising from violations of the Act or CFTC regulations." The CFTC appealed to the United States Supreme Court.

2) **Issue.** Is CFTC's adjudication over common law counterclaims a violation of Article III of the Constitution?

3) **Held.** No. Judgment affirmed.

   a) Article III of the Constitution guarantees an impartial and independent judiciary. As a personal right, the guarantee is subject to waiver. Schor decided to forgo his right to proceed in state or federal court and sought relief in the CFTC. This constituted a waiver.

   b) The adjudicatory power of the CFTC departs from the power ordinarily given to administrative agencies, only in that it has jurisdiction over common law counterclaims. The CFTC could only rule on a "[p]articularized area of law." Additionally, its decision is subject to review.

   c) The CFTC has a limited jurisdiction over a "[n]arrow class of common-law claims as an incident to the CFTC's primary, and unchallenged, adjudicative function. . . ." In addition, the parties' decision to use this forum is voluntary and does not preclude the right to litigate in state or federal court. Granting of this power does not unconstitutionally expand the power of the Legislative Branch, or restrict or undermine that of the Judicial Branch.

4) **Dissent** (Brennan, Marshall, JJ.). The majority decision is an unfair encroachment on Article III. It violates judicial independence and separation of powers.

b. **"Private right/public right" distinction and the role of Article III courts.** The United States Supreme Court addressed the distinction between private and public rights in *Northern Pipeline Construction Co. v. Marathon Pipe Line Co.*, 458 U.S. 50 (1982). At issue was the Bankruptcy Act of 1978, which conferred on bankruptcy courts jurisdiction over all "civil proceedings arising under" the Act. In the midst of a bankruptcy reorganization, Northern filed a breach of contract claim against Marathon. The bankruptcy court heard the claim. The Supreme Court held that Congress could not confer Article III adjudicatory power on a non-Article III court, such as the bankruptcy court.

1) **Bankruptcy courts.** The bankruptcy courts are not Article III courts, because bankruptcy judges do not have life tenure.

2) **Adjudicatory powers.** Non-Article III courts may only be given adjudicatory powers in very limited circumstances, such as grants to territorial courts, military courts, or issues involving public rights.

3) **Public rights.** These are controversies involving rights between the government and others. Where the right is of legislative creation, it may be vested in a non-Article III forum, even where an analogous function has historically been performed by an Article III court. Such powers may be vested in a legislative court or an administrative agency.

4) **Private rights.** These are controversies between two individuals. Although bankruptcy involves a public right, a common-law contract claim between two parties is a private right, which must be adjudicated by an Article III court.

c. *Crowell v. Benson* **distinguished.** A federal workers' compensation claim in *Crowell v. Benson*, *infra*, that was found to be constitutional was distinguished. The claim in *Crowell* was created by statute, even though it involved a dispute between private parties and would have otherwise been decided by the courts. The agency in *Crowell* made narrow findings, while the bankruptcy court has wide jurisdiction over an infinite number of questions. The agency in *Crowell* had to use the courts to enforce its orders; the bankruptcy court could enforce its own. The standard of judicial review is more stringent in the former case than in the latter.

d. **Public rights.** Where public rights are being litigated, the legislature may assign initial adjudication thereof to an administrative agency where a jury would be incompatible. [Atlas Roofing Co. v. Occupational Safety & Health Review Commission, 430 U.S. 442 (1977)]

D. THE PLACE OF AGENCIES IN GOVERNMENT

1. **Political Branches' Controls over Administrative Action.**

   a. **Federal standing committees.** Standing committees of the House and Senate keep abreast of agency activities in particular areas and sponsor legislation necessary to make necessary changes.

   b. **Investigations.** Other congressional committees concerned with general governmental operations may investigate the conduct of particular agencies. Occasionally, Congress appoints watchdog committees to examine the operation of particular agencies and to publicize controversial administrative actions.

   c. **Appropriations.** In making appropriations, Congress may likewise impose limitations on spending by the agency.

d. Appointments. The Senate must approve presidential appointments of high-level administrative and executive positions.

e. Veto of rules. Congress is increasingly enacting statutes which provide that either House of Congress may veto agency regulations within a specific period of time after they are adopted. The constitutionality of this procedure is not yet settled.

f. Miscellaneous.

    1) The Administrative Conference of the United States. The Conference analyzes federal agencies and administrative law and presents recommendations for improvement to Congress.

    2) Ombudsmen. Ombudsmen are officials who investigate and correct public complaints about specific administrative actions. Ombudsmen are used in a number of states.

    3) Legislators. Legislators sometimes attempt to intercede in administrative matters involving their constituents. This raises serious ethical questions and problems for administrators.

2. Executive Controls over Administrative Action.

a. Removal power.

    1) Executive agencies. Some statutes expressly authorize the President to remove administrators for specific causes. However, the power to remove executive administrators has been implied even where the statute is silent on this issue. [*See* Myers v. United States, *infra*—removal of postmaster *inherent* in Executive Branch as essential element of presidential power, to insure that laws are favorably executed; removal power cannot be limited by Congress]

    2) Independent agencies. On the other hand, discharge of administrators of independent agencies is limited where statutes specify the sole causes for removal.

        a) FTC. Thus, removal of a federal trade commissioner was overturned where the relevant statute provided that the commissioner could be removed only for "inefficiency, neglect of duty, or malfeasance in office," none of which had been charged. [*See* Humphrey's Executor v. United States, *infra*]

        b) Rationale. The FTC is an independent quasi-judicial agency created by Congress to effectuate specific legislative policies. Consequently, it could not be considered an arm of the executive over which the president had broad removal powers, especially since its independence would thereby be jeopardized.

        c) Board of Claims Commission. Similarly, removal of a member of the Board of Claims Commission was overturned on the ground that the Commission had a judicial function (adjudicating claims of persons suffering damage from the enemy during

World War II) which prevented presidential removal. [*See* Wiener v. United States, 357 U.S. 349 (1958)]

d) **Loophole—removal for cause.** If the statute provides a power of removal for cause, and such cause is alleged to exist, there would apparently be *no* judicial review of the removal. This seemed to provide an easy escape from the *Humphrey's* case.

e) **Fiscal power.** The President (through the Office of Management and Budget ("OMB")) can control administrative requests to Congress for appropriations or changes in legislation.

f) **Organization power.** Finally, the President has extensive statutory powers to create, abolish, and reorganize agencies within the Executive Branch.

3. **Constitutional Position of the "Independent" Agencies.** Beginning with the ICC in 1887, a number of administrative agencies have been established outside the Executive Branch. These include the CAB, FTC, SEC, NLRB, and FPC. The President's ability to remove individuals appointed to these collegial bodies without cause is circumscribed.

a. **Executive Branch agency--Myers v. United States, 272 U.S. 52 (1926)**

Myers v. United States

1) **Facts.** Myers (P) had been appointed postmaster at Portland, Oregon, and was removed prior to the expiration of his term by President Wilson, despite a statutory requirement that postmasters could only be removed with the "advice and consent of the Senate." The United States (D) argued that this statutory requirement violated the President's power to remove Executive Branch officials.

2) **Issue.** Is the power to remove subordinates in the Executive Branch inherently a part of the executive powers vested by the Constitution in the President?

3) **Held.** Yes.

a) Because the President is vested with the power to enforce the laws of the land, it is imperative for the adequate implementation of that constitutional directive that he be deemed to have disciplinary powers to remove his subordinates whenever "he loses confidence in their intelligence, ability, judgment, or loyalty."

b) The ability to control subordinates is manifest under the executive powers conferred upon the President by the Constitution, so that the statutes subject to his direction may be faithfully executed.

4) **Dissent** (Holmes, J.). Because Congress created the office and may abolish it at will, it may impose any limitations upon that office, such as preconditions of removal.

5) **Dissent** (Brandeis, J.). This is a lower federal office. Congress attempted to shield this office from discretionary removal in order to alleviate the adverse effects of the "spoils system." Prohibiting discretionary removal would effectuate constitutional policies of separation of powers and checks and balances.

6) **Comment.** In dictum, the Court stated that there may be duties exercised by subordinates that are of a discretionary or quasi-judicial nature, over which the President may exercise no control. Nevertheless, the President is free to remove subordinates who make decisions of which he disapproves.

Humphrey's **b.** **Independent regulatory agency--Humphrey's Executor v. United States,** 295
Executor v. U.S. 602 (1935).
United States

1) **Facts.** Humphrey was appointed to the FTC for a seven-year term by President Hoover. The Federal Trade Commission Act provides that a commissioner may be removed from office by the President for "inefficiency, neglect of duty, or malfeasance in office." Prior to the expiration thereof, President Roosevelt asked for Humphrey's resignation. Humphrey declined to resign and was fired by the President. Humphrey's heirs (Ps) brought this action for back pay against the United States (D), alleging that he was wrongfully removed from office. D relied on *Myers v. United States, supra*.

2) **Issue.** Does the Act limit the President's power of removal to the causes enumerated and, if so, is the Act constitutional?

3) **Held.** Yes to both questions.

a) The decision of *Myers* applies only to executive officers, such as postmasters. While its dictum may have been broad enough to encompass all federal officers, it has no application to an agency outside the Executive Branch that exercises quasi-judicial and quasi-legislative powers.

b) Whether Congress may limit the President's prerogative of removal depends upon the character of the office. The FTC was established outside the Executive Branch to exercise legislative and judicial responsibilities. Here, restrictions upon the President's removal power are constitutionally proper.

c. **Nomination and appointment.** When selecting nominees for posts on the federal judiciary, the Department of Justice seeks the advice of the American Bar Association's ("ABA's") Standing Committee on the Federal Judiciary. The issue in *Public Citizen v. United States Department of Justice*, 491 U.S. 440 (1989), was whether this relationship unconstitutionally violates the Federal Advisory Committee Act ("FACA") by violating separation of powers and usurping the President's role to nominate and appoint officers of the United States. The Court held that the relationship was not a violation of the FACA. The FACA was established as an oversight act to "assess the need for the numerous committees, boards, [etc] which have been established to advise" the government. Under the FACA, the ABA group did not expressly meet the requirements of an "advisory committee." However, the Court also examined whether the ABA was used by the President and the Department of Justice such that the ABA could be considered an "advisory committee" within the FACA's meaning. Read literally, the FACA would thus apply to the ABA. However, "[a] literalistic reading would catch far more groups than Congress could have conceivably intended." The legislative history of the FACA also seems to imply that the ABA would not be included.

4. **Congressional Control of Executive Functions.** As with the President's power to remove officials in independent agencies, Congress's power to remove officials performing executive duties also may violate the separation of powers principle.

a. **Congressional self-aggrandizement--Bowsher v. Synar,** 478 U.S. 714 (1986).

Bowsher
v. Synar

1) **Facts.** Congressman Synar (P) filed a declaratory judgment action that challenged the constitutionality of the grant of executive power to the Comptroller General ("CG"), a legislative official. The grant of that power was contained in the Gramm-Rudman-Hollings Act, which was enacted to balance the federal budget. In the Act, the CG was given the authority to make certain final decisions as to what budget reductions should be made to achieve a balanced budget. The CG's decisions under the Act were to be carried out by the President without discretion. The CG is subject to removal by joint resolution of Congress "at any time" for cause. P contended that this congressional power to remove an official charged with executive duties was a violation of the doctrine of separation of powers. A special district court appointed pursuant to the Act held for P. The Supreme Court granted certiorari.

2) **Issue.** Does the congressional power to remove an official who performs executive duties constitute a violation of the doctrine of separation of powers?

3) **Held.** Yes. Judgment affirmed.

a) To allow Congress the power to remove an official charged with executive duties, except by the impeachment process, amounts to a legislative veto. Legislative vetoes were held to be unconstitutional in *INS v. Chadha, infra.*

b) The legislation which created the office of CG provides for his removal "for any number of actual or perceived transgressions." This broad removal power serves to make his tenure subject to the whim of Congress.

c) The Act gives the CG the final authority to decide what budget reductions will be made, and the President is compelled by the Act to carry out that decision. This is clearly an executive function that is incompatible with the broad removal power possessed by Congress. Congress may not place the responsibility for the execution of legislation in the hands of an official who can be removed only by himself.

d) Congress has limited removal powers over officers of the United States—they can only be removed by impeachment and for "Treason, bribery or other high crimes or misdemeanors." Any removal powers beyond these would violate separation of powers. The vesting of the Act's powers in the CG, who is only answerable to Congress, is violative of Constitution, as it "would . . . reserve in Congress control over the execution of the laws." Since Congress has removal powers over the CG, he cannot be given executive powers (he interprets the 1985 Act to make budget recommendations, uses judgment in determining Act's applicability).

4) **Concurrence** (Stevens, Marshall, JJ.). The CG's duties under the Act serve to circumvent the lawmaking procedures found in Article I of the Constitution. In short, this is an unconstitutional delegation of legislative power.

5) **Dissent** (White, J.). This Court has never held and does not now hold that Congress may not grant executive power to officials unless they are subject to removal by the will of the President. The grant of authority to the CG under the Act is the accepted legislative function of appropriation of funds. The President has not been deprived of any function that is normally his or that is required by him to fulfill his duties. Furthermore, Congress's power to remove the CG is carefully circumscribed and can be carried out only with the compliance of the President. If the President wishes to veto that removal legislation, the veto can only be overridden by a two-thirds vote in both Houses, a larger vote than that required for impeachment.

5. **Appointment.** All officers of the United States must be appointed by the President with the "Advice and Consent of the Senate." Congress may vest the appointment of interior officers in the President alone, the courts, or the heads of departments. [U.S. Const. art. II, §2]

Buckley
v. Valeo

a. **Federal Election Commission--Buckley v. Valeo,** 424 U.S. 1 (1976).

1) **Facts.** In 1974, Congress amended the Federal Election Campaign Act to create an eight-member Federal Election Commission ("FEC"). Two members were to be appointed by the President pro tempore of the Senate, upon recommendations of the Senate majority and minority leaders. Two were to be appointed by the Speaker of the House upon recommendations of the House majority and minority leaders. Two were to be appointed by the President, and the Secretary of the Senate and Clerk of the House filled the last two seats as ex officio, nonvoting members. The six voting members were required to receive confirmation by a majority vote of both Houses of Congress. The SEC held wide-ranging rulemaking and enforcement powers. Senator James Buckley (P) contended that the nature of the FEC duties made its members "officers of the United States" within the meaning of the United States Constitution Article II, section 2, and hence their appointment by individuals other than the President was improper. Valeo and the FEC (Ds) argued that this clause of the Constitution should not be read to exclude the "inherent power of Congress" to appoint its own officers.

2) Issues.

    a) Are members of the FEC "officers of the United States?"

    b) If so, must they be appointed by the President, with the advice and consent of the Senate?

3) Held. a) Yes. b) Yes. Judgment reversed.

    a) Any appointee exercising significant authority under federal law is an officer of the United States and must be appointed pursuant to the United States Constitution, Article II, section 2.

    b) The United States Constitution specifies only two means of appointment (one for "officers of the United States" and the other for inferior officers), and all persons who hold appointed office in the federal government must be included within one or the other of these two categories.

    c) Although Congress is free to establish new "offices" under the Necessary and Proper Clause of the United States Constitution, the method of appointment must conform to Article II, section 2.

6. **Congressional Regulation.** In *Hechinger v. Metropolitan Washington Airports Authority*, 36 F.3d 97 (1994), a statute placed Washington National and Dulles International Airports under the ownership of an authority, operated by Maryland, Virginia, and the District of Columbia. The authority was overseen by a review board, also created by the statute, which was originally made up of members of Congress. This make-up was held unconstitutional for violating separation of powers by the Supreme Court. The new configuration of the board was comprised of nine "frequent" travelers, selected from candidates supplied by Congress. The district court, on remand, held that this configuration still exhibited that Congress retained control over the board. Furthermore, even though the amended board was no longer given veto power over authority actions, it still retained several powers over the authority, including the ability to force issues for authority consideration, and had temporal control over decision-making.

7. **The Civil Service System.** In 1883, Congress established the Civil Service System so as to reduce abuses of the "spoils system" of political patronage appointments. Under the system, appointment is ostensibly determined by merit, and removal is severely circumscribed. Almost 85% of federal employees fall under its umbrella. Excessive job security has been criticized as breeding lethargy among low-level and mid-level government workers.

8. **The Legislative Veto.** A large number of legislative veto provisions have been incorporated into the enabling legislation of administrative agencies since 1932. They differ in the ways that they provide for the reversal of administrative or executive action. Some provide for veto by one or both Houses of Congress, while others allow reversal by a congressional committee. A dark cloud on their constitutionality has been cast by the Supreme Court decision in *INS v. Chadha, infra.*

a.   **Wisdom of the "regulatory" veto.** Because of the necessities of modern government, the legislature found itself vesting increasingly broad powers in administrative agencies, and the judiciary found it desirable to uphold such broad delegations. Nevertheless, Congress became concerned that its power was becoming diluted and that there were insufficient "checks" on aberrant administrative behavior, and seized upon the legislative veto as a mechanism to reassert its power and rein in the agencies. But there are problems with the veto, including obstruction of the agency's ability to implement its statutory mandate, the opportunity of strong lobbies in Washington to block agency actions, and the disruption of the procedural protections afforded under the APA.

b.   **Constitutionality of the veto--INS v. Chadha,** 462 U.S. 919 (1983).

1)   **Facts.** Chadha (P), an East Indian born in Kenya, stayed in the United States beyond the expiration of his visa. His order of deportation was suspended by the Attorney General under the Immigration and Nationality Act. One provision of the Act allows either House of Congress to pass a resolution disapproving such suspension of deportation, which the House of Representatives did, without explanation.

2)   **Issue.** Is this legislative veto provision constitutional?

3)   **Held.** No. Judgment affirmed.

a)   Before a bill may become law, it must be passed by both Houses of Congress and presented to the President for his signature or veto. In the latter case, the bill fails unless both Houses override the veto with a two-thirds-majority vote. This provision was incorporated into the Constitution to allow a presidential check on the legislature's enactment of "oppressive, improvident, or ill-considered measures."

b)   By requiring both Houses' approval of a bill before it can become law, the constitutional framers assured that no statute would be enacted unless it had been carefully considered by the nation's elected representatives.

c)   By dividing the federal government into three branches and providing for a system of checks and balances, the framers assured that the government would not take imprudent action. The bicameral requirement, the Presentment Clauses, the President's veto, and Congress's power to override a veto were intended to erect enduring checks on each branch and to protect the people from improvident exercise of power by mandating certain prescribed steps. The disapproval of the Attorney General's suspension order involving P was an unconstitutional effort at lawmaking.

4)   **Dissent** (White, J.). Some 200 statutes include legislative veto provisions. Rather than serving as an opportunity for legislative tyranny over the executive, they serve as a necessary check on the expanding power of administrative agencies.

5) **Comment.** In *E. Donald Elliott, INS v. Chadha: The Administrative Constitution, the Constitution, and the Legislative Veto*, 1983 Sup. Ct. Rev. 125, Elliott's concern is that the Court's reasoning in *Chadha* is too conceptual and formalistic. The legislative veto alters "legal rights," merely because the Court's formalized approach characterizes it as such. In addition, Elliott points out that the Court never addressed the issue of why Congress should not retain supervision over the exercise of power it has not delegated.

c. **Alternatives to the legislative veto.** In order to exert control over administrative agencies, Congress has opportunities available to it that raise fewer constitutional problems. For example, it could draft legislation more precisely, giving the agency less discretion. It could also circumscribe the agency's budget to express disapproval.

d. **Congressional power.** In *American Federation of Government Employees v. Pierce*, 697 F.2d 303 (D.C. Cir. 1982), an annual appropriations bill for the Department of Housing and Urban Development had a proviso which prohibited the Department from implementing any reorganization plan without prior approval of the Committee on Appropriations. The court found that the proviso was a "means for Congress to control the executive without going through the full lawmaking process, thus unconstitutionally enhancing congressional power at the expense of the executive power." In addition, to let the agency apply for funds under one plan intrudes on the strong interest Congress has in appropriating such funds.

e. **Severability.** The problem of severability, or alternatives for the legislative vetoes, has yet to be solved. Some courts have held a veto provision severable, others have not.

f. **Sunset.** There are alternative means to control the structure of administrative agencies. One method is the "sunset legislation," which calls for a review of an agency's performance and purpose to determine whether the agency should continue. Advantages are that it keeps employees from becoming complacent and allows legislatures to determine whether an agency or its structure has become obsolete. Disadvantages are the possibility that the agency may upset a key legislator and therefore not be renewed. Also, sunset legislation may have a negative impact on morale and result in lack of long-term planning by the agency and its personnel.

g. **Congressional review of court decisions.** In 1991, Congress enacted section 27(a) of the Federal Deposit Insurance Corporation, which allowed for the reopening of several cases based on whether and when they were dismissed. The Court in *Plaut v. Spendthrift Farm*, 115 S. Ct. 1447 (1995), held that this violated separation of powers, thus affirming the appellate court. In essence, the Court found that Article III had given the courts the duty to determine the law, subject to review "only by superior courts in the Article III hierarchy." By allowing Congress to reopen judgments, this principle was violated.

h. **Presidential encroachment?--Morrison v. Olson,** 487 U.S. 654 (1988).

Morrison
v. Olson

1) **Facts.** The Ethics in Government Act, Title IV, provides for independent investigations of high ranking government officials. The procedure is as follows: the Attorney General conducts a preliminary investigation; if there

is information sufficient to constitute an investigation, the D.C. Court of Appeals Special Division must be notified within 90 days. If the court finds grounds for an investigation, the Special Division appoints an independent counsel. The counsel has the authority to "exercise all investigative and prosecutorial functions . . . of the Department of Justice [and] the Attorney General." The Attorney General ("AG") has the power to remove the special counsel for "good cause." In this case, Olson (P), an assistant AG, was accused of giving false and misleading testimony in a House investigation of the EPA. Two of his co-workers were accused of obstructing the House investigation. The AG found sufficient evidence to proceed with independent counsel (Morrison (D)) against P, but not his co-workers. D was given permission to expand her investigation with respect to P to any evidence of other violations by him. During her investigation, she requested material on the other accused workers; the AG refused and the Special Division held that the AG's earlier decision regarding these co-workers was final and unreviewable. However, it held that D's mandate was broad enough to inquire into P's connection to his co-workers's charges. P contends that the independent counsel provisions of the Ethics Act are unconstitutional.

2) Issues.

    a)   Is D an "inferior officer" under the Article II Appointments Clause?

    b)   Does Congress have the power to place authority to appoint the special prosecutor outside of the Executive Branch?

    c)   Because an executive officer (AG) can remove a judicially appointed officer, is the Act invalid because it violates separation of powers?

3) Held. a) Yes. b) Yes. c) No. Judgment reversed. (Act held to be constitutional.)

    a)   D is an inferior officer. She is subject to removal by higher executive officers, she has limited and specific duties, and she has limited tenure and jurisdiction.

    b)   Congress has discretion, based on the "as they think proper" language in the Appointments Clause and the fact that there is no incongruity in having courts appoint prosecutorial officers.

    c)   The removal power is vested entirely in the Executive Branch, with no need for congressional approval (no *Bowsher*-type of problem, *see supra*). D can only be removed for "good cause." This standard does not impede the executive, as his powers should not be more expansive (*e.g.,* at will). The removal powers do not impede the executive's power to supervise the independent counsel, as ample authority to remove is retained. There is no "undue interference" with the Executive Branch powers to remove and the Act does not undermine executive powers because it does not prohibit the executive from carrying out constitutional powers.

i. **The Inspector General--Burlington Northern Railroad Co. v. Office of Inspector General,** 983 F.2d 631 (5th Cir. 1993).

Burlington
Northern
Railroad Co.
v. Office of
Inspector
General

1) **Facts.** The Railroad Retirement Board ("RRB") was established to provide retirement and survivor benefits to workers and families (Railroad Retirement Tax Act) and to provide unemployment and sickness benefits to workers (Railroad Unemployment Insurance Act). Both programs were funded by employer taxes, based on a system of "creditable compensation." The RRB was given the authority to audit employers to insure correct payments have been made for benefit programs; the RRB had never exercised this right, instead relying on IRS audits. The Office of the Inspector General ("OIG") was created to consolidate agency auditing procedures and to eliminate any fraud and waste. In 1983, an OIG was created for the RRB. Feeling that the IRS audits were inadequate, the OIG sought to investigate the railroads itself. In 1990, it set out to audit Burlington, which argued that the audit was not within the statutory authority of the OIG. The OIG issued a subpoena duces tecum, ordering Burlington to present records "in aid of an audit." The district court held that the OIG's audit was regulatory in nature and not within its oversight powers, and thus held that the OIG did not have the authority to conduct a regulatory audit, denying the subpoena.

2) **Issue.** Was conducting an audit within the scope of the OIG's powers?

3) **Held.** No. Judgment affirmed.

   a) The intent of the OIG was not to conduct "spot checks" on railroad operators, but instead to take on a regulatory function, insuring tax compliance "and perhaps assume a tax collecting function." It did not have the statutory authority to do this. The Inspector General Act gave the OIG investigatory and subpoena powers, but no authority to conduct regulatory compliance activities. If otherwise, the integrity and objectivity of the OIG would be compromised. Congress simply wanted OIG to have oversight authority to combat fraud and other abuses.

III. THE EXERCISE OF ADMINISTRATIVE POWER: RULEMAKING AND ADJUDICATION

A. SOURCES OF PROCEDURAL REQUIREMENTS

This chapter examines the procedural requirements that agencies must employ for adjudication and rulemaking in the areas of regulation and taxation. These requirements have five sources.

1. **The Organic Statute.** The organic statute creating the agency, which may specify the procedures it is to utilize.

2. **Procedural Regulations.** The procedural regulations promulgated by the agency itself.

3. **The Administrative Procedure Act.** The APA, which establishes procedural requirements for most federal agencies.

4. **Federal Common Law.** Federal common law created by judges to facilitate judicial review.

5. **The United States Constitution.** The United States Constitution, particularly its Fifth and Fourteenth Amendment due process requirements, as interpreted by the courts.

B. THE FUNDAMENTAL PROCEDURAL CATEGORIES OF ADMINISTRATIVE ACTION

1. **The Constitution.** Constitutional due process requirements may create a hearing obligation where a "relatively small number of persons are exceptionally affected, in each case, upon individual grounds." In *Londoner v. Denver*, below, a case involving the assessment of a tax imposed upon individual property owners for the benefit realized from the paving of their street, the Supreme Court held that, at some time before the tax becomes irrevocably fixed, the taxpayer must be given the opportunity to have a hearing. But in *Bi-Metallic Investment Co. v. State Board of Equalization of Colorado*, *infra*, the Court also held that, conversely, where a large number of persons are affected by an agency action essentially analogous to that performed by the legislature, a formal hearing is not required.

Londoner
v. Denver

   a. **Oral hearing required--Londoner v. Denver, 210 U.S. 373 (1908).**

      1) **Facts.** Londoner (P), a property owner, objected to a tax assessment by the City of Denver (D) based upon street improvements. Under Colorado statutes, the Board of Public Works might order the paving of a street, followed by an apportionment of its costs among property owners. Before assessment, D was required to afford parties notice and an opportunity to file written objections. P contended that these procedures were constitutionally deficient.

2) **Issue.** Does the Fourteenth Amendment require an oral hearing prior to the assessment of a tax for street improvements?

3) **Held.** Yes. Judgment reversed.

    a) No hearing is required for the paving of a street.

    b) However, assessment of a tax based upon such street improvements does require that D offer the parties notice and an opportunity to be heard at some point before the tax becomes irrevocably fixed.

    c) Few constitutional restrictions are imposed upon the legislature's power to tax; but when the legislature delegates the function of determining the amount of the tax to an administrative agency, due process obligations must be observed.

    d) Although a full, formal, trial-type hearing is not required, P is entitled to support his position by oral argument and proof.

b. **Formal hearing not required--Bi-Metallic Investment Co. v. State Board of Equalization of Colorado, 239 U.S. 441 (1915).**

    1) **Facts.** Bi-Metallic Investment Company (P) owned real estate in Denver and sought to enjoin the State Board of Equalization of Colorado (D) from increasing the valuation of all taxable property in the city by 40%. P argued that since he was given no opportunity to be heard, his constitutional right to due process had been violated.

    2) **Issue.** Do all property owners in a municipality have a right to be heard before their property can be revalued?

    3) **Held.** No. Judgment affirmed.

        a) Where a large number of individuals are affected by an agency action, it is impractical that they each be given a hearing. The machinery of government would grind to a halt if all aggrieved parties were given a formal hearing.

        b) The action taken here is analogous to that regularly performed by the legislature. Even though the legislature can significantly affect the property of individuals "sometimes to the point of ruin," there is no constitutional requirement that a hearing be held before such action is taken.

c. **Distinction between adjudication and rulemaking.** *Londoner* and *Bi-Metallic* illustrate the fundamental distinctions between adjudication and rulemaking. As the Supreme Court has subsequently noted, there is "a recognized distinction in administrative law between proceedings for the purpose of promulgating policy-type rules or standards on the one hand, and proceedings designed to adjudicate disputed facts in particular cases on the other."

d.   **Adjudicative and legislative facts.** Professor Davis has argued that the appropriate distinction is that between adjudicative facts and legislative facts. Adjudicative facts are those surrounding the actors in an agency proceeding (*e.g.,* what happened, who did it, when, where, why, and how). Legislative facts, in contrast, are the general facts to which the agency looks in deciding questions of law and policy. Adjudications generally focus on the former; rulemaking on the latter.

e.   **Exceptions to *Londoner*.** In spite of the fact that the proceeding is adjudicatory in nature, no hearing will be required in cases of (i) mathematical rule or formula (*e.g.,* where there is no agency discretion except the application of a reasonably precise standard to uncontroverted facts, no hearing need be held), (ii) inspections, (iii) tests, and (iv) elections.

f.   **Participation.** In *Minnesota State Board for Community Colleges v. Knight*, 465 U.S. 271 (1984), the issue was whether the argument for a constitutional right to participate in a rulemaking process would be stronger if premised on the political rights found elsewhere in the Constitution (*i.e.,* stronger than *Bi-Metallic*). The Court held it was not. Justice O'Connor stated, "Nothing in the First Amendment or in this Court's case law interpreting it suggests that the rights to speak, associate, and petition require government policymakers to listen or respond to individuals' communications on public issues."

g.   **Adversary hearing.** The court in *Burr v. New Rochelle Municipal Housing Authority*, 479 F.2d 1165 (2d Cir. 1973), held that there is no requirement of an adversary hearing before a general rent increase. Tenants must be given adequate notice, but no oral presentation is required by the Due Process Clause.

h.   **Notice.** The state has no obligation to give persons notice of a statute that may have a harmful effect on them. By enacting and publishing a law, the public should be aware of such laws.

i.   **Evaluating procedures.** One author suggests criteria for evaluating procedural systems that he feels are more helpful than "fairness" or "due process." The first is "accuracy" in determining relevant facts and issues. This also encompasses giving equal treatment to similarly situated persons. The second is "efficiency," emphasizing time, effort, and expense. The third is "acceptability"—the system must be fair to the agency, the participants, and the general public. [Roger C. Cramton, *A Comment on Trial-Type Hearings in Nuclear Power Plant Siting*, 58 Va. L. Rev. 585 (1972)]

2.   **The Fundamental Statute.**

a.   **Introductory note on procedural provisions of the APA.** The following chart provides a summary of the three major means of announcing new policy (*i.e.,* adjudication, rulemaking, and statements of policy), the principal procedural obligations for each (*i.e.,* formal trial-type, hybrid, or informal legislative procedures), and the provisions of the APA in which they are found.

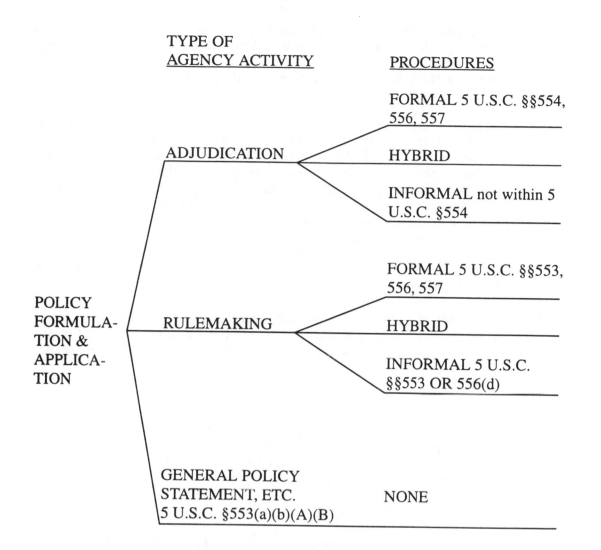

TYPE OF
AGENCY ACTIVITY   PROCEDURES

FORMAL 5 U.S.C. §§554, 556, 557

ADJUDICATION   HYBRID

INFORMAL not within 5 U.S.C. §554

POLICY FORMULA-TION & APPLICA-TION

FORMAL 5 U.S.C. §§553, 556, 557

RULEMAKING   HYBRID

INFORMAL 5 U.S.C. §§553 OR 556(d)

GENERAL POLICY STATEMENT, ETC. 5 U.S.C. §553(a)(b)(A)(B)   NONE

b.   Notice and comment rulemaking. Section 553 of the APA defines the procedural obligations applicable to most rulemaking proceedings.

1)   **Notice.** Notice of proposed rulemaking must be published in the Federal Register, unless relevant parties have actual notice. [5 U.S.C. §553(b)]

a)   **Exceptions.** Interpretive and procedural rules, as well as general statements of policy, are exempt from the requirement of publication. Also exempt are situations in which the agency finds it "impracticable, unnecessary, or contrary to the public interest." [5 U.S.C. §553(b)(3)]

2)   **Notice and comment procedures.** Parties have a right to participate through submission of written pleadings, with or without the opportunity to advocate their position or introduce evidence orally. More formal procedures are available only if the "rules are required to be made on the record after opportunity for an agency hearing." [5 U.S.C. §553(c)]

3) **Publication.** Publication or service of a substantive rule must ordinarily be accomplished 30 days prior to its effective date. [5 U.S.C. §553(d)]

Vermont Yankee Nuclear Power Corp. v. Natural Resources Defense Council

c. **The *Vermont Yankee* litigation--Vermont Yankee Nuclear Power Corp. v. Natural Resources Defense Council,** 435 U.S. 519 (1978).

1) **Facts.** Vermont Yankee Nuclear Power Corporation (D) sought permits from the Atomic Energy Commission ("AEC") to build nuclear power facilities as early as 1967. The Natural Resources Defense Council (P) objected to the issuance of a license, and hearings were held thereon in 1971. In 1972, the AEC instituted rulemaking proceedings to assess the environmental consequences surrounding the spent fuel cycle. The AEC did not offer the opportunity for formal, trial-type proceedings under 5 U.S.C. sections 556 and 557, but appeared to offer more than the de minimis procedures specified for informal rulemaking under 5 U.S.C. section 553. The lower courts nevertheless concluded that the procedures offered were inadequate. D appeals.

2) **Issue.** May the judiciary insist that federal agencies offer procedures beyond those expressed in the APA where the substantive issues under consideration are complex, technical, or involve "issues of great public import?"

3) **Held.** No. Judgment reversed.

    a) The APA expresses the maximum procedural requirements that Congress was willing to have the judiciary place upon agencies. While agencies are free to offer greater procedural opportunities, the courts are not free to insist that they do.

    b) Exceptions may exist where:

        (1) The agency is deciding a controversy involving a small number of persons, each of whom is exceptionally affected upon individual grounds (this is essentially a *Londoner* type of situation, *see supra*);

        (2) The agency makes a "totally unjustified departure from settled agency procedures of long standing;"

        (3) Constitutional due process may require more procedural opportunities than those specified in the APA; or

        (4) Exceptionally compelling circumstances exist.

4) **Comment.** *Vermont Yankee* is among the most significant, and frequently cited, decisions in administrative law.

d. **The scope of review of agency factfinding in rulemaking.**

1) **Formal rulemaking.** For formal rulemaking, utilizing the "trial-type" procedures in an "on the record" proceeding pursuant to 5 U.S.C. sections 556 and 557, the scope of review is whether the agency's decision is supported by "substantial evidence." [5 U.S.C. §706(2)(E)]

2) Informal rulemaking. The APA is silent as to what the appropriate scope of review is for informal or hybrid rulemaking. Courts ordinarily apply the "arbitrary or capricious" standard of 5 U.S.C. section 706(2)(A).

e. Procedural requirements and the scope of review in adjudication.

1) Formal adjudication. Under 5 U.S.C. section 554(a), "Every case of adjudication required by statute to be determined on the record after opportunity for agency hearing" requires formal, trial-type procedures under sections 556 and 557, unless it falls within one of the exemptions specified by statute. The scope of review for formal adjudication is "substantial evidence."

2) Informal adjudication. Almost 90% of agency actions taken with respect to individuals are done in the context of informal adjudication. Although the agency need not prepare a contemporaneous record for purposes of potential judicial review, many now do. Here, the scope of review is "arbitrary and capricious."

3) De novo review. De novo judicial review under 5 U.S.C. section 706(2)(E) has been circumscribed by the decision of the United States Supreme Court in *Overton Park, infra,* to two situations: (i) where agency fact-finding was inadequate; and (ii) where new factual issues are raised in actions for judicial enforcement of agency sanctions.

f. Comments on *Vermont Yankee*.

1) Justice Antonin Scalia. In discussing the court of appeals in *Vermont Yankee*, Justice Scalia stated "the crucial factual issue in [*Vermont Yankee*] was the adequacy of existing high-level waste disposal techniques." The evidence offered to the appeals court to sustain the suggested techniques was vague, had little detail, and left several questions unanswered. The court of appeals declined to let the petitioner cross-examine, as this is not necessary under the APA, 5 U.S.C. section 553. The petitioner offered general comments of several procedures. Justice Scalia stated that "the Commissioners' statement of basis and purpose for the rule did not respond specifically to any of these objections." The court of appeals set aside the portions of the rule pertaining to waste disposal and reprocessing issues. [Antonin Scalia, *Vermont Yankee: The APA, the D.C. Circuit, and the Supreme Court,* 1978 Sup. Ct. Rev. 345]

2) Clark Byse. Clark Byse states three reasons why courts should not order an agency to use additional procedural devices to produce what, in their view, is an adequate record for review. First, procedures are a means to an end. There may be several alternative procedures to produce the same end. Second, the courts have a duty to defer judgment to the agencies. Third, legislative history indicates that any additional procedural devices are an agency question, not a judicial question. [Clark Byse, *Vermont Yankee and the Evolution of Administration Procedure: A Somewhat Different View,* 91 Harv. L. Rev. 1823 (1978)]

g. The role of findings and reasons in formal administrative proceedings.
Formal proceedings conducted by administrative agencies must be published. The APA, 5 U.S.C. section 557(c), holds that the publication must include a

statement of "findings and conclusions, and the reasons or basis therefor, on all the material issues of fact, law, or discretion presented on the record." This allows a record for a reviewing court to determine constitutional issues and whether the agency has acted within its power. It also results in intra-agency uniformity.

1) **Purpose.** In *New Jersey Bell Telephone Co. v. Communications Workers of America*, 75 A.2d 721 (N.J. 1950), the court stated that the reason for keeping a record of administrative decisions is more than merely technical; it is to insure that the decision was not arbitrary, *i.e.,* to insure that justice be administered according to the facts and the law.

2) **Illustration.** *Elite Dairy Products, Inc. v. Ten Eyck*, 3 N.E.2d 606 (N.Y. 1936), involved a determination by the Commissioner of Agriculture that denied an application for a license to "purchase, handle, sell, or distribute milk." The court annulled the order of denial, holding that "the applicant is entitled to an opportunity to challenge a determination against him." He is entitled to the findings showing why the particular matter was decided against him.

3) **State law.** Most state statutes say something about the necessity for administrative decisions to be accompanied by findings of fact, etc. The Revised Model State Administrative Procedure Act, section 12, states that each decision must contain findings of fact and conclusions of law, and the findings of fact must be accompanied by a concise and explicit statement of the underlying facts supporting the findings.

4) **APA provisions.**

   a) **Adjudication.** APA section 557(c) governs adjudication, providing that "[a]ll decisions, including initial, recommended, and tentative decisions, are part of the record and shall include a statement of (i) findings and conclusions, and the reasons or basis therefor, on all the material issues of fact, law, or discretion presented on the record; and (ii) the appropriate rule, order, sanction, relief, or denial thereof."

   b) **Rulemaking.** APA section 553(c) provides, "After consideration of relevant matter presented, the agency shall incorporate in the rules adopted a concise general statement of their basis and purposes." These and the provisions above relating to state law reflect pre-APA law, which also required findings and conclusions.

5) **The purpose for findings.**

   a) **To insure that decisionmaker complies with requirements of relevant statutes.** In *Wichita Railroad & Light Co. v. Public Utilities Commission*, 260 U.S. 48 (1922), the Court reversed a Public Utilities Commission order to increase rates, because nowhere was it stated that the basis of the order was that existing rates are "unjust, unreasonable, unjustly discriminatory, or unduly prejudicial," as the relevant statute required.

   b) **To emphasize relevant factors.** Findings as to certain matters may be critical to an agency's jurisdiction or use of its powers. Examples:

      (1) *Yonkers v. United States*, 320 U.S. 685 (1944), involved the ICC and its authority to permit abandonment of street railways, but only if the

railway was part of a general steam railroad system. The ICC allowed discontinuance of a branch line, but it made no findings on the issue of whether a general system was involved. The Court reversed. The ICC must make the specific finding required, because otherwise, if the railway is not part of a general system, it remains within state control.

(2) *Elite Dairy Products, Inc. v. Ten Eyck, supra*, involved the Commissioner of Agriculture, who could deny an application for a milk license on three specific grounds. Elite Dairy Products, Inc. sought a license and was turned down. The court sent the case back to the Commissioner for specific findings of the basis for the denial, so that Elite would have the opportunity to challenge the determination against it.

c) **To provide a proper basis for review.** In *New Jersey Bell Telephone Co. v. Communications Workers of America, supra*, the statute allowed a seizure by the state in case of a public utility strike; then the matter went to compulsory arbitration. The Board was to make specific findings in its recommendation of five matters. The Board decided the issue by raising employee wages, citing recent wage increases in similar industries. The court reversed on the basis that the Board had not responded to the five matters on which findings were to be made, so that judicial review as to whether substantial evidence existed to support each of the required findings was impossible.

d) **To insure that decisionmaker examines the relevant issues and statutory policies.** In *Schaffer Transportation Co. v. United States*, 355 U.S. 83 (1957), the ICC turned down a trucking line's request for authority to provide service in an area served only by the railroad. There was substantial evidence that the trucker could provide the service cheaper and faster for certain types of customers. The ICC based its decision on the ground that the service to the area was already adequate. The Court reversed, citing the controlling National Transportation Policy, which required that the "inherent advantages of each mode of transportation be considered" in passing on any request for authority.

6) **Absence of rationale.** The absence of explanation by an agency even of nonadjudicatory proceedings may so frustrate judicial review as to warrant reversal.

a) **Informal adjudication--Pension Benefit Guaranty Corp. v. LTV Corp.,** 496 U.S. 633 (1990).

Pension Benefit Guaranty Corp. v. LTV Corp.

(1) **Facts.** Under the Employment Retirement Income Security Act ("ERISA"), a government insurance program was established to protect workers against termination of pension plans. Pension Benefit Guaranty Corporation (P) was the administrator of the program. When LTV Corporation (D) filed for bankruptcy in order to restructure the pension plans of its subsidiaries, P sought to terminate the pension plans of D in order to insulate ERISA from a large loss. After P took several actions to restore its fiscal health, P issued "a notice of restoration" to restore the terminated plans, which is authorized by section 4047 of the ERISA. D would not comply. P issued an enforcement action, which was vacated by the district court and

affirmed by the court of appeals, which held that the restoration decision was arbitrary and capricious. The Supreme Court granted certiorari.

    (2) Issue. Was P's restoration decision arbitrary and capricious in violation of the APA?

    (3) Held. No. Judgment reversed.

        (a) First, as to the appellate court holding that P failed to consider all areas of the law (specifically labor law and bankruptcy law) "the [appellate] court deemed relevant to the restoration decision," P had no obligation to consider these areas, particularly since they were not within P's expertise.

        (b) As to the appellate court's contention that P's policy was not explicit within the text of the statute, the policy was based on a permissible construction of the statute.

        (c) Finally, P's actions were not otherwise arbitrary and capricious.

C. THE PROCEDURAL CATEGORIES IN ACTION

    1. Formal Adjudication as an Administrative Procedure.

        a. Insufficient evidence--FTC v. Cement Institute, 333 U.S. 683 (1948).

FTC v.
Cement
Institute

        1) Facts. The FTC (D) instituted a complaint against members of the Cement Institute (Ps) on grounds that Ps restrained competition. D had refused Ps' requests to disqualify themselves. D had also made public statements to Congress while the complaint was pending that the activities of Ps were the "equivalent of a price-fixing restraint of trade in violation of the Sherman Act."

        2) Issue. Do these public statements suggest that D is impermissibly biased to conduct this enforcement proceeding?

        3) Held. No.

          a) The statements made by D do not suggest that the commissioners' minds were irrevocably closed. In fact, Ps had an opportunity to correct any erroneous impressions that D may have by introduction of evidence and argument at the agency hearing.

          b) Sustaining Ps' contention would require disqualification of the only tribunal which has jurisdiction over these matters, and would thereby frustrate the intent of Congress.

4)   Comment. This case seemed to be more illustrative of the process of administrative review than any novel legal concept.

b.   Opportunity to present evidence--Castillo-Villagra v. INS, 972 F.2d 1017 (9th Cir. 1992).

1)   Facts. Castillo-Villagra (P), a Nicaraguan citizen, sought asylum due to fear of reprisals from Sandinistas, of whom she had been critical. While her case was pending, the Sandinista government was defeated; the INS (D) took administrative notice of the change of government and concluded that the threat to P no longer existed. Notice was not given to P of the decision not to grant asylum, and she was not allowed to present evidence that a threat might still exist and asylum may be justified.

2)   Issue. Because D did not afford P the opportunity to present evidence that the threat to her may still exist, did the agency's decision violate her due process rights?

3)   Held. Yes.

a)   The Board of Immigration appeals should not have resolved the issue without giving notice and an opportunity for presentation of evidence.

b)   P does not argue with the administrative notice taken of the fact that the election had taken place or that Violetta Chamorra won the election. However, she argues that because the Sandinistas continue to control the police and the army, she still has a fear of reprisals (this fact was confirmed by a State Department report).

c)   The scope of notice in administrative hearings is broader than in trials, as it potentially impacts a larger group of people. The problem in this case is that P was denied a fair opportunity to rebut the proposition on which notice was taken, thus violating her due process rights. Such a rebuttal was unnecessary regarding facts (*e.g.,* election results), but was necessary for the issue in dispute, for which P had reasonable claim.

c.   Burden of proof--Director, Office of Workers' Compensation Programs v. Greenwich Collieries, 512 U.S. 267 (1994).

1)   Facts. The Department of Labor ("DOL") utilized a "true doubt" rule when examining benefits claims under the Black Lung Benefits Act and the Longshore and Harbor Workers' Compensation Act. This rule shifts the burden of persuasion to the party opposing the benefit claim; if the evidence is evenly balanced, the claimant wins.

2)   Issue. Because section 7(c) of the APA provides that the proponent of a rule or order has the burden of proof, does the use of the "true doubt" rule violate the APA?

3)   Held. Yes.

a)   The DOL may not allocate the burden of persuasion such that it conflicts with the APA.

b)   The case hinges on the meaning of "burden of proof" under the APA. When the APA was passed in the 1940s, the term meant the "obligation which rests on one of the parties to an action to persuade the trier of facts . . . of the truth of a proposition," thus analogous to the term "burden of persuasion." Thus, burden of persuasion as used by the DOL is the same as burden of proof under the APA. Even though Congress has recognized that benefits claimants often have problems with proof gathering and an agency may act to ease this burden, the "true doubt" rule is too extreme.

Armstrong v. Commodity Futures Trading Commission

d.   **Agency adoption of ALJ initial decision--Armstrong v. Commodity Futures Trading Commission,** 12 F.3d 401 (3d Cir. 1993).

1)   **Facts.** Armstrong (P) seeks review of the Commodity Futures Trading Commission's (D's) finding that he was the controlling person of a corporation in violation of the regulations and thus was individually liable. He argues that D did not comply with the APA, as D did not supply a "statement of . . . findings and conclusions, and the reasons or basis therefor."

2)   **Issue.** Because D did not "clearly" adopt the decision of the ALJ in P's proceeding, and did not include a separate statement of findings, conclusions, and reasonings, did it meet with APA standards?

3)   **Held.** No.

a)   The legislative rationale for including the requirement of specific reasoning for decisions was to prevent arbitrary decisions, establish a record for the Court, and give the parties an explanation. An agency does not need a specific statement if it "adopts" the decision of the ALJ. Here, D did not clearly adopt the ALJ decision, stating that it found the ALJ's decision "sufficiently correct," and noted that the ALJ's views did not equal D's views. The court noted that the agency "must leave no guesswork regarding what the agency has adopted."

e.   **Determining facts in administrative decisionmaking.** Administrative agencies are different from courts. These differences should be recognized in the procedures that are used for factfinding. For example, the agency factfinders are not jurors; the types of decisions that are being made are often different; administrative procedures may have to be more efficient to handle the workload; demeanor evidence and cross-examination may not be as relevant; basic investigation procedures may be more helpful than trial-type proceedings (*e.g.*, the chemical composition of a drug compound is best ascertained by a scientific test); etc. In summary, the best possible procedure may vary with different circumstances.

f.   **Investigation as a substitute for adversary process.**

1)   **Introduction.** Traditionally, courts have been inert—the lawyers in an adversary proceeding bring the evidence before the court, and the most convincing side wins. Administrative agencies do not necessarily follow this model. They investigate and research in an attempt to arrive at the best solutions. In this search, they use experts of all types. The issue is to

what extent an agency can accept and act on information it deems reliable, even though this information is not gathered in the conventional judicial manner and is not subjected to cross-examination.

2) **Requirements of review.** In *Hunter v. Zenith Dredge Co.*, 220 Minn. 318 (1945), the agency board found that an injury did not result from an accident. The board was required by statute to refer the issue of whether the employee had an "occupational disease" to a medical board whose findings were conclusive. The medical board did not have to make a formal record, and the employee did not appear before it or cross-examine its witnesses. The medical board held against the employee, the Commission affirmed, and the employee petitioned for review. The issue before the court was whether the medical board in a workmen's compensation case must expressly indicate the evidence on which it bases its findings. The court, reversing the agency determinations, held that it must, because due process requires that evidence on which an agency bases its findings be ascertainable; in no other way can guaranteed judicial review be carried out.

g. **Hearsay and other "incompetent" evidence.**

1) **Introduction.** The hearsay rule and other technical rules of evidence were developed for jury trials. Many criticize the unnecessary technicality of these rules even in the jury setting. In the nonjury setting (such as administrative agencies), there is even more criticism and support for a standard that evidence to support a finding should be the kind of evidence on which responsible persons are accustomed to rely in serious matters.

2) **The APA rule.** It is clear that hearsay (out-of-court statements offered to prove the truth of the matter being asserted in court) is admissible in administrative hearings as long as it is relevant. The APA provides, "Any oral or documentary evidence may be received, but the agency as a matter of policy shall provide for the exclusion of irrelevant, immaterial, or unduly repetitious evidence." [APA §556(d)]

3) **Reliance on hearsay evidence.** The real issue is whether a result can be based on hearsay evidence alone. Without some support from surrounding circumstances, a result probably cannot be based purely on hearsay. If there is some other minimum evidence to support the hearsay, this would be sufficient. Where the other evidence was consistent with the hearsay, the hearsay was not inconsistent with common knowledge, or the evidence (although technically hearsay) was still probative, then such evidence will also support an agency finding.

4) **The right to confront witnesses.**

   a) **Introduction.** One of the bases for the hearsay rule is that a party should have the right to confront and cross-examine the witnesses against him. The idea of relying on hearsay evidence for a decision is related to the issue of whether a result is permissible where a party had no opportunity to confront the witnesses giving evidence against him.

b) General rule. In situations where the credibility of the witnesses is a major factor, a result based purely on hearsay should not be allowed. Where credibility of the witnesses is not an issue, however, a result may be based on hearsay (or hearsay plus some residuum of other evidence).

5) Use of hearsay testimony.

a) Liberal rules. The technical rules of evidence (including in particular the hearsay rule and its multitude of exceptions) are generally inapplicable in administrative proceedings.

b) Legal residuum. Under the rule of *Carroll v. Knickerbocker Ice Co.*, 113 N.E. 507 (N.Y. 1916), agency findings are insufficient unless supported by a residuum of evidence beyond mere hearsay. Many states follow this rule.

Richardson
v. Perales

c) Substantial evidence--Richardson v. Perales, 402 U.S. 389 (1971).

(1) Facts. Perales (P) claimed that he became disabled when he injured his back while lifting an object at work, and filed a claim for disability insurance with Richardson (D). D had several doctors review P's condition and D sought to introduce their reports at the hearing. The reports were admitted into evidence.

(2) Issue. Do written reports of medical examiners constitute substantial evidence to support a finding of nondisability when contradicted by evidence from live witnesses?

(3) Held. Yes.

(a) Substantial evidence is "more than a mere scintilla. It means such relevant evidence as a reasonable mind might accept as adequate to support a conclusion."

(b) The administrative burden on agencies like the Social Security Administration is severe. The cost to provide live medical testimony in each of the several thousand proceedings would significantly deplete the resources required to satisfy the needs of the truly needy.

(c) Truthfulness and veracity are not at issue here. The doctors conclusions can adequately be assessed on the basis of the written record.

(d) P did not exercise his right to subpoena the doctors and thereby avail himself of the opportunity to cross-examine them. If P had genuinely wanted to challenge their testimony, he should have insisted on the presence of the doctors at the hearing.

h. The use or misuse of official notice.

1) **Introduction.** Administrative agencies have greater discretion in taking notice of factual matters than do courts. But there are limitations to this discretion.

2) **Opportunity to contradict official notice.**

   a) **Facts not supported by evidence.** APA section 556(e) provides that "[w]hen an agency decision rests on official notice of material fact not appearing in the evidence in the record, a party is entitled, on timely request, to an opportunity to show the contrary."

   b) **Possible reversal.** Accordingly, if no opportunity to dispute the facts which are officially noticed is given, there is a substantial chance that the agency's decision will be reversed, particularly if the noticed facts are adjudicative in nature, are disputable, and are critical to the outcome of the agency's decision.

   c) **Exclusive record for decision.** In formal proceedings, the transcript of the hearing testimony and all of the exhibits, together with all of the papers filed in the proceedings, constitutes the exclusive record. [5 U.S.C. §556(e)] Hence, agency decisions utilizing formal procedures must be based on the record.

   d) **Official notice.** However, an agency may take official notice of matters of common knowledge not within the record, *i.e.,* facts that are commonly known or that can be referred to by administrative agencies. Ordinarily, such facts must be set forth in the record in formal rulemaking or adjudication, and opposing parties must be given an opportunity to rebut them. [5 U.S.C. §556(e)]

   e) **Illustration: price trends--Ohio Bell Telephone Co. v. Public Utilities Commission of Ohio,** 301 U.S. 292 (1937).

   Ohio Bell Telephone Co. v. Public Utilities Commission of Ohio

      (1) **Facts.** The Public Utilities Commission of Ohio (D) set rates for Ohio Bell Telephone Company (P) on the basis of a valuation adjusted by price trends of which it took official notice, but did not put into the record.

      (2) **Issue.** May the agency rely on information not placed in the record?

      (3) **Held.** No.

         (a) By relying on information secretly collected and not disclosed to P, a fair hearing was not provided. This is condemnation without a trial.

         (b) We cannot discern whether D's conclusions were supported by the evidence.

i. **Determining facts of a general nature.**

   1) **Introduction.** An issue exists as to whether an agency may use statistical data that has been published or is gathered in regard to an agency matter

without the person compiling the report or developing the statistical data coming before the agency to be cross-examined.

2) **General rule.** The general rule seems to be that courts look at the practical side of things and decide whether it is feasible for an agency to admit evidence of a statistical nature only in cases where the compiler is available for cross-examination. For example, the court in *In re New England Power Corp.*, 103 Vt. 453 (1931), permitted the ratemaking agency to use evidence concerning assets that had been compiled by a number of employees not before the court. Also, in *Opp Cotton Mills v. Administrator of Wage & Hour Division*, 312 U.S. 126 (1941), the Court allowed the agency to rely on statistics from the Bureau of Labor in settling a minimum wage question.

2. **Informal Rulemaking as a Sui Generis Administrative Procedure.**

American Medical Association v. United States

a. **Notice--American Medical Association v. United States,** 887 F.2d 760 (7th Cir. 1989).

1) **Facts.** The American Medical Association (P) publishes journals in furtherance of its charitable mission. The collection of subscription fees for these journals does not present a taxable revenue problem. However, these journals also contain advertisements unrelated to P's mission, creating potentially taxable income. The IRS (D) came up with several factors and formula variations to determine what income would be taxable in situations like P's. P believed that one of the factors would allow it to avoid any allocation of dues revenues to its publications income. D, in its final decision, held that some of these dues revenues would be taxable income. P argues that D gave inadequate public notice of its final intent in the Notice of Proposed Rulemaking ("NPR") under the APA, which requires an agency to include within an NPR "either the terms or substance of the proposed rule or a description of the subjects and issues involved."

2) **Issue.** Did D give P adequate notice within the NPR?

3) **Held.** Yes.

a) Notice is sufficient under the APA if the issues to be addressed by the rule are given with clarity and specificity. The notice need not identify each proposal that the agency might ultimately adopt. Rather, the final rule is valid if it is a "natural out-growth" of the proposal.

b) An agency can change course as to how to implement a final rule as long as its actions are consistent with the original pro-posal. The main issue in this case is whether P was notified that its interests were at stake based on the NPR, thus giving P an opportunity to have say in the final rule. Such notice existed and D's final rule was a natural outgrowth of the NPR. The final rule merely eliminated some of the alternative calculation methods discussed in the NPR. P, however, knew that there was a possibility of including dues in taxable revenue.

c)   An agency "is not straitjacketed into the approach initially suggested on pain of triggering a further round of notice-and-comment," as long as the public is given a fair opportunity to respond to the agency's proposals.

b.   Inadequate notice--National Black Media Coalition v. FCC, 791 F.2d 1016 (2d Cir. 1986).

1)   **Facts.** When several AM foreign clear channels became available, the FCC (D) put out notice stating that it intended to use same technical and nontechnical (*e.g.,* establish outlets in unserved areas, consider minority ownership preferences, add noncommercial stations) criteria in determining who would get the licenses. In the notice, D invited other alternate proposals to be set forth and allowed commentary. National Black Media Coalition (P) applauded D's use of the nontechnical criteria. In its final order, however, D abandoned the nontechnical criteria, reasoning that since studies showed most of the new frequencies could only be used in unserved areas, the nontechnical criteria were unnecessary.

2)   **Issue.** Because D did not give proper notice of its decision to stop using nontechnical criteria such as minority ownership in awarding the AM foreign clear channels, and because it did not disclose its studies on which the final report was based to the public for comment, did D's actions violate the notice provisions of the APA?

3)   **Held.** Yes.

a)   Under section 4(b)(3) of the APA, an agency must give sufficient notice of a proposed rule and must allow for commentary by interested parties.

b)   The rationale for this requirement is that it promotes fairness, improves the quality of rulemaking, and establishes a record for judicial review.

c)   The final rule must be a logical outgrowth of the proposed rule.

d)   Here, the notice was inadequate, as it did not give interested parties an opportunity to respond, both to the change in course and to the evidence upon which the FCC based its final rule.

e)   The FCC did not comply with the APA's notice provisions, and its policy was thus arbitrary and capricious.

c.   Basis for decision--FCC v. National Citizens Committee for Broadcasting, 436 U.S. 775 (1978).

1)   **Facts.** The FCC (D) adopted cross-ownership rules that prohibited the transfer or ownership of radio or TV licenses to newspaper owners within the same community. However, to insure continued stability of service and continued local ownership, it only ordered divestiture of the 16 most "egregious" cases (*i.e.,* where the sole newspaper owner in a community was also the sole radio or TV license owner). The remaining existing combinations were "grandfathered" into law.

2) **Issue.** Because D regularly approves transfers and assignments of licenses, and because it did not base its divestiture actions on solid facts, was its decision "arbitrary and capricious"?

3) **Held.** No.

   a) A sweeping divestiture would not benefit the public welfare, which is the principal mandate of D. Such a divestiture would threaten the stability of current broadcast services and could lead to a decrease in local ownership.

   b) As to the forced divestiture of the 16 most egregious cases, diversification of ownership furthers statutory (FCC Act) and constitutional (free speech) goals. D has been granted the power to balance the public interest in meeting these goals. The fact that D did not have "hard" factual support for its conclusion regarding the egregious cases does not make this policy arbitrary; its actions can be based on forecasts. Finally, diversification was particularly necessary in the cases that D proscribed, as these were monopolistic situations; the "line drawing" was both essential and rational.

d. **The development of hybrid rulemaking procedures.** Prior to *Vermont Yankee, supra,* many courts insisted that agencies promulgate their rules via "hybrid" procedures—less than the formal trial-type procedures for 5 U.S.C. sections 556 and 557, but more than the informal notice-and-comment procedures of 5 U.S.C. section 553.

   1) **Judicial transformation of section 553 procedures.**

United States v. Nova Scotia Food Products Corp.

   a) **Adequate record and opinion--United States v. Nova Scotia Food Products Corp.,** 568 F.2d 240 (2d Cir. 1977).

      (1) **Facts.** The FDA (P) promulgated safety regulations under 5 U.S.C. section 553 governing the smoking of fish to avoid botulism. P sued to enjoin Nova Scotia Food Products Corporation (D) from processing whitefish in violation of the regulations. D contended that P had an inadequate administrative record upon which judicial review could be made, had failed to disclose the information upon which it relied, and had presented an inadequate "concise general statement."

      (2) **Issue.** Was P's procedure inadequate because it failed to disclose the scientific data and methodology upon which it predicated the rules and because it failed to address the question of commercial feasibility?

      (3) **Held.** Yes. Agency decision reversed.

         (a) The requirement of a record in informal rulemaking is principally imposed to facilitate judicial review. Even when review is based on the "arbitrary and capricious" standard, judicial review must be based on the "whole record."

    (b)   D was not apprised of the scientific data upon which the agency relied. Hence, D was denied the benefit of criticism thereof. Although in informal rulemaking the agency may go beyond the record, "when the pertinent research material is readily available and the agency has no special expertise on the precise parameters involved, there is [no] reason to conceal the scientific data relied upon from the interested parties." The agency must consider all relevant factors, including analysis critical of its data and methodology.

    (c)   P's opinion left important questions posed by D completely unanswered. While an agency in informal rulemaking need not address every fact or opinion raised, it must prepare a "concise general statement" that will enable a reviewing court to assess what major policy issues were before the agency and why the agency selected the conclusions it did. To allow P to address so inadequately the salient issues would be to sanction arbitrary decision-making.

  b) **The judicial development of "paper hearing" procedures.** Many courts have insisted that agencies in informal rulemaking prepare a documentary "paper hearing" for purposes of judicial review. They have also insisted that in preparing its "concise general statement," the agency must address the relevant issues of fact and policy. Otherwise, the agency will be deemed to have acted in a manner "arbitrary and capricious." Frequently, this pragmatically imposes a requirement that agencies publish successive rounds of Federal Register notices, each of which address the comments of the last.

e. **Inadequate notice of rulemaking--Independent U.S. Tanker Owners Committee v. Dole,** 809 F.2d 847 (D.C. Cir. 1987), *cert. denied*, 484 U.S. 819 (1987).

  1) **Facts.** Under the Jones Act, domestic maritime shippers are protected from competition by those fleets which operate on foreign routes and receive government subsidies for construction costs. Due to increased demand due to the opening of the Alaskan pipeline, some of these subsidized fleets were given permission to operate on domestic routes "for up to six months in a given year." At issue in this case was a ruling by the Department of Transportation which would allow a subsidized shipper to partake in domestic shipping if it repaid its subsidy plus interest.

  2) **Issue.** Was the Secretary of Transportation's (D's) decision to allow such action arbitrary and capricious, as she failed to show how the new rule would meet the objectives of the 1936 Merchant Marine Act?

  3) **Held.** Yes. Judgment reversed.

Independent
U.S. Tanker
Owners Committee v. Dole

	a) D failed to present a "sufficiently reasoned discussion" of the reasons for adopting the rule, and why alternatives were rejected in light of the Merchant Marine Act.

       b) Under the APA, an agency must provide adequate notice as to why it is taking the course of action. This notice "need not be an exhaustive, detailed account of every aspect of the rulemaking proceedings . . . [but] should indicate the major issues of policy that were raised in the proceedings," and must contain an explanation as to why the agency took the action it did. In this case, D failed to explain how the new policy was linked to the mission of the original Act under which she took action.

3.   **The Possible Requirement of More Formal Rulemaking Procedures.**

    a.   **Formal "on-the-record" rulemaking.** Courts will not ordinarily construe the agency's statutory language identifying procedural obligations for rulemaking as essentially synonymous with the "on the record" language of section 553(c), thereby triggering the formal procedures expressed in sections 556 and 557.

United States
v. Florida
East Coast
Railway Co.

    1)   **Illustration--United States v. Florida East Coast Railway Co.,** 410 U.S. 224 (1973).

        a)   **Facts.** The ICC (D) promulgated "incentive per diem" rules designed to provide an economic incentive for railroads promptly to return boxcars to their owners. The procedures employed by the agency somewhat exceeded those specified in 5 U.S.C. section 553 for informal rulemaking, but were somewhat less than the formal rulemaking procedures identified in sections 556 and 557. Various railroads (Ps) challenged the rules on grounds that formal procedures should have been utilized.

        b)   **Statute.** The Interstate Commerce Act provides that the ICC "may, after hearing," inter alia, promulgate various rules affecting rail transportation, including use of boxcars. [9 U.S.C. §1(14)(a)]

        c)   **Issue.** Is the "after hearing" language of the Interstate Commerce Act essentially synonymous with the "on the record" language of section 553(c), so as to require the full panoply of formal, trial-type procedures specified in sections 556 and 557?

        d)   **Held.** No. Judgment affirmed.

            (1) The words "on the record" of section 553(c) are not words of art; often statutory language having the same meaning could trigger the provisions of sections 556 and 557 in rulemaking proceedings.

            (2) Moreover, the APA neither limits nor repeals procedural requirements additional to those specified in the APA, such as those imposed by the "after hearing" language at issue here. [5 U.S.C. §559]

(3) But the meaning of a term such as "hearing" will vary depending upon whether it is found in the context of statutory provisions involving adjudication or rulemaking. If the former, it is more likely that formal procedures will be required. If the latter, it is a rare case in which formal procedures will be mandated.

(4) Even the modest procedural hurdles of section 553 do not apply to "interpretive rules, general statements of policy" or procedural rules, or "when the agency for good cause finds . . . that notice and public procedure thereon are impracticable, unnecessary, or contrary to the public interest." [5 U.S.C. §553]

(5) Even if sections 556 and 557 are triggered because the rulemaking statute is interpreted to require section 553(c) "on the record" procedures, nevertheless, section 556(d) allows the submission of the evidence in written form if the parties will not be "prejudiced thereby."

e) **Comment.** Although at least 15 federal statutes use the specific language "on the record" when describing the procedures to be utilized for rulemaking (thereby triggering sections 556 and 557), most do not. Nevertheless, courts do occasionally conclude that other statutory language is essentially synonymous with the "on the record" requirement.

2) **What process is due?--Harry & Bryant Co. v. FTC,** 726 F.2d 993 (4th Cir. 1984).

Harry & Bryant Co. v. FTC

a) **Facts.** In 1972, the FTC (D) began investigating national funeral practices. It published an NPR in 1976 and held hearings for a proposed rule to place controls on the industry. Extensive hearings were held and rebuttal submissions were invited. After this process, D published a finding that existing funeral practices were often unfair and deceptive to consumers. In 1980, a revised rule was published for comment, and in 1981, a final rule was issued. The rule defined unfair practices in the funeral industry and established preventative requirements, based on facts including: the requirement of purchase of "pre-packaged" funerals which included more than buyers might otherwise buy; misrepresentation; and unauthorized embalming. The preventative requirements included providing itemized services and price lists, requiring permission before embalming, and not requiring a casket in cases of cremation. Harry & Bryant Company (P) sought review of the rule.

b) **Issue.** Was D's ruling constitutionally infirm because, as P claimed, it violated P's due process rights, was based on insubstantial evidence, and violated First Amendment rights?

c) **Held.** No.

(1) P claims that by limiting the number of witnesses allowed to testify during hearings, due process was violated. However, there is no guarantee that every interested party will be afforded an opportunity to testify. An agency is allowed to restrict such hearings to insure that hearings are orderly. Furthermore, there is no right to cross examine every comment in the rulemaking record. Finally, it is

within D's statutory duty to establish rules that define unfair practices and establish preventative measures to halt these practices.

(2) There was substantial evidence on the record to support the rule.

(3) The requirement of an itemized price list does not violate commercial free speech protection under the First Amendment.

4. The Permissibility of Less Formal Adjudicatory Procedures.

a. Less formal adjudication.

1) **Use of agency experts--Seacoast Anti-Pollution League v. Costle,** 572 F.2d 872 (1st Cir. 1978), *cert. denied*, 439 U.S. 824 (1978).

a) **Facts.** The EPA held a hearing following APA procedures to determine whether to authorize the construction of a particular nuclear power plant. The EPA administrator was required to review the regional administrator's initial decision in which the regional administrator had found, among other things, that the Public Service Company of New Hampshire ("PSCO"), the seeker of the construction permit, had failed to furnish enough data on species' thermal tolerances. To assist him in his review, the administrator made use of a panel of EPA scientists who independently studied the problem and submitted their own findings and recommendations to him. Based solely on the panel's recommendation, the administrator reversed the regional administrator's decision by finding, among other things, that the "local indigenous populations will not be significantly affected" by the construction of the nuclear power plant. The Seacoast Anti-Pollution League (P) contended that the administrator's decision should be reversed because he should not have sought the help of the scientific panel at all and because the panel's report included information not in the administrative record. Appeal is to the circuit court.

b) **Issues.**

(1) May an agency administrator in a proceeding under the APA make use of a panel of scientists to assist him in reviewing a regional administrator's decision?

(2) May an agency administrator in a proceeding governed by APA section 556(e) base his decision on evidence not in the record?

c) **Held.** (1) Yes. (2) No. Decision reversed and remanded.

(1) An agency administrator charged with making highly technical decisions in fields far beyond his individual

expertise may rely upon agency experts to help him sift and analyze the evidence properly before the administrator.

(2) However, APA section 556(e) provides, "[t]he transcript of testimony and exhibits, together with all papers and requests filed in the proceeding, constitute the exclusive record for decision." Thus, to the extent a technical review panel's report includes information not in the record on which the administrator relies, section 556(e) is violated.

(3) The administrator did not err in merely relying on the EPA scientific panel to help him sift and analyze the evidence properly before him. However, to the extent the technical review panel's report included information not in the record on which the administrator relied, section 556(e) was violated. Since the regional administrator found that the PSCO had failed to supply enough data on the species' thermal tolerances, since nowhere in the hearing record is the requisite data supplied by any party, and since the only source of any data or information regarding species' thermal tolerances is supplied by the EPA scientific panel outside of the hearing, APA section 556(e) has been violated and the decision must be reversed and the cause remanded to the administrator. The administrator will have the options of trying to reach a new declaration not dependent on the panel's supplementation of the record; holding a hearing at which all parties will have the opportunity to cross-examine the panel members and at which the panel "will have an opportunity to amplify its position; or taking any other action within his power and consistent with this opinion."

d) **Comment.** In adjudicatory hearings, an agency must base its decision only on the evidence in the record. Rulemaking differs in that the agency may consider some off-the-record evidence as well as considering all of the on-the-record evidence.

2) **Informal hearing--Chemical Waste Management, Inc. v. EPA,** 873 F.2d 1477 (D.C. Cir. 1989).

a) **Facts.** The Resource Conservation and Recovery Act ("RCRA") established a "comprehensive program for the regulation of hazardous waste management and disposal." In order to operate a hazardous waste facility, a firm must get a permit; facilities in use as of 1980 can continue to operate as "interim facilities" pending review of their applications. RCRA also allows the EPA (D) to assess penalties for violations and hold public hearings (formal adjudicatory procedures) if there is a penalty assessed. In 1984, RCRA was amended (section h) to allow D to issue corrective orders if it finds that an interim facility is releasing hazardous waste. Under the amendment, a formal adjudicatory procedure is allowed only if D's order is a suspension, a revocation of interim status, or involves the imposition of civil penalties. If D's order is for the firm to take corrective action, D relies on informal adjudicatory procedure. Under this informal procedure, a facility may submit a written statement and may make an oral statement at the hearing; no cross- or direct-examination by the facility is allowed. Chemical Waste Management, Inc. (P) sought review of the amendment.

b) **Issue.** Do the informal hearing procedures outlined in the 1984 amendment to RCRA reflect a reasonable interpretation of the statutory mandate, consistent with due process?

c) **Held.** Yes. Petition for review denied.

(1) P makes three arguments to contend that the EPA must rely on formal hearings in all section h proceedings: (i) that the language in the original statute requires formal adjudication in all proceedings, (ii) that the legislative history shows that formal adjudication was intended, and (iii) that when Congress uses the term "hearing," it means "formal adjudication." Under *Chevron*, the standard for judicial review of an agency interpretation is whether "Congress has directly spoken to the . . . issue." If not, then the Court must determine if the agency's interpretation is within its "permissible construction."

(2) In this case, Congress did not speak to the issue involved. As to P's first argument, the use of the term "public hearing" does not define what type of adjudication was necessary. As to the second, the legislative history relied upon is ambiguous. Finally, as to the third argument, it is up to the agency to resolve ambiguity in the use of the term "hearing." As to whether D's interpretation was reasonable, D's rationale for a less formal proceeding in these cases will involve fewer issues of fact, and the issues that do arise will mostly concern technical matters, making the use of witnesses unnecessary. D's rationale is a reasonable basis for its interpretation.

Independent U.S. Tanker Owners Committee v. Lewis

3) **Review of findings and reasons in informal adjudication--Independent U.S. Tanker Owners Committee v. Lewis,** 690 F.2d 908 (D.C. Cir. 1982).

a) **Facts.** The United States merchant marine fleet is divided into two distinct segments: (i) the "Jones Act" fleet, owned and operated by United States citizens, which is given the exclusive right to engage in domestic trade and is not subsidized; and (ii) United States carriers engaged in foreign trade, who are heavily subsidized by the government on the condition that the carriers will operate only in foreign trade. However, the relevant statute provided that the Maritime Administration ("MarAd") could consent to the operation of a subsidized vessel in the domestic trade for up to six months in any 12-month period whenever it determined that such "transfer is necessary or appropriate to carry out the purposes of this chapter," and proportional repayment of the subsidy is required whenever such consent is granted. When the world tanker market virtually collapsed in the 1970s, there was persistent pressure from subsidized vessels for permission to enter the domestic market on a permanent basis in exchange for a total repayment of any construction subsidies received. MarAd granted a series of requests for repayment and permission to engage in domestic trade, moving competitors to bring suit challenging MarAd's authority to do so. After it was determined that MarAd did indeed have the power, MarAd published an interim rule stating that applications for repayment and permission to enter the domestic trade would be granted in "exceptional circumstances." Once MarAd approved such an application, its action was challenged by Independent U.S. Tanker Owners Committee (P).

b) **Issue.** Are an agency's findings and reasons in informal adjudication subject to review for proper procedures?

c) **Held.** Yes. Decision reversed.

(1) The distinct and steady trend of the courts has been to demand in informal adjudications procedures similar to those already required in informal rulemaking (namely, the requirements of notice, an opportunity to comment, and a concise general statement of basis and purpose). We are justified in demanding some sort of procedures for notice, comment, and a statement of reasons as a necessary means of carrying out our responsibility for a thorough and searching review.

d) **Comment.** The interim rule adopted by MarAd stated the procedures for considering applications in terms precisely matching those required for informal adjudications. The court simply found that MarAd's publishing its decision without explanation violated standards of fairness and due process in administrative law.

5. **The Permissibility of Yet-More-Informal Rulemaking--Pacific Gas & Electric Co. v. Federal Power Commission,** 506 F.2d 33 (D.C. Cir. 1974).

Pacific Gas & Electric Co. v. Federal Power Commission

a. **Facts.** Natural gas pipeline companies had contracts to supply natural gas to Pacific Gas & Electric Company (P) and other customers. Natural gas shortages required curtailment of deliveries. The Natural Gas Act, section 4, rendered unlawful curtailment plans that were preferential, discriminatory, unreasonable, or unfair and provided for a hearing concerning the lawfulness of newly filed curtailment plans. The Federal Power Commission (D) issued Order No. 467, which set forth a "statement of policy" that provided that curtailment priorities were to be based on use rather than contracts and that "full curtailment of the lower-priority volumes be accomplished before curtailment of any higher-priority volumes is commenced." The order also provided that "[p]roposed tariff sheets which conform to the policies expressed in [the Order] will be accepted for filing, and permitted to become effective, subject to the rights of intervenors to a hearing and adjudication of any claim of preference, discrimination, unjustness, or unreasonableness of the provisions contained in the proposed tariff sheets." P and other customers sought judicial invalidation of the order on the grounds that it constituted a substantive rule, lacking validity because of D's failure to issue it in compliance with the procedural requirements of APA section 553.

b. **Issue.** Must an agency comply with APA section 553 when issuing a policy statement?

c. **Held.** No.

1) An agency need not comply with APA section 553 when issuing a policy statement, although it must when issuing a substantive rule. Otherwise, such substantive rules would be invalid. A policy is distinguishable from a substantive rule in that a policy (i) is not

finally determinative of the issues and/or rights addressed, (ii) is a pronouncement of tentative intentions for the future, (iii) must be supported as if the policy had never been issued, (iv) is subject to complete attack before its application in future cases, and (v) is subject to a broader scope of judicial review.

2) P claims that Order No. 467 has an immediate and significant practical effect by shifting the burden of proof in curtailment cases from the pipeline companies (which must bear it under section 4 of the Natural Gas Act) to their customers because the Order "established a presumption that the curtailment rules prescribed in the Order are consistent with the Natural Gas Act in any and all situations." P claims that by stating that tariffs which conform to the proposed plan will become effective, the Order relieves the pipeline companies of their burden of justifying their plans, and that this change is in the nature of a substantive rule intended to have the force of law. But the argument that an agency must follow rulemaking procedures when it undertakes to formulate policy by a substantive rule is inapplicable here, because the Order does not establish a substantive rule. While D could engage in rulemaking to establish a binding rule, D can and apparently intends to establish its curtailment policies by proceeding through individual adjudications. The Order merely announces the general policy which D hopes to establish in subsequent proceedings. The Order itself provides that all curtailment plans submitted will be subject to the rights of intervenors to a hearing and adjudication of any claim in section 4 hearings. D has processed curtailment plans under section 4 in the past and we expect it to continue processing curtailment plans in section 4 proceedings, in which the pipeline company has the burden of proof and to refrain from treating Order No. 467 as anything more than a general statement of policy. We conclude that Order No. 467 is a general statement of policy and D did not err in not complying with APA section 553.

d. **Comment.** While this case clearly indicates that APA section 553 requirements do not apply to agency establishments of policy, the reader should be aware that what the agency calls "policy" may be a "rule," a rule may actually be policy, or an agency may attempt to apply what was mere policy as though it were a rule. Thus, the reader must look behind labels, carefully analyze the procedures used by the agency to create what it calls rule or policy, observe how the agency is implementing its rule or policy, and uphold or invalidate the agency action depending on conclusions drawn from such analysis. Note, too, that agencies can establish standards of conduct for regulatees by the process of adjudication as well as by rulemaking.

D. AGENCY DISCRETION IN CHOOSING BETWEEN RULEMAKING AND ADJUDICATION

1. The Extent, and Implications, of the Power to Choose Policymaking Mode.

a. **Introduction.** An agency can set forth its policy by making rules having prospective application or through individual orders on a case-by-case basis.

b. **Discretion in the agency.** The Supreme Court has held that, although rule-making has the advantage of regulating prospectively, an agency may nevertheless proceed on a case-by-case basis (unless it abuses its discretion).

c. **The *Chenery* litigation.** The *Chenery* litigation arose under the Public Utility Holding Company Act of 1935, which gave the Securities and Exchange Commission ("SEC") rather broad powers to reorganize the public utility conglomerates assembled by entrepreneurs in the 1920s. Section 7 of the Act allowed the SEC to approve a new securities issuance in a corporate reorganization, unless it concluded that "the terms and conditions of the issue or sale of the security are detrimental to the public interest or the interest of investors or consumers." Section 11 allowed the SEC to approve a plan of reorganization that it deems to be "fair and equitable to the persons affected by such plan."

d. **Decision must be rationally based--SEC v. Chenery Corp. (I),** 318 U.S. 80 (1943).

SEC v. Chenery Corp. (I)

    1) **Facts.** The Chenerys (Ds) were officers, directors, and controlling directors of a public utility holding company ("Federal"). During the course of Federal's reorganization, Ds purchased over 12,000 shares of Federal's common stock, the exchange of which for common stock in the reorganized corporation would give them a controlling interest. The SEC (P) did not allege fraud or lack of disclosure but nevertheless found that Ds were fiduciaries and therefore were under a "duty of fair dealings" not to trade in Federal's securities during its reorganization. P stated that it was merely applying the "broad equitable principles enunciated" in prior cases.

    2) **Issue.** Does the agency's reliance on judicial precedent sustain its conclusion that Ds should be prohibited from trading stock during a corporate reorganization?

    3) **Held.** No.

        a) Existing judicial precedent does not sustain P's new policy. While an agency is not bound by existing common law in construing a statutory grant of authority, P did not rely on its "special administrative competence" in corporate reorganization but professed to rely on existing judicial precedent.

        b) "[B]efore transactions otherwise legal can be outlawed, they must fall under the ban of some standards of conduct prescribed by an agency of government authorized to prescribe such conduct—either the courts or Congress or an agency to which Congress has delegated its authority." The statute does not explicitly prohibit such purchases, P has not promulgated a rule prohibiting them, and there is no common law proscribing such conduct.

        c) An agency decision cannot be upheld unless it expresses a proper rationale. Here, the common law upon which P ostensibly predicates its new standard fails to support it. P has misconceived the law.

4) Dissent (Black, J.). Administrative agencies should be free to announce new policy on an ad hoc, case-by-case basis, and not be required to promulgate a general rule of prospective application.

Federal Water
Service Corp.

e. **On remand--Federal Water Service Corp.,** 18 S.E.C. 231 (1945).

1) **Facts.** *See* preceding case. On remand of *Chenery I*, the SEC explicitly disclaimed any reliance on the common law and instead predicated its decision on its accumulated experience in corporate reorganizations.

2) **Issue.** Is the proposed transaction inconsistent with the standards of sections 7 and 11 of the Act?

3) **Held.** Yes.

a) Those controlling a corporation during reorganization can direct its affairs in such a way as to increase or decrease the value of its stock. Thus, if they purchase its stock, they have both an opportunity and an incentive to maximize their profits. Even in the absence of evidence of abuse, when purchasing stock during a reorganization, management's personal interests are in conflict with those of other shareholders whose interests management has a fiduciary duty to protect.

b) The burden of proving that a stock purchase satisfies the "fair and equitable" requirements of section 11 rests with those in control.

c) All cases of first impression may have effects that are unforeseen or unforeseeable. We are not required to announce new policy only through the vehicle of rulemaking, for that would unduly constrict our flexibility. We may later determine that a rule is desirable, but that does not affect our duty to protect other investors in this proceeding.

SEC v.
Chenery
Corp. (II)

f. **Agency's reliance on its accumulated experience--SEC v. Chenery Corp. (II),** 332 U.S. 194 (1947).

1) **Facts.** *See* preceding case. On remand, the SEC has avoided relying on common law, which does not sustain its decision. It has instead "drawn heavily upon its accumulated experience in dealing with corporate reorganizations." It has also explained the rationale for its decision adequately, applying its informed expert judgment.

2) **Issue.** Does the SEC's reliance on its accumulated expertise sustain its order?

3) **Held.** Yes.

a) We refuse to hold that the announcement of new policy must always be accomplished prospectively through the promulgation of rules. While the vehicle of rulemaking should be employed as often as possible, we refuse to impose any rigid requirement that rulemaking must be employed.

b) "Not every principle essential to the effective administration of a statute can or should be cast immediately into the mold of a general rule." The agency must have flexibility to decide by ad hoc adjudication questions that it could not foresee, problems with which it had insufficient experience "to warrant rigidifying its tentative judgment into a hard and fast rule," or problems "so specialized or varying in nature as to be impossible of capture within the boundaries of a general rule."

    c)   An agency must have sufficient flexibility to announce new policy prospectively via rulemaking or retroactively through ad hoc adjudication, and the choice of which vehicle to employ lies principally within the informed discretion of the agency.

    d)   "Every case of first impression has a retroactive effect, whether the new principle is announced by a court or by an administrative agency. The adverse impact of such retroactivity must be weighed against the mischief of producing a result which is contrary to a statutory design or to legal and equitable principles." As long as the deleterious effects of retroactive application are outweighed by such mischief, there is no prohibition against the imposition of new or unexpected standards of behavior.

4) **Dissent** (Jackson, Frankfurter, JJ.). The SEC has essentially reexpressed its justification for the same result. The real reason the SEC is now upheld is the change in composition of the Court that has occurred since our earlier remand. The majority upholds the SEC on the basis of its accumulated expertise with a problem with which it has never before been confronted. No prior legislative, judicial, or agency pronouncement imposes the fiduciary standard to which the Chenerys are held.

g. **Pre-rulemaking procedures--Bell Aerospace Co. v. NLRB,** 475 F.2d 485 (2d Cir. 1973).

    Bell Aerospace Co. v. NLRB

    1) **Facts.** Bell Aerospace Company (D) refused to negotiate with buyers at one of its plants because it felt they were managerial employees and were not included in a collective bargaining agreement under the National Labor Relations Act ("NLRA"). Upon review, the NLRB (P) held that the buyers could unionize. The decision was controversial because it signaled a change in course within P, which had previously held all managerial employees excluded under the NLRA, and because P had always treated buyers as managerial. Under this new course, P held that only those managers whose duties with the employer would cause a conflict of interest if they were to unionize would be excluded.

    2) **Issue.** Can P alter its administration tradition to expand the groups allowed to unionize without following rulemaking procedures?

    3) **Held.** Petition for review granted.

        a)   P is precluded from reinterpreting the NLRA to exclude only some managerial employees, due to "congressional understanding of long-standing agency practice."

        b)   P is not precluded from determining that some buyers are not managerial employees as long as proper proceedings are utilized. In order to institute such a change, P must inform industry and labor organizations of the change and allow some commentary, and then it must make an "informed" decision, taking into account all available information, before engaging in rulemaking. Such procedure was absent in this case.

NLRB v. Bell Aerospace Co.

h. Agency discretion to proceed via rulemaking or adjudication--NLRB v. Bell Aerospace Co., 416 U.S. 267 (1974).

1) **Facts.** A union petitioned the NLRB (P) for an election to represent 25 buyers in the purchasing and procurement department of Bell Aerospace Company (D). D objected on grounds that the buyers were "managerial employees" and therefore not subject to the NLRA. P disagreed, and an election was held in which 15 of the buyers voted to affiliate with the union. Upon D's refusal to bargain with the union as certified, P found that D had engaged in unfair labor practices in violation of the NLRA. On appeal, the court of appeals denied enforcement, concluding that while P could overrule its existing precedent and find that "managerial employees" were within the purview of the NLRA, it could do so only by promulgating a rule.

2) **Issue.** Must an administrative agency utilize rulemaking as the means of defining important statutory terms in its enabling legislation before imposing new and unexpected liability upon industries subject to its jurisdiction?

3) **Held.** No. Judgment affirmed in part, reversed in part, and remanded.

a) Both *Chenery, supra,* and *NLRB v. Wyman-Gordon Co.,* 394 U.S. 759 (1969), make it clear that agencies are generally free to announce new policy either prospectively, via rulemaking, or retroactively, via adjudication. The decision as to which means are employed to announce new policy lies within the informed discretion of the administrative agency.

b) This flexibility is essential to guarantee that agencies are free to address problems as they arise and adjust the solutions as the agency gains experience.

c) Reliance by the parties on the NLRB's existing precedent does not mandate a different result. This is not a situation in which "some new liability is sought imposed on individuals for past actions which were taken in good faith reliance on Board pronouncements. Nor are fines or damages involved here."

2. Time Frame: Issues of Retroactivity and Prospectivity.

Bowen v. Georgetown University Hospital

a. Retroactivity of rules--Bowen v. Georgetown University Hospital, 488 U.S. 204 (1988).

1) **Facts.** Under the Medicare Act, the Secretary of Health and Human Services ("HHS") is authorized to establish reimbursement procedures to hospitals that provide care for Medicare recipients. In June

of 1981, the HHS developed a new schedule, which was struck down by the district court, as it did not provide notice and an opportunity for comment. The HHS reverted back to the old schedules, and began a notice process in 1984. Meanwhile, Congress amended the Act such that a new schedule was instituted in 1983 retroactively. The HHS issued a rule that for 1981 and 1982, it would apply the invalidated schedule retroactively. Georgetown University Hospital (P) challenged the agency action. The district court and the court of appeals held the retroactivity was unjustified. The supreme Court granted certiorari.

2) **Issue.** Because the Medicare Act does not contain express language allowing for HHS to apply rules retroactively, may HHS do so if there is justification for its actions?

3) **Held.** No. Judgment affirmed.

   a) Generally, retroactive application of rules is disfavored by the law. For retroactivity to be applied, the statute must expressly state that such action is allowable.

   b) In this case, there was no such express language. Part of the Act allows for retroactive application, but only in case-by-case adjudications, and not in rulemaking. The general rulemaking power of the HHS to establish cost limit rules contains no retroactivity provisions. Since Congress allowed for retroactivity expressly in part of the statute, HHS cannot even rely on implicit authorization vis-a-vis rulemaking.

b. **Retroactivity of new policy--Clark-Cowlitz Joint Operating Agency (CCJOA) v. Federal Energy Regulatory Commission (FERC),** 826 F.2d 1074 (D.C. Cir. 1987), *cert. denied*, 485 U.S. 913 (1988).

Clark-Cowlitz Joint Operating Agency (CCJOA) v. Federal Energy Regulatory Commission (FERC)

   1) **Facts.** CCJOA (P) formed to apply for a license to operate a power project, which was owned by a private utility whose license was about to expire. P sought the benefit of the "municipal preference" under the Federal Power Act, which gives preference to municipal agencies. In the *Bountiful* case, FERC (D) had held that this preference was applicable to all licensing proceedings. However, it reversed its holding, deciding that the preference was contrary to legislative intent. It thus held the preference inapplicable **unless** the incumbent licensee sought a preference for an existing project. D awarded the license to another group and P appealed. Congress then removed all municipal preferences by amendment.

   2) **Issue.** Because D applied a different standard regarding preferences in *Bountiful* than it did in the P licensing proceeding, did this action violate the principles of retroactivity?

   3) **Held.** No. This action was within the scope of D's powers.

      a) A retroactive application of a new interpretation may only be withheld if the application of the interpretation would "manifest injustice." In determining whether to allow an exception to the general rule allowing retroactive application, five factors must be examined, factors first enunciated in *Retail, Wholesale & Department Store Union v. NLRB*, 466 F.2d 380 (D.C. Cir. 1972):

(1) Is the issue one of first impression? Here, it is, thus favoring retroactive application.

(2) Is the new rule an "abrupt departure" from the established practice? Here, the need for reinterpretation by D is increased by the need to have congruence with congressional intent. Also, the prior practice by D was not an established practice.

(3) What is the degree of reliance by the party against whom the rule is applied to the old rule? Here, there was not much reliance, as the application was made prior to the *Bountiful* decision.

(4) How much of a burden does the retroactive rule impose on the party? Here, P lost its preference, but was still able to compete for a license, albeit on equal grounds.

(5) What is the statutory interest in applying the new rule? If D did not use the retroactive application, it would be giving a preference to a group which it feels does not deserve preference, and could obfuscate the public interest of insuring that the best service provider gets the license.

3. Impact of Statutory Rights to an Individualized Hearing.

Heckler v. Campbell

a. Awarding disability benefits--Heckler v. Campbell, 461 U.S. 458 (1983).

1) **Facts.** In 1978, the Secretary of Health and Human Services ("HHS") promulgated regulations defining "disability." Those persons falling within the definition of "disability" were eligible for disability payments. Particular medical-vocational guidelines were established to determine eligibility. These guidelines consisted of four factors: physical ability, age, education, and work experience. If work existed that a claimant could perform, the claimant was not eligible for benefits. In 1979, Campbell (P) applied for disability benefits. Her application was denied. She then had a hearing before an ALJ, who concluded that she was not disabled. The decision was upheld by the Social Security Appeals Council and the District Court for the Eastern District of New York. The Second Circuit reversed, and the Supreme Court granted certiorari.

2) **Issue.** May the Secretary of HHS rely on published medical-vocational guidelines to determine a claimant's right to Social Security disability benefits?

3) **Held.** Yes. Judgment reversed.

a) The Secretary's reliance on medical-vocational guidelines "is not inconsistent with the Social Security Act."

b) "The Court has recognized that even where an agency's enabling statute expressly requires it to hold a hearing, the agency may rely on its rulemaking authority to determine issues that do not require case-by-case consideration."

c) The regulations allow claimants an opportunity to present evidence of their own ability and to show that the guidelines do not apply to them.

d) When the accuracy of facts has been tested during the rulemaking process, sufficient procedural safeguards have been ensured.

4) Comment. Footnote 6 in *Heckler* discusses the "safety valve," which allows a claimant to show that the guidelines do not apply because they fail to describe that particular claimant's circumstances. In *FCC v. WNCN Listeners Guild*, 450 U.S. 582 (1981), the Court sustained a statute that allowed the FCC to approve an application or renewal of a license only if "the public interest, convenience, and necessity" will be served. Such policy statements would be determined by market forces rather than regulatory forces. Justices Marshall and Brennan, in dissent, felt that it was necessary to have the opportunity in certain cases to show that market forces would not work. The majority was unconcerned with the "safety valve." The Court has not required an agency to adopt a waiver requirement.

b. Transaction costs. Transaction costs are one of the primary reasons a complex, transparent grid system of guidelines is used (such as in the above case). There are also "hidden" transaction costs such as the human costs of deprivation of benefits through delay. Another "hidden" cost is that of decentralization. There is also inadequate control of decisionmakers—state agencies that make their own decisions. Tighter, more centralized controls are needed and use of a grid system is one response to that problem.

E. THE ROLE OF PRIVATE PARTIES IN SHAPING ADMINISTRATIVE PROCEEDINGS

1. Party Initiation of Formal Proceedings. The statute establishing an administrative agency will normally give that agency the power to bring administrative charges. The power will normally include prosecutorial discretion. The question becomes: "When is the prosecutorial discretion subject to judicial review?"

a. Type of proceedings. In criminal proceedings, the agency is typically given deference. The result may be different when civil proceedings are involved. In *Dunlop v. Bachowski*, 421 U.S. 560 (1975), the Court did not allow for an unreviewable exercise of prosecutorial discretion. "To begin with, we believe that the doctrine of prosecutorial discretion should be limited to those civil cases which, like criminal prosecutions, involve the vindication of societal or governmental interest, rather than the protection of individual rights." The Court went on to find that the "language and purpose of section 482 of the LMRDA indicate that Congress intended the Secretary to file suit." Justice Rehnquist dissented in the opinion. In *Heckler v. Chaney*, *infra*, the Court, in Justice Rehnquist's majority opinion, held that "an agency's decision not to prosecute or enforce, whether through civil or criminal process, is a decision generally committed to an agency's absolute discretion." The Court distinguished these two cases on the grounds that the language of the statute in *Dunlop* rebutted the presumption of unreviewability.

2. **Party Initiation of Rulemaking.** Rulemaking proceedings may be commanded by Congress. In *Pulido v. Heckler*, 758 F.2d 503 (10th Cir. 1985), the court held that the Secretary of the Department of Health and Human Services had a duty under the Social Security Act to promulgate detailed rules relating to reimbursement for travel expenses required to attend a hearing. The statute relating to that issue used the language "shall adopt," and the court held that such terminology was intended to be mandatory.

3. **Expansion of Public Participation.** Traditionally, only those directly affected by agency action were deemed eligible to participate in the agency's proceeding and to secure judicial review thereof. The focus during this period was on the judiciary's limitation of the coercive power of government. More recently, the rights of public interest individuals or groups have been expanded to include standing to participate in and appeal agency decisions. This interest representation model seeks to insure the equitable exercise of power by administrative agencies by requiring that a wider spectrum of interests be represented in agency proceedings.

4. **The Rationale of Expanded Standing to Obtain Judicial Review.** Modern courts have been very generous in allowing a wide spectrum of interests to be represented before administrative agencies, including those suffering technological interference, economic injury, consumer injury, and aesthetic or ecological injury. The issue of standing to intervene is related to the question of standing to appeal adverse agency action, discussed in the last chapter. In either case, one who suffers an adverse effect is ordinarily deemed to have standing.

Office of Communication of the United Church of Christ v. FCC

5. **Television Audience--Office of Communication of the United Church of Christ v. FCC,** 359 F.2d 994 (D.C. Cir. 1966).

   a. **Facts.** The FCC (D) granted an applicant's application for renewal of its television license, while denying a religious group's (P's) petition seeking to intervene to oppose the application on grounds of racist programming and excessive commercials.

   b. **Issue.** Do consumers have standing to intervene before an administrative agency in pending proceedings?

   c. **Held.** Yes. FCC decision reversed.

      1) Prior cases allowed standing to those who suffered electronic interference or economic injury.

      2) Standing is a practical and functional concept, which is designed to limit agency participation only to those with a legitimate interest.

Certainly, the viewing audience has an acute interest in television programming. Consumers are excellent vindicators of the public interest.

3) Although the agency need not allow *all* potential intervenors to participate, it must allow some audience participation in license renewal proceedings. But the agency should be given broad discretion to promulgate rules defining criteria governing who may participate, consonant with its needs for administrative economy and efficiency.

6. **Rights of Intervention and Participation in Agency Proceedings.** The right to intervene has gradually been expanded, so that it is today virtually coextensive with the right to seek judicial review, which itself has been construed liberally.

   a. **Illustration--National Welfare Rights Organization v. Finch,** 429 F.2d 725 (D.C. Cir. 1970).

   National Welfare Rights Organization v. Finch

      1) **Facts.** Finch, Secretary of Health, Education, and Welfare (D), threatened to cut off federal grants to Social Security for Nevada and Connecticut. Several welfare rights organizations (Ps) sought to intervene, and D denied them that opportunity.

      2) **Issue.** Should Ps have been granted the right to intervene in the agency's hearing?

      3) **Held.** Yes.

         a) The right to intervene in agency proceedings is closely related to standing to appeal agency actions. The case law on the two have been used interchangeably. Indeed, "the criteria for standing for review of agency action appear to assimilate the criteria for standing to intervene."

         b) Since D's findings of fact will be sustained if supported by substantial evidence, issues which Ps would like to raise would be foreclosed on review. Hence, Ps must be given an opportunity to intervene.

         c) We do not believe that hundreds of parties will seek intervention as a result of this precedent. The expense of participation will limit intervention. Moreover, the agencies have authority to reasonably limit participation.

7. **Discretion to Enforce--Heckler v. Chaney,** 470 U.S. 821 (1985).

   Heckler v. Chaney

   a. **Facts.** Several prisoners (Ps) sentenced to death by lethal injection of drugs under the laws of the states of Oklahoma and Texas petitioned the Food and Drug Administration (D), alleging that the use of the drugs for capital punishment violated the Federal Food, Drug, and Cosmetic Act ("FDCA"). Ps contended that the drugs used, although approved by D for the medicinal purposes stated on their labels, were not approved for use in human executions and thus were misbranded in violation of a statute requiring labels bearing adequate directions for drug use. Ps also suggested that the FDCA's requirements for approval of new drugs applied, since these drugs were now being used for a new purpose. Accordingly, Ps urged that D was required to approve the drugs as "safe and effective" for human executions before they could be distributed in interstate commerce. Ps therefore requested D to take the following enforcement actions to prevent these perceived violations of the Act: (i) affix warnings to the labels of all the drugs stating that they were unapproved and unsafe for human execution; (ii) send statements to the drug manufacturers and prison administrators stating that the drugs should not be so used; (iii) adopt procedures for seizing the drugs from state prisons; and (iv) recommend the prosecution of all those in the chain of distribution who knowingly distribute or purchase the drugs with the intent to use them for human execution. D declined, as a matter of enforcement discretion, to pursue supplies of drugs under state control that will be used for execution by lethal injection. Ps then filed suit in district court, which granted summary judgment for D. A divided panel of the circuit court reversed, and the Supreme Court granted certiorari.

b. **Issue.** May determinations by D not to exercise its enforcement authority over the use of drugs in interstate commerce be judicially reviewed?

c. **Held.** No. Judgment reversed.

1) An agency's decision not to exercise its authority to prosecute or enforce, whether through civil or criminal process, is a decision generally committed to an agency's absolute discretion. This recognition of the existence of discretion is attributable to the general unsuitability for judicial review of agency decisions to refuse enforcement. The decision is only presumptively unreviewable, however, and may be rebutted where the substantive statute has provided guidelines for the agency in exercising enforcement powers. The presumption that agency decisions not to institute proceedings are unreviewable under section 701(a)(2) of the APA is not overcome by the enforcement provisions of the FDCA. D's decision not to take the enforcement actions requested by Ps is therefore not subject to judicial review under the APA.

2) The reasons for this general unsuitability for judicial review are many. First, an agency decision not to enforce typically involves a complicated balancing of a number of factors that are peculiarly within its expertise. Accordingly, the agency must not only determine whether a violation has occurred, but also whether (i) agency resources are best spent on this violation or another, (ii) the agency is likely to succeed if it acts, (iii) the particular enforcement action requested best fits the agency's overall policies, and (iv) the agency has enough resources to undertake the action.

8. **Shift to Rulemaking.** The agencies' widespread adoption of rulemaking as a means of deciding substantive issues in the modern era was in part prompted by decisions that served as catalysts for public interest participation. Because notice-and-comment informal rulemaking procedures limited the rights of participation, the courts responded with ad hoc requirements that more process was due. But ultimately, *Vermont Yankee, supra,* checked the ability of the judiciary to impose procedures in excess of those required by statute.

9. **Refusal to Finalize Proposed Rules--Farmworker Justice Fund, Inc. v. Brock,** 811 F.2d 613 (D.C. Cir. 1987), *vacated as moot*, 817 F.2d 890 (D.C. Cir. 1987).

a. **Facts.** Under the Occupational Safety and Health Act ("OSHA"), the Secretary of Labor (D) is authorized to act to establish occupational health standards. In 1972, a 14-year battle to get D to issue an order providing sanitary drinking water and toilets for agricultural workers began. In October 1985, after going through a rulemaking process where it was established that such a regulation was necessary, D delayed federal action in the hopes that the states would take initiative and issue the regulations. According to D, state action is preferable in the area of social and welfare aid because the states' governments are more "competent" to deal with these issues, and the citizenry feel "more in touch" with state government. Farmworker Justice Fund, Inc. (P) challenged D's action as an abuse of discretion.

b. **Issue.** Can D, after completing rulemaking proceedings that show the need for an occupational health standard, refuse to act in the hope that state governments will fill the worker's needs?

c. **Held.** No.

    1) D exceeded the scope of his discretion in this action. First of all, Congress had already concluded in instituting OSHA that the federal government should lead in the area of occupational health. D must enforce this directive.

    2) D argued that the states would be able to reach more farms, as he was not authorized to regulate any with less than 10 workers. We "do not think [D] may gamble with the health and safety of those individuals whose welfare is entrusted to him by Congress in the hope that he can wield his influence over those individuals Congress has specifically placed beyond his legal jurisdiction."

    3) Finally, D may consider imminent state action in formulating decisions, but here, any reliance was "unreasonable."

IV. SCOPE OF REVIEW OF ADMINISTRATIVE ACTION

A. FRAMING THE DISCUSSION

1. **What the APA Provides.** Section 706 of the APA defines the judicial scope of review of administrative agency actions. A court may take any of the following actions:

   a. Compel agency action that has been unlawfully withheld or unreasonably delayed;

   b. Declare unlawful and set aside agency behavior that is:

      1) Arbitrary and capricious, an abuse of discretion, or otherwise not in accordance with the law;

      2) Unconstitutional;

      3) Ultra vires (beyond its statutory jurisdictional limits);

      4) Not in accordance with lawful procedures;

      5) A formal rulemaking or adjudication unsupported by substantial evidence; or

      6) Unwarranted by the facts if subject to a trial de novo.

2. **The Scope of Judicial Review—Questions of Law and Fact.**

   a. **Administrative expertise.** Despite the scope-of-review standard particular courts may articulate, one must recognize that some courts with congested dockets, when faced with an appeal of a complex agency decision, will defer to the administrative expertise that ostensibly exists over the subject matter of the dispute.

   b. **Substantial evidence rules.**

      1) **Origins.** The substantial evidence rule originated in the Supreme Court decision of *ICC v. Union Pacific Railroad*, 222 U.S. 541 (1912).

      2) **Definition.** "Substantial evidence" is more than a mere scintilla; it is such evidence as a reasonable mind might accept to support a conclusion. Mere uncorroborated hearsay or rumor is not substantial evidence. Substantial evidence is such evidence as would be sufficient to justify a refusal to direct a verdict, if the case were before a jury. [Universal Camera Corp. v. NLRB, *infra*]

      3) **APA.** The substantial evidence standard is now embraced in 5 U.S.C. section 706(2)(E). It applies to a review of formal rulemaking or formal adjudication, where the proceeding is subject to 5 U.S.C. sections 556 and 557 or is otherwise "on the record."

4) **The whole record.** In determining whether an agency decision is supported by substantial evidence, courts must evaluate the whole record in its entirety, not merely those portions on which the agency relied.

B. JUDICIAL REVIEW OF AGENCY FACTUAL DETERMINATIONS

1. **Substantial Evidence and Judicial Review--NLRB v. Universal Camera Corp. (I),** 179 F.2d 749 (2d Cir. 1950).

NLRB v. Universal Camera Corp. (I)

a. **Facts.** The NLRB (D) ordered an employee, Chairman, reinstated by his employer, Universal Camera Corporation (P). Reversing the hearing examiner's findings, D concluded that Chairman's discharge was precipitated by Chairman's adverse testimony at a NLRB hearing to determine who should be the representative of P's maintenance employees. P argued that Chairman was discharged for different reasons (*i.e.,* insubordination) having nothing to do with the unionization effort, and the hearing examiner agreed. P argued that new legislative amendments warranted a more stringent judicial review than previously available and that D's conclusion was not supported by substantial evidence.

b. **Issue.** Was D's decision supported by "substantial evidence"?

c. **Held.** Yes. D's decision affirmed.

1) The National Labor Relations Act ("NLRA") had been amended in 1947 to provide that NLRB findings "shall be conclusive . . . if supported by substantial evidence on the record considered as a whole." The requirement that the whole record be considered was included to reverse judicial conclusions that the agency's findings should be upheld "if any passage could be found in the testimony to support a finding . . . no matter how much other parts of the testimony contradicted or outweighed it."

2) The APA includes a similar provision. The APA also provides that on appeal from a decision of a hearing examiner, "the agency shall . . . have all the powers which it would have in making the initial decision." But it is silent as to what effect an agency must give the examiner's findings.

3) An agency need not accept an examiner's findings, for this would elevate the status of an examiner to that of a master. Although an agency would be wrong in failing to consider a hearing examiner's findings, the court will not consider it in reviewing the agency's final decision.

2. **More than a Mere Scintilla--Universal Camera Corp. v. NLRB,** 340 U.S. 474 (1951).

Universal Camera Corp. v. NLRB

a. **Facts.** *See* preceding case. Universal Camera Corporation (P) appeals the circuit court opinion above.

b. **Issue.** Must the reviewing court assess whether the NLRB's (D's) decision is supported by substantial evidence upon the record considered as a whole?

c. **Held.** Yes. Judgment reversed and remanded.

    1) The Wagner Act provides that "the findings of the Board as to the facts, if supported by evidence, shall be conclusive."

    2) The Wagner Act's reference to evidence means "substantial evidence." Substantial evidence is "more than a mere scintilla. It means such relevant evidence as a reasonable mind might accept as adequate to support a conclusion." It must be sufficient "to justify, if the trial went to a jury, a refusal to direct a verdict."

    3) The Attorney General's Committee issued a report in 1941 on the predecessor to the APA. Three members registered a dissent in which they argued against the traditional interpretation of the substantial evidence test. The prevailing view at that time was that the rule was satisfied if substantial evidence was found to exist anywhere in the record, irrespective of "how heavily the countervailing evidence may preponderate," so that courts could merely examine one side of the case; if substantial evidence existed there, contrary evidence could be ignored and the agency's decision could be sustained. Presumably responding to this criticism, the proposed language was subsequently amended to include the phrase "upon the whole record." Congress unanimously embraced this language when it promulgated the APA in 1946.

    4) Whether evidence is substantial must take into account whatever in the record "fairly detracts from its weight."

    5) The lower courts must assume more responsibility for the reasonableness and fairness of agency decisionmaking than they have in the past. They must keep the agencies within reasonable bounds. The agency's decisionmaking must be set aside when the evidence is not substantial when viewed on the whole record. The substantial evidence test is the standard of review to be applied by the court of appeals. The Supreme Court will intervene only where the standard has been misapprehended or grossly misapplied.

    6) Although a hearing examiner's findings should not be deemed conclusive by an agency, neither should they be ignored. And, for reviewing courts, an examiner's report is a part of the record to be considered in determining whether the agency's decision is supported by substantial evidence. "[E]vidence supporting a conclusion may be less substantial when an impartial, experienced examiner who has observed the witnesses and lived with the case has drawn conclusions different from the Board than when he has reached the same conclusion."

3. **On Remand,** *Universal Camera (II).*

a. **Judge Hand.** On remand in *NLRB v. Universal Camera Corp. (II)*, 190 F.2d 429 (2d Cir. 1951), Judge Learned Hand interpreted the Supreme Court's decision as requiring that the NLRB cannot overrule the hearing examiner's findings "without a very substantial preponderance of the evidence as recorded."

b. **Judge Frank.** Judge Frank felt that Judge Hand's interpretation went too far. He said that the Supreme Court merely reversed the Second Circuit because of its disregard of the hearing examiner's findings. It did not insist that the agency can only overrule the hearing examiner's evidentiary findings if based on credibility of testimony where they are "clearly erroneous." Judge Frank also drew a distinction between "testimonial inferences" or "primary inferences" (facts to which a credible witness testified) vis-a-vis "secondary inferences" or "derivative inferences" (facts to which there was no actual testimony, but inferences from testimony). The NLRB may reach its own secondary inferences, in the same way an appellate court can reach secondary inferences different from those of the trial court.

4. **Deference to Agency Findings--NLRB v. Curtin Matheson Scientific, Inc.,** 494 U.S. 775 (1990).

a. **Facts.** The NLRA obligates employers to negotiate with union workers in good faith. This obligation is terminated if the employer has a "good faith doubt" that the union has the support of a majority of the workers. For the first year after a union is formed, the NLRB creates an irrebuttable presumption that such doubt cannot arise. After one year, it is up to the employer to rebut the presumption. A teamsters union had formed at Curtin Matheson Scientific, Inc. (D) in 1970; in 1979, after a company lockout, the workers went on strike. D brought in non-union replacement workers, and soon refused to bargain with the workers due to a "good faith doubt" of union support, claiming that its replacement workers did not back the union and constituted a majority of its workers. The NLRB (P) instituted unfair labor proceedings. It held that D's evidence of lack of majority support for the union was insufficient. The Fifth Circuit reversed, and the Supreme Court granted certiorari.

b. **Issue.** Must P presume that replacement workers oppose the union in determining whether the employer has presented sufficient evidence of "good faith doubt" in the union?

c. **Held.** No. Judgment reversed.

1) P is the primary national actor regarding the establishment of labor policy. As long as P's decision is rational and consistent with the NLRA, the Court will uphold its decisions. To accept D's argument that the union has lost support due to lack of support by replacement workers is untenable. By disallowing such actions, P assures that objective evidence and not gross generalizations will form the basis of proof. P argues, and the Court agrees, that replacement workers may actually support the union, and that the union may not seek displacement of all replacement workers, depending on its relative bargaining position. Thus, D's generalization regarding hostility is unfounded.

2)   Also, since strike situations vary on a case-by-case basis, it would not be appropriate for P to conclude as a presumption that replacement workers are against the union. Finally, by rebutting D's argument, P is acting consistently with its mission to achieve "industrial peace," by ensuring good faith bargaining. If otherwise, an employer could chill workers' motivation to strike, as it would simply bring in enough replacement workers to establish "good faith doubt."

5.   **Principles of Judicial Review of Agency Factfinding.**

a.   **Middle course.** Judicial review of factual conclusions is essential as a means of checking agency abuse of discretion. Yet de novo review is impractical for the bulk of agency decisions. The substantial evidence standard exists as a compromise between total judicial deference and de novo review.

b.   **Clearly erroneous.** The "clearly erroneous" standard, which applies to appellate review of trial court findings, differs from the substantial evidence standard of review of administrative agency decisionmaking. The latter is a narrow standard of review, thereby permitting agencies greater discretion than that accorded trial courts. But the actual difference between them is difficult to articulate.

c.   **"Widows and orphans" issues.** The United States Supreme Court has struck down judicial review standards that require more evidence when the issue at stake is more important or sensitive.

d.   **Credibility of witnesses.** Courts usually defer to agency conclusions regarding witness credibility. But some judges have criticized the excessive emphasis that has been placed upon the ability of the trier of fact accurately to assess credibility as "myth and folklore."

e.   **Expertise.** Most judges defer to agency findings on information the analysis of which requires technical or specialized expertise.

f.   **Discretion.** Administrative agencies are given deference as to their findings of fact. These findings of fact, however, are reviewable by the courts. In *United States ex rel. Exarchou v. Murff*, 265 F.2d 504 (2d Cir. 1959), the court of appeals reversed the district court's dismissal of a decision of the Immigration and Naturalization Service ("INS"). An INS officer determined that Exarchou, a deportable alien, did not meet the standard of "good moral character" needed to be eligible for relief. The court found that the officer did not look to the credibility of Exarchou, as required; rather, the officer simply did not believe the story that Exarchou had told him. The reviewing court found that Exarchou had indeed met his burden of proof establishing "good moral character," and his application was entitled to further consideration.

g.   **Standard of proof.** A matter related to scope is that of the standard of proof an agency requires. *Woodby v. INS*, 385 U.S. 276 (1966), required "clear, unequivocal, and convincing evidence"; the dissenters would require "reasonable, substantial, and probative evidence." APA section 556(d) states: "Except as otherwise provided by statute, the proponent of a rule or order has the burden of proof . . . supported and in accordance with the reliable, probative, and substantial evidence." *Steadman v. SEC*, 450 U.S. 91 (1981) held the preponderance-of-the-evidence standard sufficient to uphold violations of the antifraud and securities laws.

h. **Burden of proof.** Another related matter is that of who bears the burden of proof. A recent Supreme Court case held the burden of proof to be synonymous with the "burden of going forward." *NLRB v. Transportation Management Corp.*, 462 U.S. 393 (1983), concerned the NLRB's treatment of "dual motivation" charges. The Court held that the employer carried the burden of proving an affirmative defense. The circuit judge felt that the issue was how much respect the NLRB's legal judgment should be given. Stating that the allocation of the burden of proof was a legal question, the judge concluded that "Congress has entrusted courts with primary responsibility for determining questions of law related to the agency's mission." The Supreme Court, however, felt that the statute was broad enough to allow the Board to allocate the burden of proof.

6. **Review of Factual Determinations in Proceedings Not Required To Be on Record--Association of Data Processing Service Organizations, Inc. v. Board of Governors of the Federal Reserve System, 745 F.2d 677 (D.C. Cir. 1984).**

Association of Data Process- ing Service Organizations, Inc. v. Board of Governors of the Federal Reserve System

a. **Facts.** The Association of Data Processing Service Organizations, Inc. (P), a national trade association representing the data processing industry, along with two of its members, petitioned the Court of Appeals for the District of Columbia Circuit for review of two orders of the Board of Governors of the Federal Reserve System (D), pursuant to the Bank Holding Company Act [12 U.S.C. §1848]. P sought review of D's July 9, 1982, order approving Citicorp's application to establish a subsidiary, Citishare, to engage in certain data processing and transmission services, and D's subsequent order of August 23, 1982, entered after notice and comment rulemaking, amending those portions of Regulation Y that dealt with the performance of data processing activities by bank holding compa- nies. As the two appeals were consolidated by the court, a situation was created in which both an adjudicatory authorization (adjudication) and an amendment of Regulation Y (rulemaking) were at issue in the same case. P contended that the substantial evidence standard governed the court's review of both orders, while Citicorp, who intervened, argued that the adjudication should be controlled by the substantial evidence standard and the rulemaking amendment should be upset only if arbitrary or capricious.

b. **Issue.** Is the substantial evidence test the only appropriate standard of review of factual determinations in proceedings not required to be decided on the record?

c. **Held.** Yes.

1) Section 1848 makes it clear that only one standard—the substantial evidence test—applies to review of all D's actions. In their appli- cation to the requirement of factual support, the substantial evidence test and the arbitrary or capricious test are one and the same; "the former is only a specific application of the latter."

2) The scope of review provisions of the APA, section 706(2), are cumulative. Thus, an agency action that is supported by the required substantial evidence may in another regard be "arbitrary, capricious, an abuse of discretion, or otherwise not in accordance with law," for example, because it is an abrupt and unexplained departure from agency precedent. Paragraph (A) of subsection 706(2)—the "arbitrary or capricious" provision—is a catch-all, picking up administrative misconduct not covered by the other more specific paragraphs. When the arbitrary or capricious standard is performing that function of assuring factual support, there is no substantive difference between what it requires and what would be required by the substantial evidence test, since it is impossible to conceive of a "nonarbitrary" factual judgment supported only by evidence that is not substantial in the APA sense—*i.e.,* not "enough to justify, if the trial went to a jury, a refusal to direct a verdict when the conclusion sought to be drawn . . . is one of fact for the jury."

7. **Jurisdictional or Constitutional Facts.** Three different categories of circumstances have been identified where the existence of constitutional or jurisdictional facts warrant de novo judicial review of the agency's determination:

a. **Admiralty.** Admiralty jurisdiction is specifically conferred to the federal courts by the Constitution. Hence, courts have been reluctant to defer to initial agency determinations in admiralty cases. [*See* Crowell v. Benson, *infra*—the district court may independently consider the issue of employment in a maritime workers' compensation claim]

b. **Confiscation.** Where a party alleges that the government is confiscating its property, such as in a rates valuation case, courts have undertaken de novo review of the agency's order. [*See* Ohio Valley Water Co. v. Ben Avon, 253 U.S. 287 (1920)]

c. **Deportation.** Both the APA and the Immigration and Naturalization Act support review of deportation orders.

d. **Jurisdictional facts.** Another possible exception to the general rule of review of findings of fact involves "jurisdictional facts."

1) **Definition.** "Jurisdictional facts" are those that must be found in order for the administrative agency to have jurisdiction over a matter.

2) **Cases and analyses.**

Ng Fung Ho
v. White

a) **Jurisdiction over the plaintiff--Ng Fung Ho v. White,** 259 U.S. 276 (1922).

(1) **Facts.** The Secretary of Labor (D) issued deportation orders for two citizens (Ps); Ps complained that they were not "aliens." The statute involved did not provide for judicial review. Review was obtained pursuant to a writ of habeas corpus.

(2) **Issue.** Where a United States statute (under which an agency acts) does not provide for judicial review of actions taken pursuant thereto, may a plaintiff affected by the statute receive judicial review of whether jurisdiction under the statute was proper?

(3) **Held.** Yes.

    (a) The issue of whether or not Ps are "citizens" is a jurisdictional fact and a trial de novo is required in making this determination.

(4) **Comment.** Note that this case goes farther than *Ben Avon*, *supra*, since it requires more than an independent review of the record; a trial de novo is required.

b) **Issues that may arise in claim--Crowell v. Benson,** 285 U.S. 22 (1932).

Crowell v.
Benson

(1) **Facts.** An administrative agency found that Benson (P) was injured while working within the scope of his employment and on navigable waters, awarding damages under the Longshoremen's and Harbor Workers' Act. The agency made a compensation award to P.

(2) **Issue.** Is de novo review required on certain issues that might arise in a claim?

(3) **Held.** Yes.

    (a) On questions of "jurisdictional facts" (here the issues of "scope of employment" and "on navigable waters") there must be a retrial and a new record from that made by the administrative agency.

(4) **Comments.**

    (a) The *Crowell* case was severely criticized, since "jurisdictional issues" are present in every administrative agency case and, if *Crowell* were followed, the power of all administrative agencies would have been curtailed.

    (b) *Crowell* has never been applied to any other context. Therefore, possibly its holding is limited to, "When a federal court is exercising the admiralty power, Congress may not constitutionally cut this power down by requiring the court to reach conclusions of fact on a record made elsewhere."

3) **Current meaning.** The "jurisdictional facts" doctrine has never been expressly overruled; but it has never been followed. Perhaps it might be resurrected at some time, possibly in the context of protecting certain personal constitutional rights.

C. JUDICIAL REVIEW OF AGENCY DETERMINATIONS BEYOND THE FACTS

    1. Historical Building-Block Cases.

        a. Review of "mixed questions" and "questions of law." While "questions of fact" are subject to limited judicial review, "questions of law" are subject to full or independent judicial review. The problem becomes determining when there are clear questions of law or clear questions of fact. Often there are mixed questions. One of the casebook authors feels that the "mixed questions" are law-applying and are primarily the agencies' responsibility. This is because the decision will affect that particular case and have little bearing on any other decisions.

O'Leary v.
Brown-
Pacific-
Maxon, Inc.

            1) Illustration--O'Leary v. Brown-Pacific-Maxon, Inc., 340 U.S. 504 (1951).

                a) Facts. This case involves a review of a compensation award under the Longshoremen's and Harbor Workers' Compensation Act. John Valek, an employee, drowned in an attempted rescue in a recreational swim area maintained by his employer for employees. His dependent mother filed a claim under the Longshoremen's Act. The deputy commissioner awarded a death benefit to his mother, finding that the death resulted as "an incident of his employment." The district court denied a petition to set aside the award. The court of appeals reversed, and the Supreme Court granted certiorari.

                b) Issue. Is the application of the Longshoremen's and Harbor Workers' Act in this case a "question of law" and therefore appropriate for independent judicial review?

                c) Held. No. Judgment reversed.

                    (1) The deputy commissioner correctly treated the question as one of fact.

                    (2) Although this case involves a combination of questions of law and fact, the question of law is not so severable as to be appropriate for independent judicial review.

                    (3) Unless the record is "unsupported by substantial evidence on the record as a whole," it is to be accepted.

        b. Applying law to fact: interpreting the terms of a statute. The test on review for an agency's factual findings is often whether the findings are supported by substantial evidence, as discussed above.

1) **Agency interpretation--NLRB v. Hearst Publications, Inc.,** 322 U.S. 111 (1944).

   a) **Facts.** Hearst Publications, Inc. (D) refused to bargain collectively with a union representing newsboys. Petitions for investigation and certification were filed by a union with the NLRB (P), which concluded that full-time newsboys were employees under the NLRA and certified the union. Upon D's refusal to bargain with the certified union, P ordered D to cease and desist from such refusal. D argued that the newsboys were not employees within the meaning of the statute, but were independent contractors. The court of appeals rejected P's conclusions and independently evaluated the issue of whether the newsboys were employees within the meaning of the statute. It found that the newsboys were not employees.

   b) **Issue.** Are the newsboys employees within the meaning of the NLRA?

   c) **Held.** Yes. Judgment reversed.

      (1) P has been entrusted by Congress with responsibility to administer the NLRA. The experience it derives from administering the statute familiarizes it with the employment relationships in various trades.

      (2) In making factual determinations, the findings of the agency, if supported by substantial evidence, are conclusive. It is not the task of the Court to substitute its judgment of factual questions for those of the agency if they are supported by evidence.

      (3) Issues of statutory interpretation are for the judiciary to resolve, giving appropriate weight to the initial legal determinations of the agency.

      (4) "[W]here the question is of specific application of a broad statutory term in a proceeding in which the agency administering the statute must determine it initially, the reviewing court's function is limited." Here, the application of the statutory term "employees" to these facts should be upheld if they have support in the record and a rational basis in law.

2) **Rational basis test.** Many modern courts apply the rational basis test, announced in *Gray v. Powell*, 314 U.S. 402 (1941). Under it, the court must uphold the agency's statutory findings if they are reasonable, even where the court might have construed the language of the statute differently. But some courts refuse to accord an agency's legal conclusions as great a deference as they ascribe to its factual findings, insisting that questions of law are for the independent judgment of the reviewing court.

3) **Plain meaning--Packard Motor Car Co. v. NLRB,** 330 U.S. 485 (1947).

   a) **Facts.** Foremen employed by Packard Motor Car Company (D) sought to organize as a union affiliated with the Foremen's Association of America. The NLRB (P) recognized them as an appropriate unit for collective bargaining under the NLRA and certified the Foremen's Association as their bargaining representative. D asserted that foremen were not "employees" within the meaning of the NLRA and refused to bargain with them. P ordered D to bargain.

    b)   **Issue.** Are foremen entitled to the collective bargaining opportunities afforded "employees" within the meaning of the NLRA?

    c)   **Held.** Yes. P's order affirmed.

        (1)   The definitional provisions of the NLRA provide that "[t]he term 'employee' shall include any employee" and "[t]he term 'employer' includes any person acting in the interest of an employer, directly or indirectly."

        (2)   Although foremen represent management in disputes with labor, their interests are nevertheless adverse to those of management on issues surrounding their own wages and working conditions.

        (3)   The statute is clear on its face that all employees fall within its scope. It is the responsibility of Congress to create exceptions contrary to its explicit provisions.

    d)   **Dissent** (Douglas, J.). The majority opinion tends to obliterate the line between management and labor and establishes one between equity and debt holders, on the one hand, and the operating group on the other. If foremen are "employees," then so must be the rest of management. When Congress passed the NLRA, it legislated against the unfair labor practices of foremen, not on their behalf.

    e)   **Comment.** Congress subsequently amended the NLRA explicitly to exclude from its definition of "employee" any person "employed as a supervisor."

  c.   **"Legislative rules" and agency interpretation.**

    1)   **Legislative rules.** Legislative rules are the product of an agency's exercise of its rulemaking powers under 5 U.S.C. section 553 to promulgate binding rules. If properly promulgated, constitutional, and within the scope of statutory authority conferred, legislative rules are binding on the parties who fall within their ambit, the agency, and the courts.

Skidmore v.
Swift & Co.

    2)   **Persuasive authority--Skidmore v. Swift & Co.,** 323 U.S. 134 (1944).

        a)   **Facts.** Seven employees (Ps) of Swift and Company (D) brought an action under the Fair Labor Standards Act ("FLSA") to recover overtime wages earned during the evenings they remained in D's fire hall to answer fire alarms. The trial court decided as a "matter of law" that the time spent by Ps in the fire hall does not constitute hours worked under the FLSA.

        b)   **Issue.** As a matter of law, are hours spent in a fire hall exempt from the requirements of the FLSA?

        c)   **Held.** No. Judgment reversed.

(1) No principle of law requires that time so spent is not working time under the FLSA. The question of whether such time falls within or without the FLSA is one of fact.

(2) Although Congress vested decisional responsibility over such questions in the courts rather than an administrative agency, it did create the office of administrator to bring an injunction action to restrain violations of the FLSA. In pursuing his responsibilities, the administrator has developed considerable experience and expertise in such questions of what constitutes working time within the meaning of the FLSA. He believes the answer requires a flexible solution and has identified several standards and examples in his bulletin. He believes the answer depends upon the extent to which the worker is "free to engage in personal activities during periods of idleness when he is subject to call." Here, the employees were rarely interrupted during their eating or sleeping time, but all of their other on-call hours were included in working time by the administrator.

(3) The administrator's interpretations, while not controlling on the courts, reflect a body of expertise to which the judiciary and litigants may resort for guidance. The weight given such interpretations depends upon "the thoroughness evident in its consideration, the validity of its reasoning, its consistency with earlier and later pronouncements, and all those factors which give it power to persuade, if lacking power to control."

3) **Interpretative rules.** Interpretative rules are not promulgated pursuant to the notice-and-comment procedures of section 553. They are not binding on the courts, but are only persuasive authority as to how the agency believes its statute ought to be interpreted.

   a) **Administrator overruled--Addison v. Holly Hill Fruit Products, Inc.,** 322 U.S. 607 (1944).

Addison v. Holly Hill Fruit Products, Inc.

   (1) **Facts.** The FLSA established minimum wage requirements, but exempted employers whose employees were engaged in the canning of agricultural products "within the area of production." The administrator (D) defined the phrase "area of production" to include employment in which there are no more than seven employees canning agricultural products raised on farms in the immediate vicinity. Holly Hill Fruit Products, Inc. (P) argues that this ceiling of seven employees is inconsistent with the statute.

   (2) **Issue.** Is D's interpretation of the statutory exemption for cannery employees working in the "area of production" as including no more than seven employees correct?

   (3) **Held.** No.

      (a) Nothing in the statute suggests that Congress intended to allow D to discriminate against larger establishments within the zone of agricultural production. The phrase "area of production" suggests geographic limitations; it is not a technical term.

(b) The legislative history clearly supports the interpretation that size is irrelevant in determining whether the exemption applies.

(4) **Dissent** (Rutledge, J.). Congress has vested in D the task of interpreting the statute and of considering complex economic factors in so doing. The interpretation here is fundamental to protecting the goal of the statute not to exempt large numbers of industrial employees from its ambit. We should defer to D's judgment.

2. The Present-Day Framework.

Citizens to
Preserve
Overton Park,
Inc. v. Volpe

a. Reasons requirement--Citizens to Preserve Overton Park, Inc. v. Volpe, 401 U.S. 402 (1971).

1) **Facts.** The Secretary of Transportation (D) authorized construction of an interstate highway through Overton Park in Memphis, Tennessee. Federal legislation prohibited federal highway construction through public parks where a "feasible and prudent" alternative route existed. The highway as authorized would consume 26 acres of the 342-acre city park. D made no formal findings explaining his decision and its consistency with federal statutes, but provided litigation affidavits asserting that the decision was his and was supportable by law. Citizens to Preserve Overton Park, Inc. (Ps) contended that D did not make an independent determination. The district and appellate courts found that formal findings by D were not required. Ps appeal.

2) **Issue.** Is D's failure to explain the rationale for his decision or its consistency with federal statutes error?

3) **Held.** Yes. Judgment reversed.

a) The case must be remanded so that the full record before D at the time he rendered his decision can be evaluated.

b) Agency officials who participated in the decision may be asked to testify. *Morgan v. United States*, *infra*, prohibits inquiry into the mental processes of decisionmakers, however, unless a strong showing of bad faith or improper behavior exists.

c) The litigation affidavits were merely "post hoc" rationalizations and therefore constitute an inadequate basis for review.

4) **Comment.** *Overton Park* is among the most frequently cited decisions in Administrative Law. Its facts depict a rather common practice in agency decisionmaking where subordinates are delegated the task of rendering many of the agency's technical decisions and the agency head dictates policy. The large number of decisions required by law to be made by administrative agencies makes such delegation necessary. But where it occurs, a prudent decisionmaker will have his subordinate prepare a written decision explaining the facts and their application to the law.

5) **Comment.** Note the *Camp v. Pitts* case, below, where the Comptroller of the Currency rejected an application to open a branch bank on the basis that there existed "no need." Review of the Comptroller's discretion was held to be on the administrative record already in existence (supporting the conclusion of "no need") and not some new record citing additional factors.

b. **De novo review.** Citing *Citizens to Preserve Overton Park, Inc. v. Volpe*, *supra*, the Court in *Camp v. Pitts*, 411 U.S. 138 (1973), held that de novo review was appropriate in two situations: (i) where inadequate factfinding procedures were used during an adjudicatory hearing; or (ii) where judicial proceedings are brought to enforce administrative actions. An inadequate explanation of a decision is not sufficient for a de novo hearing. If the explanation was not adequate, the remedy is to obtain affidavits and other information available to explain the decision. This particular case had an explanation, although it was only in the form of a letter; it was sufficient to indicate the reason for the decision. Based on that record, using the appropriate standard of review, if the finding is not substantial, the decision is to be vacated and remanded to the proper party for review.

c. **The "adequate consideration" or "hard look" approach to review of discretion.** Between the extremes of de novo review and strong deference to administrative decisionmaking, some courts have taken a "hard look" at the agency's decisional process, insuring that the agency has considered all relevant issues and policies and taken a good look at the facts, while allowing the agency the discretion to determine policy. It is the agency's process and its justification or rationale for its selection of a policy alternative that becomes the focus of this approach.

d. **The interplay between rulemaking and adjudication.** As a result of *Florida East Coast Railway*, *supra*, most agency rulemaking is through informal, legislative notice-and-comment procedures. This frequently results in the absence of an agency record for purposes of judicial review, thereby frustrating judicial challenges to agency action.

e. **Rescinding a rule--Motor Vehicle Manufacturers Association of the United States, Inc. v. State Farm Mutual Automobile Insurance Co.**, 463 U.S. 29 (1983).

1) **Facts.** Over the course of 60 rulemaking notices beginning in the mid-1960s, the Department of Transportation ("DOT") issued various rules requiring installation of seat belts. Passive restraints were, under the rules, to be installed in large cars in 1982 and in all cars by 1985. However, in 1981, President Reagan's Secretary of Transportation announced that the rulemaking would be reopened because of the deleterious economic circumstances in which the domestic automobile industry found itself. DOT's National Highway Traffic Safety Administration ("NHTSA") rescinded the earlier rules on grounds that it could no longer find that significant safety benefits would be realized therefrom. In 1977, it had anticipated that airbags would be installed in 60% of new vehicles and automatic seat belts in 40%. By 1981, it appeared that seat belts would be installed in 99% and could be detached easily. Because of the $1 billion cost that would be imposed upon the industry by the rule, the NHTSA found that anticipated safety benefits would not warrant the expenditure.

Motor Vehicle Manufacturers Association of the United States, Inc. v. State Farm Mutual Automobile Insurance Co.

2) **Issue.** Is the rule rescission arbitrary and capricious?

3) **Held.** Yes. Decision vacated and remanded.

a) Rule rescission or modification is significantly different from a failure to act. Where an agency changes direction, it must provide a reasoned analysis for the change. While an agency need not promulgate rules to last forever and must be given sufficient latitude to adjust its policies to comport with contemporary needs, deregulation is not always in the best public interest.

b) The scope of review under the arbitrary and capricious standard is narrow; the courts may not substitute their judgment for that of the agency. However, the agency must review the relevant evidence and provide a satisfactory explanation of its result, including a rational connection between the facts and its conclusion. An agency rule could be deemed arbitrary and capricious "if the agency has relied on factors which Congress has not intended it to consider, entirely failed to consider an important aspect of the problem, offered an explanation for its decision that runs counter to the evidence . . . or is so implausible that it could not be ascribed to a difference in view or the product of agency expertise."

c) The NHTSA failed to consider what benefits might be realized by an "airbag only" rule. Although a rulemaking will not be deemed inadequate merely because it failed to consider "every alternative device and thought conceivable to the mind of man," the airbag is a technological alternative within the scope of the existing rule. Also, the NHTSA was too quick to dismiss the benefits of automatic seat belts. An agency that changes its course must supply a reasoned analysis.

4) **Dissent** (Rehnquist, J.). A change in philosophy brought about by the democratic process in electing a new administration is an appropriate basis for an agency to reappraise the costs and benefits of its existing programs' regulations.

f. **Reasonable construction of statute--Chevron, U.S.A., Inc. v. Natural Resources Defense Council, Inc.,** 467 U.S. 837 (1984).

Chevron, U.S.A., Inc. v. Natural Resources Defense Council, Inc.

1) **Facts.** The Clean Air Act Amendments of 1977 allowed the Environmental Protection Agency ("EPA") to establish national air quality standards. States that did not meet these requirements could establish a program regulating "new or modified major stationary sources" of air pollution. The EPA adopted a plantwide definition of "stationary sources." Natural Resources Defense Council, Inc. (P) filed a petition in the United States Court of Appeals for the District of Columbia Circuit to set aside the regulations. That court stated that the purpose of the permit program was to improve air quality. Under such a program, a plantwide or "bubble" concept was contrary to law.

2) **Issue.** Absent congressional definition of the statutory term "stationary source," was the EPA's adoption of the "bubble" concept a reasonable construction of that term?

3) **Held.** Yes. Judgment reversed.

    a) If the statute is silent on a specified issue, the court does not adopt its own interpretation of the statute. If the agency has adopted a permissive and reasonable view of the statute, it should not be disturbed.

    b) The EPA should be given "broad discretion in implementing the policies of the 1977 amendments."

    c) In a technical and complex area such as this, the agency responsible for administering this legislation should have flexibility to implement and interpret the legislation.

g. **Less deference for proscribed conduct.** In *State Department of Insurance v. Insurance Services Office*, 434 So. 2d 908 (Fla. Dist. Ct. App. 1983), the court invalidated a rule by the Insurance Department which had extended a statute. The statute stated that the Department "may not enact a rule which shall enlarge or extend" the statute. The chief judge dissented. His feeling was that the judges were, in effect, declaring their own interpretation of the statute as the "right" one. In such situations, deference should be given to the agencies. As the number of judges and the number of combinations of judges increase, the number of "right" answers to statutory interpretation increases.

h. **Modification of regulations--MCI Telecommunications Corp. v. AT&T,** 512 U.S. 218 (1994).

    1) **Facts.** Under title 47, section 203(a) of the United States Code, all common carriers must file rate tariffs with the FCC. The FCC, under section 203(b), has the ability to "modify" these requirements. As long distance service competition became more "open," the FCC relaxed the filing requirements for non-dominant carriers (in essence, everyone except AT&T (D)).

    2) **Issue.** Was the FCC's decision to allow non-dominant long distance carriers the option of submitting rate tariffs a valid exercise of its modification authority?

    3) **Held.** No. Judgment reversed.

        a) The case turns on the meaning of "modify" as embodied in the statute. MCI (P) argues that the term allows the FCC to make fundamental changes in the regulatory regime. We find that it means "to change in a minor fashion." The case is a "battle of dictionary definitions;" ultimately, P's definition is only based on one source, as opposed to the Court's definition, which is found in "virtually all other dictionaries," and was the basis for the legislative use of the word in 1934 when the Act was instituted. Thus, the FCC's modification is only acceptable if it is not a radical change.

        b) Here, the change is radical and fundamental. It strikes at the heart of the common-carrier section of the Communications Act, as rate filings are essential to regulated industries. Such a revision would affect 40% of the industry. Congress did not intend the FCC to have such authority.

c)   The FCC is allowed to make limited changes. However here, the change is "effectively the introduction of a whole new regime of regulation which may well be a better regime but is not the one that Congress established."

D.   "ROOMS IN THE MANSION OF THE LAW"

1.   The Obligation To Be Consistent.

Shaw's Super-
markets, Inc.
v. NLRB

a.   Consistency with precedent--Shaw's Supermarkets, Inc. v. NLRB, 884 F.2d 34 (1st Cir. 1989).

1)   Facts. The NLRB (P) held that Shaw's Supermarkets, Inc. (D) had violated the NLRA, as D's vice president had made statements taken to be a threat of reprisal against unionization five days prior to a vote on unionization. The NLRA expressly provides that an employer is not allowed to make threats of reprisal if employees desire to form a union. The vice president's statements concerned the potential wages under a collective bargaining agreement, stating that D would start with an offer of minimum wage ($3.35/hour); several employees had been making up to $11.70/hour. In its investigation, no other unfair practices were discovered by P.

2)   Issue. Because P relied on statements that were ambiguous as to a threat of reprisals and had previously held similar language to not be a violation, along with the fact that there was no additional evidence of unfair practices, was P acting within its authority in penalizing D?

3)   Held. No.

a)   The statements by the vice president could "innocently represent a legal truth about how the collective bargaining process works," or inform the employees about how trade-offs must be made for union benefits. P held that these statements were "bargaining from scratch" statements; however, in previous "bargaining from scratch" cases where P held no violation of the NLRA, statements were no worse than those uttered by D. In the cases where a threat was found, there were typically other unfair labor practices discovered.

b)   Thus, the decision in this case is inconsistent with P's precedents. To depart from precedent, an agency must explain why it significantly departed from precedent; this insures that the public has a usable guide for its conduct. P did not give such explanation in this case.

2.   Responsibility for Inducing Detrimental Reliance.

a.   Estopping the government. The rule has traditionally been that good-faith reliance on an agency ruling or opinion would normally keep a person out of jail, but would not necessarily protect him against government fines, injunctions, damage actions, etc. That is, the government is not estopped by errors made by its agents.

b.   Detrimental reliance--Office of Personnel Management v. Richmond, 496 U.S. 414 (1990).

   1)   Facts. Richmond (P), a former Navy Department employee, went on disability retirement in 1981; in 1986, he had an opportunity to collect extra money through part-time employment. His annuity would cease if he were to return to an "earning capacity fairly comparable to the current rate of pay of the position occupied at the time of retirement." An agency directive had established, before 1982, that the earning capacity was restored if the earned income for two consecutive years was 80% of the current pay rate. In 1982, the period was amended to one year. P inquired at the Navy's Civilian Personnel Department as to whether his benefits would be affected; the advice given, as well as the pamphlet he was given, both referenced the pre-1982 time restriction. In 1987, he again sought and received erroneous advice. The federal Office of Personnel Management (D) discontinued his annuity based on the 1982 amendment. P challenged D's action.

   2)   Issue. Does erroneous oral or written advice given by a government employee give rise to estoppel against the government?

   3)   Held. No.

   a)   Estoppel against the government is appropriate in certain situations (*e.g.*, where the government has acted with affirmative misconduct). But if Executive Branch officers were allowed to obligate treasury funds, the control over these funds placed under Congress in the Appropriations Clause would be subverted. Thus, in this case, if estoppel were allowed and payments continued, the Appropriations Clause would become a "nullity."

   b)   One cannot estop the Constitution. Allowing this estoppel claim would be to allow "endless litigation over both real and imagined claims of misinformation by disgruntled citizens." Also, government agents, if liable for all of their statements, would give out less advice.

3.   The Obligation to Abide by Prior Judicial Determinations: Preclusion and "Nonacquiescence."

a.   Res judicata. The general principles of res judicata prohibit a subsequent suit on issues of fact or law already litigated and finally decided. Some efforts of administrative agencies to reverse prior decisions involving the same parties and facts have been struck down on grounds of being "arbitrary and capricious." Other courts allow agencies to reexamine their statutory and factual conclusions and change their minds at a later date.

b.   Against the government--United States v. Mendoza, 464 U.S. 154 (1984).

1) Facts. Mendoza (P), a Filipino national, filed a petition with the INS in 1978 for naturalization based on the Nationality Act, which had expired 32 years earlier. He claimed that the government's application of the Act denied him due process. The Act was established to provide citizenship opportunities for noncitizens who had served with honor in World War II. The problem was that the process was held up in the Philippines due to the Japanese occupation of the area and the subsequent Filipino governments. In 1975, a group of Filipinos sued the United States (D) in a California district court under terms similar to Mendoza's claim. The California court held that D's action did violate due process. The government docketed, and subsequently withdrew, an appeal, allowing only those who had sought nationalization and had filed a petition before the 1975 case was filed. The lower courts in this case held that D was collaterally estopped from relitigating the constitutional issue, and D appeals.

2) Issue. Can the government be collaterally estopped from relitigating the constitutional issue against Mendoza based on the 1975 suit?

3) Held. No. Judgment reversed.

a) With respect to collateral estoppel, the government is not identical to private litigants, due to its large geographic scope, being subject to a large number of lawsuits, being involved in issues that are typically more important to the public interest (especially constitutional issues), and being more likely to be involved in lawsuits involving similar issues by different parties. Allowing non-mutual collateral estoppel against D would "freeze the development of the law" as to issues of public import. Also, litigation by the government is not a mechanical process; subsequent administrations must be allowed to litigate similar issues as to different parties based on the policy decisions within the administration.

United States
v. Stauffer
Chemical Co.

c. Collateral estoppel--United States v. Stauffer Chemical Co., 464 U.S. 165 (1984).

1) Facts. The EPA (P), Tennessee authorities, and a private contractor employed under contract with P attempted to inspect Stauffer Chemical Company's (D's) chemical plant. D refused entry unless the private contractors would sign an agreement not to disclose trade secrets, which they refused to do. P obtained an administrative warrant to inspect the plant, which D refused to honor. P filed a contempt proceeding against D, and D moved to quash the warrant.

2) Issue. Was the government collaterally estopped from instituting a civil contempt proceeding against D due to an earlier case between P and D (*Stauffer I*) arising under similar circumstances?

3) Held. Yes. Judgment affirmed.

a) Mutual defensive collateral estoppel is applicable against a government agency to preclude relitigation of the same issue already litigated against the same party.

b)   P argues that its special role in litigating important issues of public policy warrants exception to the standard rule of collateral estoppel, as application would "freeze the development of the law." It also argues that since P is charged with administering rules nationally, the application of collateral estoppel would lead to inconsistent application of the law to similarly situated parties. Although agreeing with P in the abstract, the Court finds that the main problem in this case is that the parties are *identical* in the two cases. There is no preclusion of proceeding against different parties for similar actions.

d.   **Applicability of judicial precedent--Stieberger v. Heckler,** 615 F. Supp. 1315 (S.D.N.Y. 1985), *vacated & remanded,* 801 F.2d 29 (2d Cir. 1986).

Stieberger
v. Heckler

1)   **Facts.** This action was brought against the Social Security Administration (D), challenging D's "non-acquiescence policy" whereby D's ALJs are ordered to disregard federal court decisions within its circuit if they conflict with D's directives. A controversy arose as to the differing definitions presented by the circuit court and D regarding the weight given to the medical opinion of Claimant Stieberger's (P's) physician ("treating physician rule").

2)   **Issue.** Does D's "non-acquiescence policy" violate the APA and separation of powers?

3)   **Held.** Yes.

a)   D's policy allows either for ALJs to ignore circuit court opinions if contrary to an agency ruling or for D to direct agency workers not to follow the decision. D argues that since the agency is a "co-equal" branch of the government, it is not bound by stare decisis, and that it must adhere to its own interpretation of the laws to allow for national uniformity in agency decisions. We hold otherwise.

b)   First of all, decisions such as *Marbury v. Madison*, 5 U.S. (1 Cranch) 137 (1803), have "established the authority of the federal courts to render decisions which bind all other participants in our constitutional system." There is also no rationale for D's policy, as D does not retain discretionary decisionmaking authority.

c)   D has other alternatives available to remedy decisions it disagrees with, specifically appeals process and legislative remedies.

d)   A "nonacquiescence policy" would not be bad in all cases; it could be used where D anticipates reconsideration of a decision by a higher court, for example. However, the policy as practiced has "created a litigation burden of unprecedented proportions on the Court." Forcing claimants to go through an administrative process to collect benefits assured by court decisions has frustrated congressional intent, and has forced ALJs to choose between the law and D's orders.

E. ENFORCEMENT AND SANCTIONS

Butz v.
Glover
Livestock
Commission
Co.

1. **Scope of Review of Administrative Sanctions--Butz v. Glover Livestock Commission Co.,** 411 U.S. 182 (1973).

   a. **Facts.** The judicial officer for the Department of Agriculture, Butz (P), found that Glover Livestock Commission Company (D) had violated the Packers and Stockyards Act by falsifying weight measurements for its livestock. Investigations of D began in 1964, and D was "informally warned" of its transgressions. In the 1969 investigation that is the center of this case, the Department of Agriculture judicial officer entered a cease and desist order against D to keep correct weight records, and suspended D for 20 days. The court of appeals upheld the fact that D had violated the Packers Act, but set aside the suspension. P appeals.

   b. **Issue.** Because the court of appeals found that the suspension was "unconscionable" (since the Secretary of Agriculture had previously not suspended violators except for flagrant violations and the cease and desist order), and the negative publicity surrounding D's violations were "ample" punishment, did the court exceed its scope of judicial review of administrative sanctions?

   c. **Held.** Yes. Judgment reversed.

      1) The standard of judicial review is such that a court may only overturn an administrative penalty if there was no justification in fact for the penalty or if the punishment was unwarranted. The court of appeals found that the punishment was unwarranted because it implied a necessity for uniformity of sanctions in the Act. However, no such uniformity is statutorily required, and the Secretary of Agriculture had discretion to penalize as he saw fit.

      2) The fact that the suspension was based in part on a prior disregard of warnings is evidence of "justification in fact."

      3) Finally, it is not up to the judiciary to fashion "reasonable" remedies.

FTC v. Universal-Rundle Corp.

2. **Selective Enforcement--FTC v. Universal-Rundle Corp.,** 387 U.S. 244 (1967).

   a. **Facts.** The FTC (P) brought an action against Universal-Rundle Corporation (D) on the basis that D was selling its products at one price to one set of customers and at a higher price to others. Those who were buying at the lower price were buying in truckloads. After four years, the cease and desist order was issued. D appealed on the basis that all of its competitors were doing the same thing and that the order would put it out of business. The court of appeals found that P had abused its discretion. P appeals.

   b. **Issue.** Was the cease and desist order properly issued?

c.   **Held.** Yes. Judgment reversed.

   1)   The standard of the reviewing court for cease and desist orders is whether there has been a "patent abuse of discretion" by the agency. Here, there has not been.

   2)   P has indicated that the violation is not selling truckloads, but selling only to certain customers at a preferred price.

3.   **Application of the Law--Jacob Siegel Co. v. FTC,** 327 U.S. 608 (1946).

a.   **Facts.** The FTC (P) issued a cease and desist order against Jacob Siegel Company (D), a company manufacturing coats under the name "Alpacuna," in which no vicuna wool was included. The FTC found that the name "Alpacuna" was deceptive because consumers might assume that the coats contained vicuna wool. D sought judicial review.

b.   **Issue.** Where P conclusively determines that a regulatee's use of a trade name is "unfair or deceptive," must P choose the least drastic remedy adequate to cope with the unlawful practice?

c.   **Held.** Yes. Decision reversed and remanded.

   1)   Here, the policy of the law is to accommodate the protection of trade names with the prevention of unfair or misleading business practices. However, there is no indication that P considered the policy (instead, it considered only the misleading practice). Courts cannot review an agency determination before an agency has considered less severe sanctions and made a decision based on available alternatives.

V. THE CONSTITUTIONAL REQUIREMENT OF AN OPPORTUNITY TO BE HEARD

A. PROCEDURAL DUE PROCESS

1. **Constitution.** The Fifth and Fourteenth Amendments to the United States Constitution provide that no person may be deprived of "life, liberty, or property, without due process of law."

2. **Components.** The essential components of due process are notice and an opportunity to be heard. Notice is ordinarily a simpler question for legal resolution than is the issue of whether an aggrieved party has been accorded a sufficient opportunity to be heard. The fundamental issue is frequently how much process is "due."

B. LEGISLATIVE VS. JUDICIAL FUNCTIONS

1. **Formal Hearing Required.** The Supreme Court has recognized that a formal hearing is "required where there is a relatively small number of persons, who were exceptionally affected, in each case upon individual grounds. . . ." In *Londoner v. Denver, supra*, a case involving the assessment of a tax imposed upon individual property owners for the benefit realized from the paving of their street, the Court held that, at some time before the tax becomes irrevocably fixed, the taxpayer must be given the opportunity to have a hearing.

2. **Informal Hearing Sufficient.** The Supreme Court has also held, conversely, that where a large number of persons are affected by an agency action essentially analogous to that performed by the legislature, a formal hearing is not required. [*See* Bi-Metallic Investment Co. v. Colorado, *supra*]

3. *Londoner* and *Bi-Metallic*. These decisions illustrate the fundamental distinctions between adjudication and rulemaking. As the Supreme Court has subsequently noted, there is "a recognized distinction in administrative law between proceedings for the purpose of promulgating policy-type rules or standards, on the one hand, and proceedings designed to adjudicate disputed facts in particular cases on the other." The distinction is aptly illustrated by the landmark decisions of *Londoner* and *Bi-Metallic*.

4. **State and Federal Constitutions.** Both state and federal constitutions provide that no person may be deprived of life, liberty, or property without due process of law. Under the federal Constitution, the Fifth Amendment Due Process Clause applies to the federal government; the Fourteenth Amendment Due Process Clause governs state matters.

5. **Statutory Issues.** Before a constitutional question of due process is even reached, administrative procedure must comply with statutory requirements. But persons affected by correct procedures may then challenge them on the basis that, although they conform to the statute, they do not conform to constitutional requirements of due process.

6. **Basic Requirements.** The basic requirements are that decisions that affect life, liberty, or property must be preceded by adequate notice and an opportunity for a fair hearing.

7. **Issues.** There are many issues raised by due process. Among them:

   a. What is adequate notice and a fair hearing?

   b. What interests are included in "liberty" and "property"?

   c. Beyond these questions of what administrative procedures must be is the question of what "should" they be?

8. **Summary Administrative Action: The Timing of a Hearing.**

   a. **General rule.** Where unusual circumstances exist, courts have upheld the deprivation of property with a hearing postponed until after the government acts. Three criteria have been identified where post-hearing seizure of property has been upheld:

      1) **Important public interest.** The seizure must be necessary to satisfy an important governmental interest such as health or safety;

      2) **Promptness.** There must be a significant urgency for expeditious action; and

      3) **Control.** The government official responsible for determining the need for the seizure must be the one initiating it.

   b. **Public health--North American Cold Storage Co. v. Chicago,** 211 U.S. 306 (1908).

      North American Cold Storage Co. v. Chicago

      1) **Facts.** Health officials of the City of Chicago (D), acting under an ordinance prohibiting refrigerated warehouses from storing food unfit for human consumption, ordered the North American Cold Storage Company (P) to tender putrid poultry for destruction. P refused, and D prohibited further deliveries to the warehouse. P sought an injunction, objecting on grounds that the effort to summarily seize its property without a hearing violated the Fourteenth Amendment requirement of due process.

      2) **Issue.** In a situation where the city has a good faith belief that certain food poses a danger to public health, must it afford the parties a pre-seizure hearing before such property is confiscated?

      3) **Held.** No.

         a) Food that is unfit for human consumption poses a danger to the public health and is, therefore, a nuisance of the most dangerous kind. A pre-seizure hearing of food that is unwholesome is not required.

b)   Here, P can secure a hearing in a tort action for wrongful taking of its property.

c.   **Dismissal from government employment--Bailey v. Richardson,** 182 F.2d 46 (D.C. Cir. 1950), *aff'd* (by an equally divided Court), 341 U.S. 918 (1951).

1)   **Facts.** Bailey (P) was discharged from the civil service "due to reduction in force" after having been employed for eight years; one year later she was reinstated. Civil Service Regulations made reinstatement subject to various conditions, including disqualification if "on all the evidence, reasonable grounds exist for belief that the person involved is disloyal to the Government of the United States." Two months after her reinstatement, P was notified that she had been the subject of an investigation as part of the Federal Employees Loyalty Program, and that she would have the right to an administrative hearing before the Regional Loyalty Board. The Regional Board found P disloyal and proceeded to separate her from the service, rating her ineligible for federal employment, and barring her from competing in civil service examinations for a three-year period. The Loyalty Review Board sustained the finding of the Regional Board on appeal. P sued officials (Ds) in the Federal Security Agency and the Civil Service Commission; the district court granted Ds' summary judgment motion. P claims that she was denied reinstatement without revelation by the government of the names of those who informed against her and of the method by which her alleged activities were detected. P also claims that the Due Process Clause of the Fifth Amendment requires that she be afforded a hearing of the quasi-judicial type before being dismissed.

2)   **Issue.** Is a quasi-judicial hearing required before dismissal from government employment?

3)   **Held.** No. Judgment affirmed.

a)   P was not entitled either by executive order or statute to more process than she received. The portion of the government's orders that barred P from federal service for three years was invalid as constituting a "punishment," which could be meted out only through compliance with the Sixth Amendment. Mere dismissal from employment, however, was not such a "punishment."

b)   The Due Process Clause of the Fifth Amendment does not restrict the President's discretion or the prescriptive power of Congress in respect to executive personnel. Due process of law is not applicable unless one is being deprived of something to which he has a right, and P did not have a right to a civil service position.

4)   **Comment.** In dealing with this highly political question, the Court saw no requirement in the Constitution that the Executive Branch rely upon the services of persons in whom it lacks confidence. The criterion for retention or removal of subordinate employees is the confidence of superior executive officials; confidence is not controllable by process. (It should be noted that the affirmance by an equally divided Supreme Court bestows no precedential value to this holding.)

d. **Revocation of security clearance--Cafeteria & Restaurant Workers Union v. McElroy,** 367 U.S. 886 (1961).

    1) **Facts.** Rachel Brawner (P) had worked for more than six years at a cafeteria operated by M & M Restaurants, Inc. at the Naval Gun Factory in Washington, D.C., when the Department of Defense (D) revoked her security clearance without hearing or explanation. She was offered a job at another M & M cafeteria, but declined. The lower courts found for D. P appeals.

    2) **Issue.** Did D violate Fifth Amendment requirements of due process by failing to provide P with notice and hearing?

    3) **Held.** No. Judgment affirmed.

        a) It does not suffice to say that since P had no right to be there in the first place, she was not deprived of a liberty or property interest. "[O]ne may not have a constitutional right to go to Baghdad, but the Government may not prohibit one from going there unless by means consonant with due process."

        b) To determine what process was due, we must assess the "precise nature of the government function involved as well as the private interest affected by the governmental action." If the private interest is a mere privilege, we have traditionally held that no process is due.

        c) Here, the government's interest was in the management of the internal operations of an important military base, not in the regulation of a profession.

        d) The private interest was not D's right to follow her chosen profession, but merely the denial of the opportunity to work in one specific military installation.

        e) This is not a case where loss of employment is predicated on arbitrary or discriminatory grounds.

        f) Neither is this a case where P's reputation has been injured. D may merely have thought that P was garrulous or careless with her badge of identification.

    4) **Dissent** (Brennan, J.). D's unsustained allegation that P posed a security threat nullifies the substantive constitutional protection against discrimination and injures her reputation.

9. **The Erosion of the Privilege Doctrine.**

    a. **The right to a public school education.**

        1) **Introduction.** Does a student in a public school have a "right" to be a student? On what grounds may a student be expelled? After what procedures? Are the rights involved different for students attending private (nontax-supported) institutions?

2) **Procedural safeguards--Dixon v. Alabama State Board of Higher Education,** 294 F.2d 150 (5th Cir. 1961), *cert. denied,* 368 U.S. 930 (1961).

    a) **Facts.** Students were expelled without a hearing from a tax-supported state college. They had been involved in sit-in demonstrations.

    b) **Issue.** Does a student at a public college have a right to a hearing concerning his or her expulsion?

    c) **Held.** Yes.

        (1) Students cannot be expelled without adequate notice of charges against them and a right to a hearing, which must be more than an informal review. The students must be able to present witnesses, testimony, etc.

        (2) It makes no difference that the college rules provided that students enrolling waived any constitutional rights to such procedural safeguards.

3) **Nature of the procedural safeguards.** The court in *Dixon* indicated that the hearing need not be a full, trial-type hearing, with the right to confront witnesses, cross-examine, etc. But the students must be given notice of the witnesses against them, transcripts of their testimony, etc.

C. DUE PROCESS EXPLOSION: LIBERTY, PROPERTY, AND SOME KIND OF HEARING

1. **Summary Action.**

    a. **Introduction.** Normally, a hearing must be given before agency action is taken. However, there are a number of circumstances where the required hearing may be delayed. These are situations of "summary action pending a deliberated decision."

    b. **Provisional administrative action.**

        1) Where the agency action has no immediate adverse effect on any party, it is appropriate for the agency, without a hearing, to make a determination.

        2) Normally, a provisional order requires that interested parties take some action prior to some deadline, or the order will go into effect.

2. **Erosion of Privilege Concept.** The growth of government and its licensing and welfare functions made inevitable the result that adherence to strict notions of privilege would have onerous consequences. Justice Frankfurter argued as early as 1951 that the mere fact that the interest conferred is deemed to be a privilege does not warrant the conclusion that government may revoke it arbitrarily.

3. **Privilege-Right Distinction on the Run.** Beginning in the 1960s, several federal courts began to view the privilege-right distinction as archaic and ill-conceived. Even though a person held no right (to a liquor license, or to travel, for example), the courts held that government could not deprive an individual of a liberty or property interest without due process of law. [*See* Dixon v. Alabama, *supra*]

4. **The Due Process Explosion.** The decision in *Goldberg v. Kelly*, below, is the high-water mark holding of the United States Supreme Court on the question of what process is due and began what has since been affectionately referred to as the "Due Process Explosion."

5. **Welfare--Goldberg v. Kelly,** 397 U.S. 254 (1970).

   Goldberg
   v. Kelly

   a. **Facts.** Several welfare recipients (Ps) challenged the procedures employed by New York (D), which sought to terminate their welfare without a formal pre-termination hearing. The procedures which existed, in chronological order, were written notice, a pre-termination opportunity to submit a written response, termination of welfare payments, and a post-termination opportunity for a formal oral hearing. If the welfare recipient prevailed at the formal hearing, she would be paid all monies erroneously withheld. The district court held for Ps. D appeals.

   b. **Issues.** Do constitutional requirements of due process require a pre-termination formal hearing before the government may end a welfare recipient's benefits?

   c. **Held.** Yes. Judgment affirmed.

      1) A welfare recipient is ordinarily without financial resources beyond those provided by government. It would be unconscionable to terminate benefits without a pre-termination formal hearing in face of this "brutal need." The extent to which an individual is entitled to procedural due process is largely influenced by the extent to which the individual would be "condemned to suffer grievous loss."

      2) The government's interest in preserving finite fiscal and administrative resources must be weighed against the individual's "overpowering need." Moreover, the government's interest includes avoiding the "social malaise that may flow from a widespread sense of unjustified frustration and insecurity," as well as ensuring that a legitimate recipient is not erroneously terminated. The state can protect its economic interest by developing procedures for expeditious formal pre-termination hearings.

6. **Judge Friendly's Cost-Benefit Analysis.** Judge Friendly has argued that the cost incurred by the government in offering elaborate due process coupled with the loss of monies paid during the interim to ineligible recipients at some point will outweigh the benefits realized by eligible recipients. "[T]he expense of protecting those likely to be found undeserving will probably come out of the pockets of those deserving." During 1972 alone, some 13 million individuals received federal assistance at a cost of $10.5 billion. The most significant category was Aid to Families with Dependent Children, accounting for 10.5 million individuals and $6.5 billion in federal revenue.

Board of
Regents of
State Colleges
v. Roth

1. **Legitimate Claim of Entitlement Required--Board of Regents of State Colleges v. Roth,** 408 U.S. 564 (1972).

    a. **Facts.** David Roth (P) was hired as an assistant professor by Wisconsin State University (D) for a one-year term and was not rehired at the end of the term. Although P was not conferred tenure by D, he claimed that the failure of D to give him a hearing violated the Fourteenth Amendment and that the real motive for removal involved his exercise of his First Amendment rights.

    b. **Issue.** Have P's due process rights been violated by the failure of D to afford P a hearing prior to removal?

    c. **Held.** No. Judgment reversed and remanded.

        1) The Fourteenth Amendment speaks in terms of interests in liberty and property. When such protected interests are infringed, the right to some kind of hearing becomes paramount. To determine when due process requirements apply, we look to the nature of the interest affected. The rights-privileges dichotomy has been abandoned.

        2) Liberty interests embrace pursuits of happiness: the right to contract, to engage in one's occupation, to acquire useful knowledge, to marry, to establish a home and raise children, and to worship God. Here, P's reputation has not been injured, his right to employment elsewhere has not been infringed, and there is no proof that his right to free speech has been harmed.

        3) In order to have a constitutionally protected property interest, the individual must have more than a unilateral expectation to it. He must have a legitimate claim of entitlement. Property interests are not created by the Constitution, but stem from an independent source, such as state law. Here, P had no legitimate claim to re-employment after his one-year term.

    d. **Dissent** (Marshall, J.). "Every citizen who applies for a government job is entitled to it, unless the government can establish some reason for denying the employment." Such employment is property, the "liberty to work" is liberty, and both are constitutionally protected.

Perry v.
Sindermann

2. **Liberty/Property Interests in De Facto Tenure--Perry v. Sindermann,** 408 U.S. 593 (1972).

    a. **Facts.** Sindermann (P) was involved in a public disagreement with the Board of Regents of Odessa Junior College (D), and D voted not to renew P's contract, issuing a press release setting forth allegations of insubordination. P brought a 42 U.S.C. section 1982 action alleging that his removal was in retaliation for exercise of his First Amendment rights.

b. Issue. Did P's removal without a hearing violate his Fourteenth Amendment due process rights?

c. Held. Yes. Judgment reversed.

    1) The government may not deny a benefit to a person on a basis that infringes his constitutionally protected interests, particularly free speech.

    2) De facto tenure may constitute a constitutionally protected property interest, and does here. An implicit contract of tenure may constitute a legitimate claim of entitlement.

3. Employment. In *Bishop v. Wood*, 426 U.S. 341 (1976), a police officer who had been discharged without a hearing was found to have no Fourteenth Amendment property interest, based on the trial judge's determination that state law permitted termination "at will."

4. Prisons--Meachum v. Fano, 427 U.S. 215 (1976).

a. Facts. Fano and other prisoners (Ps) were transferred from a minimum to a maximum security prison by the state (D) after setting fires. They were permitted to testify, but were not allowed to confront and cross-examine adverse witnesses. Ps brought an action under 42 U.S.C. section 1983 alleging deprivation of liberty without due process of law. The lower courts held for Ps, and the Supreme Court granted certiorari.

b. Issue. Should Ps have been granted a more elaborate hearing before being transferred to a less desirable prison?

c. Held. No. Judgment reversed.

    1) Ps had no liberty interest that was deprived. State law does not condition a transfer. They were already deprived of liberty when convicted. A state may freely subject inmates to the rules of the prison system as long as the rules do not otherwise violate the inmates' constitutional rights (*e.g.*, to be free of cruel and inhuman punishment).

    2) Any other result would place the courts into the day-to-day business of running the prisons.

d. Dissent (Stevens, J.). The majority assumes that liberty interests to be protected must have a source in the Constitution or in state law. While the law is essential to the enjoyment of liberty, men have been endowed by their Creator with certain inalienable rights, including liberty.

5. Absence of Ascertainable Standards--Holmes v. New York City Housing Authority, 398 F.2d 262 (2d Cir. 1968).

a. Facts. The Holmeses and others (Ps) brought a class action suit under 42 U.S.C. section 1983 against the New York City Housing Authority (D), alleging that they had filed applications for low-rent public housing and had been denied without explanation or discernable criteria that might advise them in what way their applications were deficient. Ps allege that the absence of standards increases the likelihood of "favoritism, partiality, and arbitrariness" and deprives them of a fair opportunity to acquire public housing or to obtain adequate judicial review. The court took this issue on interlocutory appeal.

b. **Issue.** Does the absence of ascertainable standards for public housing violate applicants' due process rights?

c. **Held.** Yes.

1) D has adopted no standards for selection among the class of applicants to which Ps belong. Thus, it "failed to establish the fair and orderly procedure for allocating its scarce supply of housing which due process requires." Due process insists that there be ascertainable and objective standards in distinguishing among applicants for this scarce resource. Without such standards, administrators will enjoy unrestrained discretion, which constitutes an "intolerable invitation to abuse."

2) Due process requirements attach where the individual is suffering a loss of his liberty or a vested entitlement to property established by federal or state law. But no hearing is required where an entitlement does not exist and the agency has discretion to act. In such cases, there is no requirement that administrators adopt standards to constrict their discretion.

Morton v. Ruiz

6. **Substantial Individual Rights--Morton v. Ruiz,** 415 U.S. 199 (1974).

a. **Facts.** Ruiz (P) was a Papago Indian living 15 miles from the reservation. The Bureau of Indian Affairs ("BIA"), relying upon its internal manual, declared that Indians living off the reservations were ineligible for economic assistance under the Snyder Act.

b. **Issue.** Are Indians living off the reservation ineligible for economic assistance under the Snyder Act?

c. **Held.** No. Judgment affirmed and remanded.

1) An agency is free to restrict the class of eligible recipients, if necessary, to conserve finite appropriations. But substantive individual rights may not be restricted on an ad hoc basis; they must instead be limited in rulemaking.

2) The APA was promulgated in order to insure that individual rights and obligations would not be arbitrarily circumscribed by agency action via unpublished ad hoc adjudication. Here, the BIA relies on its unpublished manual, which is unavailable to the public.

3) Before an agency may constrict individual rights, it must comply with its own internal procedures, even when they are more rigorous than those required by statute.

7. **Social Security Disability Benefits--Mathews v. Eldridge,** 424 U.S. 319 (1976).

    a. **Facts.** Eldridge (P) was awarded disability insurance benefits in 1968. In 1972, after reviewing P's completed questionnaire and reports from P's physician, the Social Security Administration (D) informed P that D had tentatively concluded that his disability had ceased and offered P the opportunity to submit additional information. P was subsequently informed that his benefits would be terminated, but that he could seek a post-termination hearing. P commenced this action challenging the constitutionality of D's failure to give him a pre-termination hearing. The lower courts held for P, and D appeals.

    b. **Issue.** Must the government offer an individual a formal adjudicatory hearing prior to termination of Social Security benefits?

    c. **Held.** No. Judgment reversed.

        1) In order to determine what process is due, a court must assess the facts present and tailor the procedures to satisfy the needs thereby created. Three factors are weighed and balanced: (i) the *private interest* that will be affected by the government's action; (ii) the *procedures* utilized, the risk they pose for erroneous deprivation, and the value of increased procedures; and (iii) the *governmental interest*, including the need to protect its finite fiscal and administrative resources.

        2) Since the recipient would be awarded full retroactive compensation if he ultimately prevailed on his intra-agency appeal, the individual's interest is in the uninterrupted receipt of income pending agency disposition of his claim. Here, the deprivation will likely last more than one year. But, unlike welfare, disability benefits are not based upon need. Other public assistance may be available to the recipient if he loses his disability assistance.

        3) Here, the medical assessment of the individual's physical or emotional well-being is a "much more sharply focused and easily documented decision" than is eligibility for welfare. Disability can ordinarily be determined accurately upon assessment of medical reports rather than evaluating the truthfulness and credibility of witnesses. In welfare, the poor and uneducated would have significant difficulty in filing written pleadings. [*See* Goldberg v. Kelly, *supra*] This is not usually so in disability cases.

        4) The financial and administrative costs of requiring a formal pre-termination hearing would likely be substantial. At some point, the costs of additional procedures outweigh the benefits.

8. **Medicare Claims Hearings Conducted by Private Insurance Carriers--Schweiker v. McClure,** 456 U.S. 188 (1982).

    a. **Facts.** In order to make the administration of Part B of the Medicare program—entitled "Supplementary Medical Insurance Benefits for the Aged and Disabled"—more efficient, Congress authorized the Secretary of

Health and Human Services to contract with private insurance carriers to administer on his behalf the payment of qualifying Part B claims. Under this arrangement, the Secretary pays the participating carriers' costs of claims administration. In return, the carriers act as the Secretary's agents by reviewing and paying Part B claims for the Secretary according to a precisely specified process. Should the carrier refuse on behalf of the Secretary to pay a portion of the claim, the claimant has one or more opportunities to appeal—none of which involve an ALJ. The district court had held Ps entitled to a de novo hearing before a Social Security ALJ, such as the ALJs used to administer Part A appeals.

b.   **Issue.** Is Congress's provision that hearings on disputed claims for certain Medicare payments be held by private insurance carriers, without further right of appeal, consistent with the requirements of due process?

c.   **Held.** Yes. Judgment reversed.

1)   While the lower court is correct in its view that the private interest in Part B payments is "considerable" and that the additional cost and inconvenience of providing ALJs would not be unduly burdensome, the risk of erroneous decision by the "carrier courts" and the probable value, if any, of the additional procedure are minimal. The trial court record did not support the conclusion that the Secretary's selection criteria for hearing officers was more likely to result in the erroneous deprivation of Part B benefits.

2)   Due process is flexible and calls for such procedural protections as the particular situation demands. It was not shown that the procedures prescribed by Congress and the Secretary are not fair or that different or additional procedures would reduce the risk of erroneous deprivation.

d.   **Comment.** All claimants are first entitled to a "review determination," in which they may submit written evidence and arguments of fact and law. A carrier employee, other than the initial decisionmaker, will review the written record de novo and affirm or adjust the original determination. If the amount in dispute is $100 or more, a still-dissatisfied claimant then has a right to an oral hearing presided over by an officer chosen by the carrier. (The hearing officers do not participate personally, prior to the hearing stage, in any case that they adjudicate.) Hearing officers receive evidence and hear arguments pertinent to the matters at issue, and must render written decisions based on the record as soon as practicable. Neither the statute nor the regulations make provision for further review of the hearing officer's decision.

Gray Panthers v. Schweiker (I)

9.   **Minor Medicare Claims--Gray Panthers v. Schweiker (I),** 652 F.2d 146 (D.C. Cir. 1980).

a.   **Facts.** The Gray Panthers and three named Medicaid beneficiaries (Ps) brought suit to challenge the Secretary of Health, Education, and Welfare (D) on D's procedures for resolving disputes concerning claims for less than $100. Medicare is principally administered through insurance companies under contract with the government. Individuals submitting claims for payment or reimbursement for sums of less than $100 are not entitled to a hearing, although those filing claims exceeding $100 are given one. Ps challenged these procedures on due process grounds. D argued that the cost of additional procedures for such small claims outweighed the benefits of oral hearings. The district court found for D. P appeals.

b. **Issue.** Are informal (notice-and-comment) procedures sufficient to deny medicare claims of less than $100?

c. **Held.** No. Judgment reversed.

1) Accuracy, accountability, and fairness are all enhanced by oral procedures.

2) An oral hearing is one of several alternatives that satisfy due process requirements depending upon whether the fiscal and administrative burdens of additional procedures are outweighed by their value.

   a) Although need is not a requirement for eligibility, a disproportionate number of Medicare recipients are near the poverty level. Hence, amounts like $100 are of particular significance to them. Although in *Mathews v. Eldridge, supra*, the individual's interest was merely in uninterrupted receipt of Social Security benefits, here we are dealing with a permanent loss of amounts claimed.

   b) Insufficient notice of the specific reasons for denial accompanied by lack of opportunity to communicate personally with the decisionmaker, who may be biased, is insufficient due process.

   c) The cost imposed by giving a recipient adequate notice and an opportunity to confront the decisionmaker is not as onerous as that which might be imposed for a formal hearing.

3) "[S]implified, streamlined, informal oral procedures" consistent with the congressional concern for economic and efficient administrative justice are required here.

d. **Comment.** The ultimate procedures adopted by the Department of Health and Human Services for Medicare, and approved by the judiciary on remand [*Gray Panthers v. Schweiker (II)*, 716 F.2d 23 (D.C. Cir. 1983)], included a toll-free telephone "hearing" combined with written supplementation where only mathematical errors were alleged; but where credibility and veracity were at issue, a face-to-face hearing would be provided.

10. **Academic Dismissal--Board of Curators of the University of Missouri v. Horowitz,** 435 U.S. 78 (1978).

    a. **Facts.** Horowitz (P) was dismissed from the University of Missouri-Kansas City Medical School (D) for failure to meet academic standards during her last year of study. Among other things, P lacked a "critical concern for personal hygiene," and her clinical skills were unsatisfactory. Several efforts had been made by D to apprise P of her problems and to afford her an opportunity to correct them. P claimed the dismissal denied her due process. The district court found that P had been given all the process that was due. The court of appeals reversed. D appeals.

b. **Issue.** Does due process require a formal hearing prior to academic dismissal from a university?

c. **Held.** No. Judgment reversed.

1) We are impressed by the fact that D made several attempts to review P's progress and afford P the opportunity to respond. Although no formal hearing opportunity was given, the procedures used satisfied the Fourteenth Amendment. In *Goss v. Lopez*, 419 U.S. 565 (1975), all that was required was an "informal give-and-take" between the student and administrators. More than that was given here.

2) Less stringent procedures are required for an academic as opposed to a disciplinary suspension, such as that involved in *Goss*. Academic evaluations of student performance are not well suited for adjudicatory procedures, for they are more subjective and evaluative than are the factual issues present in a disciplinary case.

d. **Comment.** The Court was unwilling to expand the judiciary's role in the educational environment beyond *Goss*.

Ingraham
v. Wright

11. **Corporal Punishment--Ingraham v. Wright**, 430 U.S. 651 (1977).

a. **Facts.** Junior high school students (Ps) of Dade County, Florida (D) were paddled for disciplinary reasons. Ps brought a class action suit under 42 U.S.C. section 1983 alleging violation of the Eighth Amendment's "cruel and unusual punishment" prohibition and the Fourteenth Amendment's due process provisions. The district court dismissed, the court of appeals in rehearing affirmed, and the Supreme Court granted certiorari.

b. **Issue.** Does the absence of a pre-paddling hearing violate the Fourteenth Amendment?

c. **Held.** No. Judgment affirmed.

1) No Eighth Amendment violation exists here. The paddling here was not "cruel and unusual punishment."

2) Restraining the students for purposes of paddling deprived them of their liberty. Thus, the three-part test of *Mathews v. Eldridge* is applied.

3) Corporal punishment is a recognized remedy for disciplinary problems in the school under the common law, as long as it is reasonably imposed and not excessive. Under Florida law, excessive punishment creates a tort remedy for damages; malicious punishment may result in the imposition of criminal penalties.

4) Because paddlings usually respond to conduct directly observed by teachers, the likelihood of a wrongfully imposed paddling is negligible.

5) Additional procedures would not be justified by their cost and by their adverse effect upon the ability of educators to maintain discipline in the schools.

d. **Dissent** (White, J.). Tort litigation is an inadequate remedy because it provides no remedy if the disciplinarian in good faith believed that the infliction of corporal remedies was reasonable, and does not alleviate the physical pain which has already been inflicted. The disciplinarian should be required to offer skeletal due process akin to that required in *Goss v. Lopez, supra.*

12. **Injury to Reputation--Paul v. Davis,** 424 U.S. 693 (1976).

Paul v. Davis

a. **Facts.** Davis (P) was described in a flyer distributed to store owners by the Louisville Police Department (D) as an "active shoplifter." P had earlier been arrested for shoplifting, but was never convicted.

b. **Issue.** Does D's circulation of leaflets defaming P constitute a deprivation of a property interest without due process of law?

c. **Held.** No. Judgment reversed.

1) While this case states a claim for defamation, there is no constitutional protection for tort injury. Were we to conclude otherwise, the opportunity for due process litigation would exist for every injury inflicted by a state official.

2) Reputation, standing alone, is neither a "liberty" nor a "property" interest within the meaning of the Fourteenth Amendment. There must be a government action depriving the individual of something, such as his job.

3) Here, the state has not conferred any right to the enjoyment of reputation. This is merely one of a number of interests the state may protect under its tort law.

d. **Dissent** (Brennan, J.). An individual's interest in a good name and reputation is a constitutionally protected liberty interest, and is sufficient, in and of itself, to sustain a due process claim.

13. **For Cause Employees--Cleveland Board of Education v. Loudermill,** 470 U.S. 532 (1985).

Cleveland Board of Education v. Loudermill

a. **Facts.** In 1979, the Cleveland Board of Education (D) hired respondent Loudermill (P) as a security guard. On his job application, P stated that he had never been convicted of a felony. Eleven months later, as part of a routine examination of his employment records, D discovered that in fact P had been convicted of grand larceny in 1968. By letter dated November 3, 1980, D's business manager informed P that P had been dismissed because of his dishonesty in filling out the employment application. P was not afforded an opportunity to respond to the charge of dishonesty or to challenge his dismissal. On November 13, D adopted a resolution officially approving the discharge. Under Ohio law, P was a "classified civil servant." Such employees can be terminated only for cause, and may

Administrative Law - 101

obtain administrative review if discharged. Pursuant to this provision, P filed an appeal with the Cleveland Civil Service Commission on November 12. The Commission appointed a referee, who held a hearing on January 29, 1981. P argued that he had thought that his 1968 larceny conviction was for a misdemeanor rather than a felony. The referee recommended reinstatement. On July 20, 1981, the full Commission heard the argument and orally announced that it would uphold the dismissal. Although the Commission's decision was subject to judicial review in the state courts, P instead brought the present suit in district court. The district court dismissed, but the court of appeals reversed and remanded. The Supreme Court granted certiorari.

   b.   **Issue.** Must some pre-termination process be accorded a public employee who can be discharged only for cause?

   c.   **Held.** Yes. Judgment affirmed.

   1)   We have described the root requirement of the Due Process Clause as being that an individual be given an opportunity for a hearing before he is deprived of any significant property interest. This principle requires some kind of a hearing prior to the discharge of an employee who has a constitutionally protected property interest in his employment. The pre-termination hearing, though necessary, need not be elaborate. The hearing need not definitively resolve the propriety of the discharge; it should be an initial check against mistaken decisions—essentially, a determination of whether there are reasonable grounds to believe that the charges against the employee are true and support the proposed action.

   2)   The essential requirements of due process are notice and an opportunity to respond. The tenured public employee is entitled to oral or written notice of the charges against him, an explanation of the employer's evidence, and an opportunity to present his side of the story. To require more than this prior to termination would intrude to an unwarranted extent on the government's interest in quickly removing an unsatisfactory employee.

   d.   **Dissent** (Rehnquist, J.). Because I believe that the Fourteenth Amendment of the Constitution does not support the conclusion that Ohio's effort to confer a limited form of tenure upon P resulted in the creation of a "property right" in his employment, I dissent.

   e.   **Comment.** The need for some pre-termination hearing is evident from a balancing of the competing interests at stake. These are the private interests in retaining employment, the governmental interests in the expeditious removal of unsatisfactory employees and the avoidance of administrative burdens, and the risk of an erroneous termination.

O'Bannon v.
Town Court
Nursing
Center

14. **Nursing Homes--O'Bannon v. Town Court Nursing Center,** 447 U.S. 773 (1980).

   a.   **Facts.** In 1976, the Department of Health, Education, and Welfare (D) certified Town Court Nursing Center (P) as a "skilled nursing facility" eligible for government subsidies. In 1977, D revoked the designation.

P and six Medicaid recipients brought suit, arguing that their due process rights had been violated and that the individuals would suffer both a loss of benefits and serious emotional and physical harm. The court of appeals concluded that D's procedures did not deny P due process, but did deny due process to the Medicaid recipients. The Supreme Court granted certiorari.

b.   **Issue.** Are residents of a nursing home entitled to a hearing before the home's subsidies may be revoked?

c.   **Held.** No. Judgment reversed.

1)   The statute did not confer a right to residence in a specific nursing home, but gave only the opportunity to select one of a number of qualified providers of nursing home care.

2)   No direct benefits of the Medicaid recipients are infringed upon here. The indirect and incidental impact of the government's decision to decertify the nursing home does not constitute deprivation of life, liberty, or property, and hence no constitutional due process rights are infringed.

d.   **Concurrence** (Blackmun, J.). I would draw the *Bi-Metallic* distinction in this case: "When government action affects more than a few individuals, concerns beyond economy, efficiency, and expedition tip the balance against finding that due process attaches."

15. **Statutory Attorney Fee Limitation--Walters v. National Association of Radiation Survivors,** 473 U.S. 305 (1985).

a.   **Facts.** Two veterans organizations, three individual veterans, and a veteran's widow (Ps) had convinced the court below that the administrative scheme set up to hear veterans' benefit claims violated the Due Process Clause. The district court entered a "preliminary injunction" enjoining the enforcement of statutory provisions dating from 1864 which limit the fees payable to agents or attorneys engaged by a veteran to pursue benefits to $10 per claim. The statute also provides for criminal penalties for any person charging fees in excess of the $10 limit. The limits were originally intended to protect claimants' benefits from being unnecessarily diverted to unscrupulous lawyers.

b.   **Issue.** Does the statutory fee limitation, as it bears on the administrative process in operation, deprive a rejected claimant or recipient of "life, liberty, or property, without due process of law" by depriving him of representation by expert legal counsel?

c.   **Held.** No. Judgment reversed.

1)   The very nature of the due process inquiry indicates that the fundamental fairness of a particular procedure does not turn on the result obtained in any individual case; rather, procedural due process rules are shaped by the risk of error inherent in the truth-finding process as applied to the generality of cases, not the rare exceptions. (In reaching its conclusions the court below relied heavily on the problems

presented by what it described as "complex cases," which apparently included those in which a disability was slow-developing and therefore difficult to find service-connected, as well as other cases involving difficult matters of medical judgment.)

2) The system for administering benefits should be managed in a sufficiently informal way that there should be no need for the employment of an attorney to obtain benefits to which a claimant was entitled, so that a claimant would receive the entirety of the award without having to divide it with a lawyer. It would take an extraordinarily strong showing of probability of error under the present system—and the probability that the presence of attorneys would sharply diminish that possibility—to warrant a holding that the fee limitation denies claimants due process of law.

3) The procedure was established in this manner to allow for "informality and solicitude for the claimant." The government also wanted to insure that the claimant would not have to share benefit awards with an attorney. It is not within the Court's discretion to overrule the congressional purpose. By eliminating the fee cap, the process would also become more complex. Even simple cases would require an attorney, driving up administrative costs. Where the due process interest is a "property interest in the continued receipt of Government benefits, which interest is conferred and terminated in a non-adversary proceeding," the requirement of an attorney is not significant. Finally, the Court holds that the evidence upon which the district court based its holding, regarding success rates of cases involving attorneys versus the use of other forms of representation, did not show enough of a disparity to implicate due process concerns.

   d. **Dissent** (Stevens, Brennan, Marshall, JJ.). The paternalistic and bureaucratic governmental interests relied on by the majority in upholding the validity of the statutory fee limitation are inadequate. The kind of paternalism reflected in this statute as it operates today is irrational. It purports to protect the veteran who has little or no need for protection and it actually denies him assistance in cases in which the help of his own lawyer may be of critical importance. We are not considering a procedural right that would involve any cost to the government. We are concerned with the individual's right to spend his own money to obtain the advice and assistance of independent counsel in advancing his claim against the government.

Brock v.
Roadway
Express, Inc.

16. **Reinstatement of Discharged Employee--Brock v. Roadway Express, Inc.,** 481 U.S. 252 (1987).

   a. **Facts.** Roadway Express, Inc. (P), a trucking company, fired an employee for allegedly breaking a vehicle light to earn extra money while having to wait for the light to be repaired. The employee had previously reported alleged safety violations by P to the government, and alleged he was fired for his "whistleblowing." An Occupational Safety and Health investigator interviewed the employee and other employees to determine whether the termination was protected by the whistleblower provisions of the Surface Transportation Assistance Act. Section 405 of the Act provides that employees may not be discharged for refusing to operate a vehicle that fails to comply with state and federal safety regulations or for reporting such violations. Under this section, Secretary of Labor conducts an investigation of an alleged violation, and if he finds that an employee was discharged in violation of the Act, the employee may be reinstated. The employer may thereafter request an evidentiary hearing. Without detailing the evidence leading to his decision, the investigator found "reasonable cause" to believe the employee, and the Regional Administrator of the Department of Labor ordered the employee's reinstatement. Prior to the reinstatement, P was able to meet with the inspector and submit a written statement, but was not allowed access to the witnesses or their statements. P filed this action, seeking to enjoin enforcement of the reinstatement order and seeking a declaratory judgment that section 405 is unconstitutional to the extent that it does not allow for a pre-reinstatement evidentiary hearing. The district court granted summary judgment for P, and the Secretary appealed directly to the Supreme Court.

b.   **Issues.**

    1)   Did the procedures followed by the Secretary unconstitutionally deprive P of due process because they did not provide P with the evidence supporting the employees' complaint?

    2)   Is section 405 unconstitutional to the extent that it fails to allow an employer an evidentiary hearing and an opportunity to cross-examine witnesses prior to the reinstatement of an employee?

c.   **Held.** 1) Yes. 2) No. Judgment affirmed in part and reversed in part.

    1)   Section 405 was developed to protect so-called whistleblowers, in the hopes of encouraging reporting of safety violations. Congress found that for the section to be the most effective, it had to allow for reinstatement prior to evidentiary review, as to give an employee incentive to act. P argues that it has been deprived of a property right to terminate employees for cause. As P is correct that P has such a property right, the question remains of what process is due.

    2)   A procedural due process determination requires a balancing of the employer's interest in controlling the makeup of its workforce, the government's interest in highway safety and protection of employees from retaliatory discharge, and the employee's interest in not being discharged for proper whistleblowing.

    3)   The balancing test does not allow for a full evidentiary hearing before reinstatement if the government procedures allow for an adequate "initial check against mistaken decisions," and eventual complete and expeditious review. P was entitled to (i) access the government's supporting evidence, (ii) meet with the investigator, and (iii) submit statements and argue its position orally.

        a)   The government's preliminary reinstatement order was invalid because P was not provided with the relevant evidence supporting the complaint, hindering its ability to prepare a meaningful response to the complaint.

          b)   However, P was not entitled to a full pre-reinstatement hearing or the opportunity to cross-examine witnesses.

    4)   A prior evidentiary hearing under these circumstances would be a significant burden, as it would delay an employee's reinstatement, unfairly burdening the employee.

d.   **Dissent in part** (Brennan, J.). An employer should be provided the opportunity to cross-examine witnesses before preliminary reinstatement when there are factual disputes as to the validity of a deprivation of due process rights.

e.   **Dissent in part** (White, Scalia, JJ., Rehnquist, C.J.). The government has a strong interest in preventing disclosure of information supporting its decisions; we should allow withholding of witnesses' names and statements prior to preliminary reinstatement.

f.   **Dissent in part** (Stevens, J.). I disagree with the Court's finding that a full hearing is not required before reinstatement, particularly in light of the fact that the preliminary investigations themselves are often lengthy and during that time, there would be ample time to conduct a full pre-reinstatement hearing without further burdening the employee.

VI. AGENCY ACQUISITION OF INFORMATION

A. INTRODUCTION

As decisional bodies, agencies require adequate information upon which to base conclusions that best serve legitimate public interest concerns. The means of acquiring such information fall into three categories: (i) requiring reports, (ii) inspection of documents or facilities, and (iii) subpoena of documents and witnesses.

B. RECORDS AND REPORTS

Many substantive legislative enactments conferring jurisdiction upon administrative agencies include record-keeping requirements. An agency's authority to secure those records is seldom challenged.

1. **Self-Incrimination.** It has been argued that the Fifth Amendment privilege against self-incrimination prohibits government acquisition of business records.

   a. **Private business records.** In *Shapiro v. United States*, *infra*, the United States Supreme Court held that private business records required to be kept by a fruit and produce wholesaler were not protected by the Fifth Amendment from forced disclosure, on grounds that the records involved were the appropriate subjects of governmental regulation, and they were of a kind normally kept in the course of business.

   b. **Records of illegal activities.** But in *Marchetti v. United States*, *infra*, the Supreme Court struck down requirements that gamblers register and file reports regarding their illegal gambling activities, as violating the individual's Fifth Amendment protection against self-incrimination. In distinguishing *Shapiro*, the Court noted that (i) Marchetti was not required to keep records "of the same kind as he has customarily kept," (ii) there were no "public aspects" in such records, and (iii) these requirements were directed at a "selective group inherently suspect of criminal activities."

C. COMPULSORY INFORMATION GATHERING PROCESSES

Most of the information sought by agencies is given voluntarily. The issues here, however, deal with the powers of an agency to gather information which persons will not turn over voluntarily.

1. **Methods Used.** Many agencies (but not all) are authorized to use the following methods to obtain information:

   a. Hearings;

   b. Subpoena power to obtain testimony and documents;

   c. Periodic or special reports; and

   d. Inspections.

2. **Enforcement.** Some agencies may enforce their orders for information. For example, some agencies can revoke licenses or take other actions that will punish a person who will not comply. However, most agencies must go through the courts for enforcement. The normal sanctions for noncompliance are penal and contempt.

D. PHYSICAL INSPECTIONS

1. **Introduction.** It is routine for governmental officials to inspect homes and businesses in connection with such health and welfare matters as health and fire laws. The issue is whether such "searches" violate the Fourth Amendment.

2. **Cases and Comments.**

   a. **Residential searches.** In *Camara v. Municipal Court*, 387 U.S. 523 (1967), the Court held that the Fourth Amendment requires that a warrant procedure be employed, in the absence of an emergency situation (such as involved in the seizure of unwholesome food), for administrative inspections of commercial and residential premises pursuant to fire, health, and housing regulations, unless the consent of the occupant has been obtained.

      1) **Probable cause not necessary.** Such a warrant need not be based on a finding that there is "probable cause" to believe that conditions in a particular dwelling violate the regulations; rather, warrants may issue (usually only after the occupant refuses entry, unless there has been a citizen complaint or there is other satisfactory reason for securing immediate entry) on reasonable need to conduct periodic, area-wide inspections.

      2) **Reasonable need.** What is "reasonable need" for such area inspections, according to the Court, "will vary with the municipal program being enforced, and may be based on the passage of time, the nature of the building, or the condition of the entire area."

Marshall v.
Barlow's, Inc.

   b. **Business property--Marshall v. Barlow's, Inc.,** 436 U.S. 307 (1978).

      1) **Facts.** The Occupational Safety and Health Act empowered agents of the Secretary of Labor ("Secretary") to search work areas of any employment facility within the Act's jurisdiction to inspect for safety hazards and violations of OSHA regulations. No search warrant or other process is expressly required under the Act. An OSHA inspector entered the customer service area of Barlow's, Inc. (D), an electrical and plumbing installation business, displayed his credentials, and informed D's manager that he wished to conduct a search of D's working area. After learning that no complaint had been received concerning D and that the inspector had no search warrant, the manager refused the inspector admission to D's working area. The Secretary petitioned for and obtained from the district court an order compelling D to admit the inspector. D again refused

admission and sought injunctive relief from the warrantless searches assertedly permitted by the Act. The district court declared the warrantless search provisions of the Act unconstitutional and granted D relief. The case ultimately came before the Supreme Court.

2) Issues.

    a)   Except for pervasively regulated businesses, must a federal regulatory agency inspector have a search warrant to search working areas of commercial buildings not usually accessible to the public?

    b)   If a warrant is needed, need the inspector demonstrate probable cause in the criminal law sense to obtain an administrative search warrant?

3) Held. a) Yes. b) No. Judgment affirmed.

    a)   Except for pervasively regulated businesses, a federal regulatory agency inspector must have a search warrant to search working areas of commercial buildings not usually accessible to the public, unless the party in charge of such buildings consents to such a search without a warrant.

    b)   A federal regulatory agency inspector need not demonstrate probable cause in the criminal law sense to obtain an administrative search warrant. He need only show that a specific business has been chosen for a search on the basis of a general administrative plan for the enforcement of the Act derived from neutral sources such as, for example, dispersion of employees in various types of industries across a given area, and the desired frequency of searches in any of the lesser divisions of the area.

    c)   The basic purpose of the Fourth Amendment is to safeguard the privacy and security of individuals against arbitrary invasions by government officials. Its enactors intended the Fourth Amendment Warrant Clause to protect commercial buildings in civil as well as criminal investigations. Thus, the Fourth Amendment prohibits OSHA agents from entering a place of business from which the public is restricted and to conduct their own warrantless search.

    d)   However, even though an inspector must obtain a search warrant to inspect if the party in charge refuses admission, for purposes of an administrative search such as this, probable cause justifying the issuance of a warrant may be based not only on specific evidence of an existing violation but also on a showing that reasonable legislative or administrative standards for conducting an inspection are satisfied with respect to a particular establishment.

    e)   The warrant will provide assurances from a neutral officer that the inspection is reasonable under the Constitution, is authorized by statute, and is pursuant to an administrative plan containing specific neutral criteria. Also, a warrant will then and there advise the owner of the scope and objects of the search, beyond which limits the inspector is not allowed to proceed. The Act is unconstitutional insofar as it purports to authorize inspections without warrant or its equivalent, and we affirm the district court's injunction enjoining the Act's enforcement to that extent.

4) **Dissent** (Stevens, Blackmun, Rehnquist, JJ.). The Court's approach disregards the plain language of the Warrant Clause and is unfaithful to the balance struck by the framers of the Fourth Amendment. Our constitutional fathers were not concerned about warrantless searches, but about overreaching warrants. Since the general warrant, not the warrantless search, was the immediate evil at which the Fourth Amendment was directed, in order to put limits on its issuance, the framers required that a warrant only issue on a showing of particularized probable cause. Fidelity to the original understanding of the Fourth Amendment leads to the conclusion that the warrant clause has no application to routine, regulatory inspections of commercial premises. If such inspections are valid, it is because they comport with the ultimate reasonableness standard of the Fourth Amendment. The Court's holding adds little to the protections already available under the Act and pertinent regulations, and any benefit is insufficient to identify a constitutional violation or to justify overriding Congress's judgment that the power to conduct warrantless inspections is essential. The test of whether a warrantless search is permissible is not whether the search is to be made on a pervasively regulated business long subject to government regulations in which proprietors will be aware of and consent to routine, regulatory inspections; rather, the test is whether Congress has limited the exercise of the inspection power to those commercial premises where the evils at which the statute is directed are to be found. The Act is directed at health and safety hazards in the work place, and the inspection power granted to the Secretary extends only to those areas where such hazards are likely to be found.

5) **Comment.** The Court here appears to be playing compromise politics rather than interpreting law. The Court says a warrant is required, but that the warrant may be based on administrative necessity. The case seems to change nothing.

3. **Warrantless Searches.** The Fourth Amendment prohibition against unreasonable searches and seizures has been interpreted as not barring warrantless searches of certain highly regulated industries.

Donovan
v. Dewey

a. **Illustration--Donovan v. Dewey**, 452 U.S. 594 (1981).

1) **Facts.** Secretary of Labor Donovan (P) sought an injunction against Dewey (D), who had refused to allow a warrantless inspection by a federal mine inspector of D's quarry. The Federal Mine Safety and Health Act of 1977 requires federal mine inspectors to inspect underground mines four times a year and surface mines two times a year. It grants inspectors "a right of entry" onto mine premises and provides that "no advance notice of any inspection shall be provided to any person." The district court held for D, finding that the statute violates the Fourth Amendment. P appeals.

2) **Issue.** Does this statute, which authorizes warrantless inspection of mines, violate the Fourth Amendment?

3) Held. No. Judgment reversed.

    a) The Fourth Amendment protects a property owner only against *unreasonable* searches. Searches may be unreasonable if they are not authorized by law, not required to satisfy governmental interests, or so random and unpredictable that the owner has no real expectation that he will be inspected.

    b) Where Congress has authorized an inspection but identified no standards to govern the inspector, a warrant may be required to protect the owner from the unbridled discretion of the inspector.

    c) Certain industries are subject to pervasive regulation (*e.g.,* sale of alcohol, guns), and no warrant is required for their inspection. Individuals who enter these businesses have already subjected themselves to pervasive governmental regulation.

    d) This statute embodies a substantial federal interest in protecting the health and safety of individuals working in a hazardous industry. If inspection is to be a deterrent to unlawful activity, unannounced inspections are essential. This statute limits the discretion of inspectors as to when they may inspect and under what circumstances such inspections are to be performed.

4) Dissent (Stewart, J.). The Court in *Marshall v. Barlow's, Inc.,* *supra,* emphasized the requirement that a warrant must be obtained for inspection of all but two industries—alcohol and guns. The rationale for these exceptions was implied consent of the individuals engaging in such enterprises.

4. Plain View. Government officials are free to enter areas open to the public and to take enforcement action based upon what they observe.

    a. Limiting *Marshall* and *Camara*. *Wyman v. James,* 400 U.S. 309 (1971), upheld the conditioning of welfare benefits on periodic home visits after advance notice by caseworkers. Although the purpose of these visits was "both rehabilitative and investigative," the Court held that they were not "searches" under the Fourth Amendment "in the traditional criminal law context," because the recipient's denial of permission was not a criminal act, but merely a barrier to receiving welfare.

        1) Reasonableness of search. Even if the visits were searches without a warrant under the Fourth Amendment, the Court held that they were not unreasonable because of their limited nature and the public interest in assuring the objectives of its welfare program.

        2) Admissibility of evidence at criminal trial. The Court expressed no opinion as to whether evidence discovered during the home visit would be admissible in a criminal prosecution against the recipient.

E. ACQUIRING DOCUMENTS

1. **Required Forms and Reports.** In many instances, agencies are autho-
    rized to require those they regulate to keep certain records. The issue is
    whether these records can be subpoenaed even if they are incriminating.

2. **Required Records and the Fifth Amendment.**

    a. **Self-incrimination--Braswell v. United States,** 487 U.S. 99 (1988).

        1) **Facts.** Braswell (D) ran a business as a sole proprietorship until
            1980, when he formed a corporation. In 1981, he formed a
            second corporation, funded by a 100% interest in the first
            corporation. He was ordered by a grand jury in 1986 to pro-
            duce records from the corporations. He refused, arguing that
            production would violate his Fifth Amendment right to avoid
            self-incrimination.

        2) **Issue.** May the custodian of a corporation refuse a subpoena to
            produce records based on the Fifth Amendment right to avoid
            self-incrimination?

        3) **Held.** No.

            a) For the sake of Fifth Amendment analysis, corporations
                are treated differently from individuals. Under the "col-
                lective entity" rule, a corporation does not have the power
                to refuse to submit documents under subpoena.

            b) The issue in this case is slightly different, examining
                whether a corporate officer can refuse a subpoena by
                raising a personal privilege. Court precedent has held that
                the corporate custodian holds the records as a corporate
                representative and not in a personal capacity. As a corpo-
                rate officer, he has duties to produce these documents.
                Furthermore, extension of the personal privilege to corpo-
                rations would create a non-existent privilege. The custodi-
                an, even though he must produce the records, cannot be
                compelled to incriminate himself through oral testimony.
                The government may not, however, use the custodian's act
                of producing the records against the individual, since
                he/she is acting as a corporate officer.

            c) Allowing such a privilege would hamper government
                efforts to fight white-collar crime.

        4) **Dissent** (Kennedy, Brennan, Marshall, Scalia, JJ.). The ma-
            jority's holding that a corporate agent must incriminate himself
            even when he is named in the subpoena and is a target of the
            investigation, and even when compliance requires compelled,
            personal, testimonial, incriminating assertions, is not supported
            by any precedent. The fact that the government designates a
            specific individual in the subpoena belies the agency rationale
            behind the court's decision. The Fifth Amendment does not

provide for exceptions to make it easier for the government to investigate organizations at the expense of the individual employee's right against self-incrimination.

b. Unprivileged records--Shapiro v. United States, 335 U.S. 1 (1948).

1) **Facts.** During World War II, the Price Control Act permitted the Administrator to regulate the maximum price of fruit and to require that wholesalers keep records pertaining to their business (such as sales invoices, etc.). Shapiro's (D's) records showed that he violated the Act, and he was convicted of a criminal offense. D argued that the records could not be discovered and used against him.

2) **Issue.** In this situation, are D's business records immune from discovery and use in a prosecution against D?

3) **Held.** No.

   a) There is no Fifth Amendment protection to the records—they were required to be kept and related to activity that Congress could lawfully regulate.

   b) The immunity provisions of the statute, which incorporated the Compulsory Testimony Act, did not apply, as the record information was unprivileged. No immunity results from supplying unprivileged information.

c. Privileged records--Marchetti v. United States, 390 U.S. 39 (1968).

1) **Facts.** The federal statute required that gamblers register, pay an occupational tax, and keep detailed information about their activities. Marchetti (D) argued that the statute required him to incriminate himself by providing information about his gambling activities.

2) **Issue.** In this situation, can D's business records (which were required to be kept on D's gambling business—often an illegal business) be discovered and used in a prosecution against him?

3) **Held.** No.

   a) In *Shapiro*, the records kept were those normal to a business. D, on the other hand, was required to keep records he would not ordinarily keep as a businessman.

   b) There were "public aspects" to Shapiro's records; there was no public aspect to D's situation.

   c) This case involves a tax on a selective group of people inherently suspect of criminal activity, while *Shapiro* arose from a normal regulatory activity (price control).

3. **Compulsory Process.** Subpoenas require the giving of information, either in the form of written documents (subpoena duces tecum) or in the form of oral testimony (subpoena ad testificandum).

a. **Statutory origins.** For an agency to possess subpoena power, such authority must have a statutory origin. Only courts are free to issue subpoenas without a statutory basis. Most regulatory agencies have been given such power explicitly in their enabling legislation. Even when statutory authority has been vested in the agency head, such power has usually been subdelegated to a subordinate.

b. **Scope and effect of subpoenas.** No agency subpoena has a coercive effect until the judiciary enforces it. However, unlike judicial subpoenas, federal agency subpoenas are ordinarily valid throughout the United States. But, again, agencies look to the courts to enforce agency subpoenas.

c. **Defense of ultra vires.**

1) **General rule.** Most courts appear to view a defense that the information sought deals with matters beyond the scope of authority conferred as an insufficient defense to a subpoena of documents.

2) **Relevancy of material sought--Endicott Johnson Corp. v. Perkins,** 317 U.S. 501 (1943).

a) **Facts.** Secretary of Labor Perkins (P) issued a subpoena requesting payroll records of Endicott Johnson Corporation (D), alleging that P had reason to believe that D's employees were engaged in the performance of government contracts under the Walsh-Healey Act and, hence, entitled to its minimum wage requirements. D argued that the plants under investigation did not fall within the Act and were therefore beyond the agency's jurisdiction. The district court denied P's request for an enforcement order, but the court of appeals reversed. D appeals.

b) **Issue.** Must a court first conclude that the matters subpoenaed fall within the agency's jurisdiction before it allows the subpoena to be enforced?

c) **Held.** No. Judgment affirmed.

(1) The evidence sought was neither incompetent nor irrelevant to the agency's lawful purposes on its face, and the issue of whether the plants fell under the agency's jurisdiction would be reached after the documents were reviewed.

3) **Jurisdiction over defendants--Oklahoma Press Publishing Co. v. Walling,** 327 U.S. 186 (1946).

a) **Facts.** Walling (P), the Wage and Hour Administrator, sought enforcement of his subpoenas of records of Oklahoma Press Publishing Company newspaper publishers, and others (Ds) to determine whether Ds were violating the Fair Labor Standards Act ("FLSA"). Ds argued that the FLSA was not applicable to

Endicott
Johnson
Corp. v.
Perkins

Oklahoma
Press Publish-
ing Co. v.
Walling

them, that the issue of whether they are subject to its provisions must be adjudicated before the subpoenas may be enforced, and that issuance of the subpoenas would allow P to engage in a general fishing expedition. On appeal of several judgments, the courts of appeals held for P. Ds bring this consolidated appeal.

b) **Issue.** Must the issue of whether Ds are subject to the provisions of the FLSA be adjudicated before enforcement of the subpoenas will be allowed?

c) **Held.** No. Judgment affirmed.

(1) The subpoena power in the FLSA has been conferred so that P can discern whether Ds have violated the FLSA.

(2) No violation of the Fifth Amendment protection against self-incrimination is involved where, as here, the only records sought were ordinary business records of a corporation.

(3) The issuance of a subpoena does not violate Fourth Amendment prohibitions, because no question of actual search and seizure is involved.

(4) The issuance of a warrant or subpoena need not be premised on an allegation that Ds have violated the law. It is sufficient that the investigation is pursuant to a lawfully authorized purpose. "Probable cause" is satisfied where there exists a lawfully authorized inquiry of a type the legislature can command and where the documents sought are relevant to the inquiry.

4) **Ultra vires limitation on subpoena powers.** One issue that has arisen is whether an administrative agency's subpoena powers may be limited because the information sought and/or the parties from which the information is sought lie beyond the agency's jurisdiction. Several courts have refused to limit the agency's subpoena power where the information or persons fall within the general authority of the agency, liberally construed, and refuse to rule on the agency's substantive jurisdictional parameters in subpoena enforcement actions. [*See* Freeman v. Brown Brothers Harriman & Co., 357 F.2d 741 (2d Cir. 1966)]

d. **The judicial role in compulsory process.** The following principles govern the role of the judiciary in enforcing administrative subpoenas:

1) The subpoena must be issued in pursuit of an authorized objective;

2) The agency must not be acting in bad faith or for purposes of harassment;

3) The evidence must be germane to a lawful subject of inquiry;

4) The demands for evidence must not be unduly vague or unreasonably burden-some;

5) The administrative command must not ignore applicable privileges; and

6) The administrative command must be in a proper form.

VII. OPEN GOVERNMENT AND THE FREEDOM OF INFORMATION ACT

A. FREEDOM OF INFORMATION AND GOVERNMENT NEEDS FOR CONFIDENTIALITY

1. **The Freedom of Information Act.** The Freedom of Information Act ("FOIA"), 5 U.S.C. section 552, amended the APA in 1966 (and subsequently) to insist that federal agencies promptly provide requested information, unless the information sought falls within one of the nine specific exemptions of section 552(b).

   a. **Time limits.** Agencies must decide whether to release requested information within 10 working days and decide an appeal of an adverse determination within 20 working days. A 10-day extension may be had under "unusual circumstances." [5 U.S.C. §552(a)(6) (A), (B)]

   b. **Segregation.** Even when one of the nine specified exemptions of section 552(b) applies to a portion of the document requested, any reasonably segregable portion thereof that does not fall within the exemption shall be provided to the requesting party.

   c. **Judicial review.** FOIA appeals take precedence on the docket of the federal district court, which shall determine the issues de novo. The burden of proof is upon the agency to justify its refusal to make the documents available. [5 U.S.C. §552(a)(4)(B)] The courts possess full contempt powers to enforce their determinations and may assess reasonable attorneys' fees against the government should the complainant prevail. [5 U.S.C. §552(a)(4)(E), (G)] Disciplinary proceedings may be initiated against the agency individual who wrongfully withheld the requested information. [5 U.S.C. §552(a)(4)(F)] The reviewing court is also free, pursuant to the 1974 amendments of the FOIA, to perform an in-camera inspection of the disputed document. [5 U.S.C. §552(a)(4)(B)]

   d. **Specific exemptions.**

      1) **Secrecy exemption.** The first exemption under the FOIA is for matters secret in the interest of national defense and foreign policy and which "are, in fact, properly classified pursuant to executive order." [5 U.S.C. §552(b)(1)(A), (B)] The quoted language was added as a 1974 amendment, largely in order to overrule the decision of *EPA v. Mink*, 410 U.S. 73 (1973). In *Mink*, the Supreme Court rejected claims (asserted by 32 congressmen) that the legitimacy of executive security classification of government documents was subject to judicial review at the request of a citizen, or that such documents were subject to an in-camera inspection so that the court could segregate the legitimately secret from the nonsecret components thereof.

      2) **Internal personnel rules and practices exemption.** This exemption serves to protect the personal privacy of agency

employees and shield the agencies from excessive harassment. [5 U.S.C. §552(b)(2)]

3) **The exemption for documents governed by statutes which specifically direct nondisclosure.** This exemption was narrowed in 1976. [5 U.S.C. §552(b)(3)]

4) **The private business information exemption.** Information is confidential if its disclosure would be likely to injure the competitive position of one who filed it or if its release would impair the ability of the agency to obtain such information in the future. [5 U.S.C. §552(b)(4)] Trade secrets and commercial or financial information obtained from a person and privileged or confidential communications are included in this exemption.

5) **The exemption for agency memoranda.** The purpose of this exemption is to protect the candor of internal agency discussions. [5 U.S.C. §552(b)(5)]

6) **The personal privacy exemption.** This exemption is designed to protect the individual's right to privacy. [5 U.S.C. §552(b)(6)] Personnel and medical files and similar files, the disclosure of which would constitute a clearly unwarranted invasion of personal privacy, are included in this exemption.

7) **The investigatory records exemption.** This exemption precludes the release of information that might interfere with enforcement proceedings, deprive a defendant of a fair trial, disclose the identity of a confidential source, etc. [5 U.S.C. §552(b)(7)]

8) **The financial institution and geological exploration exemptions.** These are rarely litigated. [5 U.S.C. §552(b)(8), (9)]

9) **Reverse-FOIA litigation.** Information acquired by an administrative agency is often secured under an implicit or explicit promise that the tendered data will remain confidential. But parties who tendered such information have generally been unsuccessful in their attempts to enjoin release thereof by the agency. [*See* Chrysler Corp. v. Brown, *infra*]

2. **Government Needs for Confidentiality.**

NLRB v. Sears, Roebuck & Co.

a. **Scope of agency memoranda exemption--NLRB v. Sears, Roebuck & Co., 421 U.S. 132 (1975).**

1) **Facts.** Sears, Roebuck & Company (P) had unsuccessfully urged a Regional Director of the NLRB (D) to file an unfair labor practice complaint against a labor union with which it was engaged in collective bargaining. The Regional Director refused, the company was told, because P had delayed taking certain steps in the bargaining; he was guided in his judgment by internal advice received from D's General Counsel. His refusal was appealable to the General Counsel. While preparing its appeal, P requested disclosure of various memoranda and indices generated by the Office of the General Counsel in

deciding whether to issue unfair labor practice complaints. The General Counsel refused, principally on the ground that the fifth exemption to the FOIA, 5 U.S.C. section 552(b)(5), permitted him to resist disclosure of "inter-agency or intra-agency memoranda or letters which would not be available by law to a party other than an agency in litigation with the agency." P brought suit in the United States District Court for the District of Columbia, claiming that the documents it sought were disclosable both as "final opinions" or "instructions to staff that affect a member of the public" [5 U.S.C. §552(a)(2)] and as "identifiable records" not within any exemptive category [5 U.S.C. §552(a)(3)]. After the General Counsel failed in efforts to settle the dispute, the district court granted P sweeping relief, and the court of appeals affirmed without opinion. D appeals.

2) **Issue.** Does the fifth exemption of the FOIA call for disclosure of all opinions and interpretations embodying the agency's effective law and policy, while at the same time withholding all papers that reflect the agency's group thinking in the process of working out its policy and determining what its law shall be?

3) **Held.** Yes. Judgment affirmed in part and reversed in part.

a) "Exemption 5" does not apply to those appeals and advice memoranda that conclude that no complaint should be filed and which have the effect of finally denying relief to the charging party; but exemption 5 does protect from disclosure those appeals and advice memoranda which direct the filing of a complaint and the commencement of litigation before the Board. In addition, if an agency chooses expressly to adopt or incorporate by reference an intra-agency memorandum previously covered by exemption 5 in what would otherwise be a final opinion, that memorandum may be withheld only on the ground that it falls within the coverage of some exemption other than exemption 5.

b) D claims that its intra-agency opinions and attorney-client and attorney work product materials were privileged. The purpose of exemption 5 is "to prevent injury to the quality of agency decisions" by protecting the agency's decisionmaking process. However, the privilege does not apply to communications made after a final decision has been rendered or materials which explain a decision. "Exception 5, properly construed, calls for 'disclosure of all opinions and interpretations—which embody the agency's effective law and policy. . . .'" All materials that embody an agency's final decision (*e.g.*, an order not to file a complaint) are subject to disclosure, as the agency's decisionmaking process is not impeded; the decision is already made. On the other hand, any agency materials concerning the filing of complaints and litigation status before a final decision are privileged. Finally, if otherwise protected materials are referenced in the final opinions, they are subject to discovery as long as another exemption does not apply.

4) **Comment.** Since exemption 5 withholds from a member of the public documents that a private party could not discover in litigation with the agency, it is reasonable to construe exemption 5 to exempt those documents, and only those documents, normally privileged in the civil discov-

ery context. While recognizing the two privileges claimed by the government as legitimate—namely, executive privilege (to prevent injury to the quality of agency decisions) and attorney work product privilege—the Court distinguished between pre-decisional communications, which are privileged, and communications made after the decision and designed to explain it, which are not.

B. FREEDOM OF INFORMATION AND PRIVATE NEEDS FOR CONFIDENTIALITY

1. Proprietary Information.

Critical Mass Energy Project v. Nuclear Regulatory Commission

a. **Voluntarily submitted information--Critical Mass Energy Project v. Nuclear Regulatory Commission,** 975 F.2d 871 (D.C. Cir. 1992), *cert. denied,* 507 U.S. 984 (1993).

1) **Facts.** The Critical Mass Energy Project (P) attempted to obtain access to safety reports prepared by the Institute for Nuclear Power Operations ("INPO") under the FOIA. The INPO, an independent group that collects "candid" information from nuclear plant workers across the country, had voluntarily given this information to the Nuclear Regulatory Commission (D) on the condition that it would not be disclosed without permission of the INPO.

2) **Issue.** Because the INPO voluntarily gave information to D that it did not intend for public disclosure without its permission, is the material privileged under exemption 4 of the FOIA?

3) **Held.** Yes.

   a) As long as the information is provided voluntarily and is the type that the INPO would normally withhold, it must be kept confidential.

   b) Under the test in *National Parks & Conservation Association v. Morton*, 498 F.2d 765 (D.C. Cir. 1974), material is deemed confidential and privileged under exemption 4 of the FOIA if disclosure is likely to "impair the government's ability to obtain necessary information in the future; or to cause substantial harm to the competitive position of the person from whom the information was obtained." Because the INPO provided the information voluntarily, the government's interest is in retaining future access to material. Disclosure would harm this interest and harm INPO's desire to keep material discreet.

4) **Comment.** The court adds a new element to *National Parks*: the material is confidential under exemption 4 if it is the type of information not normally released to the public.

b. **Incidental disclosure of trade secrets--Chrysler Corp. v. Brown,** 441 U.S. 281 (1979).

1) **Facts.** The Department of Defense Logistics Agency ("DLA"), pursuant to regulations of the Department of Labor's Office of Federal Contract Compliance Programs ("OFCCP") and for the purpose of insuring compliance with Executive Orders 11,246 and 11,375 mandating observance of nondiscriminatory hiring practices, required Chrysler Corporation (P) to furnish reports and other information about its programs, some of which is commercially sensitive data. OFCCP regulations provided that even if such information was exempt from disclosure under the FOIA, "records obtained or generated pursuant to Executive Order 11,246 (as amended) shall be made available for inspection and copying if it is determined that the requested inspection or copying furthers the public interest and does not impede any of the functions of the OFCCP or the Compliance Agencies, except in the case of records disclosure of which is prohibited by law." Parties desiring to monitor P's employment practices filed FOIA requests for reports regarding two of its facilities. The DLA notified P of the requests and, later, of its intention to honor them. P filed an action in federal district court to enjoin the disclosure of information on the ground that its release was precluded by the fourth exemption of the FOIA. P prevailed in district court. The Third Circuit Court of Appeals reversed, and the Supreme Court granted certiorari.

2) **Issues.**

   a) Does the fact that a particular request for information fits under a FOIA exemption prohibit the requested agency from voluntarily disclosing the information despite the reporting party's objections to such disclosure?

   b) When applicable, will section 1905 of the Trade Secrets Act prevent an agency from disclosing mandatorily reported information, the disclosure of which is requested under the FOIA?

   c) Does section 1905 of the Trade Secrets Act afford a mandatorily reporting party about whom information has been requested under the FOIA a private right of action to obtain injunctive relief?

3) **Held.** a) No. b) Yes. c) No. Judgment vacated and remanded for further proceedings consistent with this opinion.

   a) The legislative history of the FOIA indicates that there was sentiment that government agencies should have the latitude, in certain circumstances, to afford the confidentiality desired by these submitters. But the congressional concern was with the agency's need or preference for confidentiality; the FOIA by itself protects the submitters' interest in confidentiality only to the extent that this interest is endorsed by the agency collecting the information. Congress did not design the FOIA exemptions to be mandatory bars to disclosure. Thus, the fact that a particular request for information fits under a FOIA exemption does not prohibit an agency from voluntarily disclosing requested information despite a submitter's objection to such disclosure.

b) Section 1905 of the Trade Secrets Act provides, inter alia, that any officer or employee of the United States who discloses to any unauthorized extent any information coming to him in the course of his employment or official duties that relates to confidential statistical data, amount or source of income, profits, losses, or expenditures, of any person, will be fined in an amount not more than $1,000 or imprisoned not more than one year, or both, and will be removed from office or employment. A disclosure is "authorized by law" only if the agency regulation authorizing it is "substantive"; *i.e.,* affects individual rights and obligations, is a *product of a congressional grant* of legislative authority, and conforms with any procedural requirements imposed by Congress.

   (1) The regulations relied upon by the government in this case as providing "authorization by law" within the meaning of section 1905 certainly affect individual rights and obligations; they govern the public's right to information in records obtained under Executive Order 11,246 and the confidentiality rights of those who submit information to OFCCP and its compliance agencies.

   (2) However, when Congress enacted these OFCCP statutes, it was not concerned with public disclosure of trade secrets or confidential business information, and it is simply not possible to find in these statutes a delegation of the disclosure authority asserted by the government here. Furthermore, when the Secretary of Labor published the regulations pertinent in this case, he stated that they related solely to interpretive rules, general statements of policy, and rules of agency procedure and practice and, consequently, neither notice of proposed rulemaking nor public participation was required by the APA; nor were such procedural requirements followed.

   (3) When such regulations are not properly promulgated as substantive rules, they are not the products of procedures which Congress prescribed as necessary prerequisites to giving a regulation the binding effect of law. An interpretative regulation or general statement of agency policy cannot be the "authorization by law" required by section 1905.

c) This Court has rarely implied a private right of action under a criminal statute and, where it has done so, "there was at least a statutory basis for inferring that a civil cause of action of some sort lay in favor of someone." Nothing in section 1905 prompts such an inference. Thus, section 1905 does not afford P a private right of action for injunctive relief. Besides, a private right of action under section 1905 is not necessary to make effective the congressional purpose, because the review of the DLA's decision to disclose is available under the APA section 10(a). The applicable scope of review set forth in APA section 10(e) is that a reviewing court shall hold unlawful and set aside agency action, findings, and conclusions found to be arbitrary, capricious, an abuse of discretion, or otherwise not in accordance with the law. Therefore, we vacate the court of appeal's judgment and remand for further proceedings consistent with this opinion so that the court of appeals may consider whether the contemplated disclosures would violate the prohibition of section 1905.

4) **Comment.** The FOIA disclosure exemptions create in the agency the right—not the obligation—to withhold information. However, even if an exemption exists, the agency may still disclose at its discretion. No right to prevent disclosure exists in others under the FOIA. However, a right to prevent agency disclosure may exist in another party (*i.e.,* a third party) under an act separate from the FOIA.

2. Individual Privacy.

a. **Unwarranted invasions of privacy--United States Department of Justice v. Reporters Committee for Freedom of the Press,** 489 U.S. 749 (1989).

1) **Facts.** The Federal Bureau of Investigation ("FBI") compiles and maintains criminal "rap sheets," which contain information regarding personal description, arrest history, charges, convictions, and incarcerations of over 24 million persons. The rap sheet information is voluntarily exchanged between the FBI and local, state, and federal law enforcement agencies to aid in detection and prosecution of offenders and assist court sentencing and parole decisions. Rap sheets are generally confidential and restricted to government uses; however, subjects of the rap sheet are allowed a copy and rap sheets may be used to prepare press releases and publicity to help apprehend wanted persons or fugitives. Exemption 7(C) of the FOIA excludes from disclosure records or information compiled for law enforcement purposes to the extent that production of the information "could reasonably be expected to constitute an unwarranted invasion of personal privacy." Respondent news correspondents and reporters requested disclosure under the FOIA of the rap sheet for one member of the Medico family, a family linked with corruption and organized crime. The district court held that the rap sheet was exempt from disclosure, the court of appeals reversed, and the Supreme Court granted certiorari.

2) **Issue.** Is disclosure of a rap sheet by the FBI to a requesting third party an "unwarranted invasion of personal privacy" and thus exempt from the disclosure requirements of the FOIA under section 552(b)(7)(C)?

3) **Held.** Yes. Judgment reversed.

a) Although the events summarized in the rap sheet of Medico have been previously disclosed to the public, the privacy interest in the rap sheet as a summary of information is substantial.

(1) Federal funding of the preparation and maintenance of the rap sheets suggest that the summarized information would not be "freely available," in light of the fact that the rap sheet contains computerized information about the subject compiled over the course of up to 80 years.

(2) There is a strong privacy interest supporting nondisclosure of rap sheet information under the Privacy Act, which prohibits agency disclosure of records within a system of

records without written consent of the individual to whom the record pertains.

    b)   Invasion of Medico's privacy is not "warranted" under exemption 7(C), since disclosure of information about private citizens in governmental files does not assist citizens' right to be informed about what their government is "up to." Disclosure of a rap sheet does not reveal much concerning the agency's conduct.

b.   **Government in the Sunshine Act.**

1)   **General rule.** The Government in the Sunshine Act, 5 U.S.C. section 552b, provides that meetings of a sufficient number of agency members to transact business generally must be open to the public.

2)   **Exemptions.** Where the agency votes that the public interest so requires and the matters under discussion fall within one of the 10 specified exemptions, the meetings need not be public. Among the exemptions are discussions of:

    a)   Matters properly classified as secret;

    b)   Internal personnel rules;

    c)   Matters exempt from disclosure by statute;

    d)   Trade secrets and commercial and financial information;

    e)   Discussions involving an individual accused of a crime;

    f)   Information the disclosure of which would constitute a clearly unwarranted invasion of personal privacy;

    g)   Investigatory records compiled for law enforcement purposes;

    h)   Information involving the regulation or supervision of financial institutions;

    i)   Financial information, the premature disclosure of which would lead to financial speculation, endanger the stability of a financial institution, or frustrate implementation of agency action; or

    j)   Matters involving agency issuance of a subpoena or the agency's participation in a judicial proceeding.

3)   **Judicial review.** The federal district courts have jurisdiction over disputes arising under the Sunshine Act. [5 U.S.C. §552b(h)]

c.   **Advisory group--Association of American Physicians & Surgeons, Inc. v. Hillary Rodham Clinton,** 997 F.2d 898 (D.C. Cir. 1993).

1)   **Facts.** Clinton (D) was named by the President to head the Task Force on National Health Care Reform. To assist the Task Force, an "interdepartmental working group" was set up, comprised of members of the Executive Branch, Congress, and "special government employees." This working group gathered information and established options for the Task Force. The Task Force would in turn report to the President. In the spring of 1993, the Task Force held one public and 20 closed meetings. The Association of American Physicians and Surgeons, Inc. (P) sought access to the meetings under the Federal Advisory Committee Act ("FACA"). The district court held first that D was not a federal government officer or employee merely because she was the First Lady, and that therefore the Task Force was not exempt from FACA as an "advisory group composed solely of 'full-time officers or employees' of the government." However, recognizing the need to protect the President's right to seek confidential advice, the court entered an injunction that required the Task Force to meet all FACA requirements *except* when meeting to prepare advice for the President. The court then held that the "interdepartmental working group" also was not an advisory group. D appeals.

2)   **Issue.** Was P entitled to access the meetings because of D's participation on the Task Force and the working group falling under FACA?

3)   **Held.** Judgment reversed and remanded for further proceedings.

a)   Even though D was on the Task Force and was not a government official, the problem with applying FACA is the Task Force's proximity to the President. Applying FACA would "seriously burden [the President's] power," impeding confidentiality.

b)   As to the working group, it would fall under FACA if "it is asked to render advice or recommendations, as a group, and not a collection of individuals" (*e.g.*, have a fixed membership).

c)   The record is not developed enough to resolve the issues in this case, so the case is remanded.

4)   **Comment.** Obviously, there is room for plenty of conflict between the disclosure objective and the exemptions stated. Also, there are tremendous logistical problems in actually getting disclosure accomplished and in judicial supervision of disclosure. But the general trend of the Act is clear—more and more disclosure of government records is being allowed.

VIII. THE PROCESSES OF AGENCY DECISION

A. ON-THE-RECORD ADJUDICATION

1. **Introduction.** Some administrative agencies combine many functions within their agencies: they may formulate policy, administer it, and adjudicate particular cases. They may also investigate, prosecute, and try cases. Normally, these functions are allocated among divisions of the agency. But even this separation has not silenced the critics of administrative agencies, who have argued that the combination of functions has resulted in poor or biased decisions. Various theories have been advanced to separate the functions of agencies, including the following:

   (i) Divorce the judicial from the administrative functions.

   (ii) Separate the prosecutor from the agency.

   None of these suggestions has worked in practice.

2. **The Administrative Law Judge.**

   a. **Functions.** Generally, the hearing officer presides at the first hearing and makes an initial decision. This is appealed to the heads of the agency or sometimes to an intermediate review board.

   b. **Stature.** Initially, hearing officers, who were installed to begin the process of hearing and to gather basic facts, were not highly regarded. However, over the years they have gained substantial stature. Their jobs have become circumscribed, they have gained a degree of independence from superiors above them in the agency organization, they have become civil service employees (removable only by the Civil Service Commission and with pay rates set by the Commission), and they have gained stature in name (they are now called Administrative Law Judges).

   c. **Problems.** The growing importance and prestige of hearing officers has also brought some problems: How can the agency work effectively, combining into a whole the various departments of the agency, if the hearing officers are totally independent of the agency (as a separate type of "judicial" system)? To what extent should the hearing officer's determinations be final? What is the review relationship between the hearing officer and the heads of the agency?

Nash v.
Bowen

   1) **Independence of ALJs--Nash v. Bowen,** 869 F.2d 675 (2d Cir. 1989).

      a) **Facts.** Nash (P), an ALJ who had over 30 years' experience in the Social Security Administration, protested policies implemented by the Director of the Bureau of Hearings and Appeals (D). The policies included a "Peer Review Program," monthly production goals, and a "Quality Assurance System" that contained provisions to encourage ALJs to decrease reversal rates. The reforms were adopted to ease the backlog of over 100,000 cases. P challenged the reforms, arguing that the reforms would impair an ALJ's "right to 'decisional independence'" under the APA. The district court found for D.

b) Issue. Under the APA, the Social Security Act, and the Due Process Clause of the Fifth Amendment, did D interfere with the "decisional independence" of ALJs by instituting the administrative reforms?

c) Held. No. Judgment affirmed.

(1) The "Peer Review Program" did not infringe upon the decisional independence of the ALJs since the basis for the program was to improve the quality and efficiency of ALJ decisionmaking and the program did not directly interfere with the "live" decisions of the ALJs.

(2) The monthly production goals, which set a minimum number of decisions an ALJ must decide, did not infringe on the decisional independence of the ALJs. The large backlog of cases was sufficient justification for the Secretary to regulate efficiency levels, and the monthly minimum number only reflected ALJ goals, not quotas.

(3) D's reversal rate policy in the "Quality Assurance System," although suspect, did not constitute an infringement on the decisional independence of the ALJs. The policy did not "coerce" ALJs into lowering reversal rates; rather, the goal of the policy was to improve the decisional quality and consistency of ALJs. (The court relied on evidence that correlated ALJs' decisional errors with extreme reversal rates.)

(4) D properly exercised discretion in adopting reasonable administrative measures to improve the ALJ decisionmaking process.

d. Removal or suspension of ALJs--Social Security Administration, Office of Hearing & Appeals v. Anyel, 58 M.S.P.R. 261 (1993).

Social Security Administration, Office of Hearing & Appeals v. Anyel

1) Facts. The Social Security Administration (P) wanted to remove Anyel (D) as an ALJ because (i) it was alleged that she did not have an acceptable level of professional and legal competence and (ii) she frequently refused to follow administration policy which assured a right to counsel in pro se claimant hearings. As to the first charge, the Chief ALJ held that it was inappropriate to punish D for these transgressions, as this would usurp the function of the appellate process. As to the second, he felt that the charge warranted a 90-day suspension, as her actions regarding the granting of counsel did not concern her case decisions, but the fulfillment of the hearing function. The Merit Systems Protection Board ("MSPB") appeals this decision.

2) Issue. Did P show good cause for suspending D?

3) Held. No. Case remanded for determination on the merits.

a) The standard of review is that an "[a]gency generally may remove or suspend an ALJ 'only for good cause established and determined by the MSPB'." The agency is not required to show that the ALJ's errors were more egregious than those of other ALJs.

b) The removal of an ALJ for performance does not have a chilling effect on the decisionmaking authority of an ALJ. The APA gives ALJs a "qualified right of decisional independence." However, in cases such as this, where the ALJ does not follow binding interpretations of the law by an agency leading to inconsistency of the application of the law, sanctions may be appropriate.

c) The Chief ALJ must show that his decision was based on "good cause."

e. **Bias as to the defendant or party.**

1) **Introduction.** Where it is shown that the decisionmaker has actual bias toward a party to the proceeding, there must be a disqualification.

2) **The issue.** The issue is: How close a contact with the matter previously is too much? It is a difficult question to answer. All one can do is review the cases and get some "feel" for how the courts react to various situations. But note that normally, it is not bias and a new tribunal is not needed when a case is reversed by a court and remanded to the same agency for further proceedings.

3) **Prejudgment.** Many cases fall into the situation where the decisionmaker has made public pronouncements that seem to indicate his "prejudice" toward a matter that he will have to pass on. For example, in *Texaco, Inc. v. FTC*, 336 F.2d 754 (D.C. Cir. 1964), *vacated and remanded on other grounds*, 381 U.S. 739 (1965), the FTC Chairman made a speech in which he indicated that certain practices by tire companies were illegal, and named the companies engaging in such practices. The very issues were before the agency in the *Texaco* case. The court held that the FTC had already prejudged the case.

Central Platte Natural Resources District v. Wyoming

4) **Bias--Central Platte Natural Resources District v. Wyoming,** 513 N.W.2d 847 (Neb. 1994).

a) **Facts.** Central Platte Natural Resources District (P) filed six applications to remove water from the instream flows of the Central Platte River, in order to preserve upstream food and habitats for five species of birds. After hearings held in 1991, the Department of Water Resources granted three applications, granted in part and denied in part another, denied another, and dismissed another. During the hearing, the principle issue was whether the river could meet both the new requests and established water rights. To this end, models predicting the water supply and the economic and environmental tradeoffs of the decision were utilized. The agency called Dr. Ann Bleed as an expert witness to discuss these controversial models. Bleed served as the examining officer during the hearing, and had previously assisted in the preparation of a report favoring instream flows. Wyoming (D), which contended that Bleed was biased, appeals the decision.

b) **Issue.** Did the fact that one of the agency's witnesses during the hearing served as the hearing officer during the hearing and had previously published material which showed a bias towards a probable resolution require her disqualification as a witness?

c) **Held.** No.

   (1) Bleed should not be disqualified because she had previously issued an opinion as to the facts underlying the scientific theory in the case. Although due process "requires disqualification when the administrative adjudicator has actually prejudged the precise facts at issue, due process does not require the disqualification of one who has merely been exposed to or investigated the facts at issue."

   (2) Also, any prejudgment she may have about the issues is not disqualifying; otherwise it would preclude all ALJs from trying the same or similar issues more than once.

5) **Duality of functions.** Merely because an agency performs dual functions does not mean that it has bias in performing the latter function (which may depend on the findings of the former function).

   a) **Separation of functions--Grolier, Inc. v. FTC,** 615 F.2d 1215 (9th Cir. 1980).

   Grolier, Inc. v. FTC

      (1) **Facts.** Grolier (D) is engaged in the door-to-door and mail order sale of encyclopedias and related reference publications. The FTC (P) issued an administrative complaint charging D with unfair methods of competition and unfair or deceptive acts or trade practices in connection with its sales activities, pricing representations, promotional techniques, recruitment practices, debt collection, and mail order operations. After the original ALJ assigned to the case retired and a second ALJ recused himself, ALJ von Brand began hearings and decided to recall many of the witnesses who had testified previously. ALJ von Brand later informed the parties that he had served as an attorney-advisor to a former Commissioner of P during the period in which D was intermittently investigated and charged by P. Upon learning of von Brand's advisory responsibilities, D requested that the judge disqualify himself from further participation; von Brand refused, stating that he did not recall working on matters involving D while serving as legal advisor to the Commissioner. D then filed a formal motion with P for disqualification and removal of ALJ von Brand, at the same time requesting P to permit discovery of specified records which would have tended to show the nature and extent of the ALJ's contact with D's case. P denied both the motion for disqualification and the requested discovery.

      (2) **Issue.** Does section 554 of the APA mandate an internal separation of the investigatory-prosecutorial functions from adjudicative responsibilities?

(3) Held. Yes. Decision reversed and remanded.

    (a)   In an effort to minimize any unfairness caused by the consolidation of executive, legislative, and judicial responsibilities, section 554 of the APA mandates an internal separation of the investigatory-prosecutorial functions from adjudicative responsibilities. To violate section 554, an agency employee must, in the same or a factually related case, (i) engage in investigative or prosecutorial functions and (ii) participate or advise in the decision.

    (b)   By forbidding adjudication by persons engaged in the performance of investigative or prosecutorial functions, Congress intended to preclude from decision-making in a particular case not only individuals with the title of investigator or prosecutor, but all persons who, in that or in a factually related case, had been involved with ex parte information, or who had developed, by prior involvement with the case, a "will to win." Those courts that have considered the question have focused not upon the former position of the challenged adjudicator, but upon his actual involvement, while in that former position, with the case he is now deciding.

3. Agency as Decisionmaker.

a. The intermediate report by the hearing officer.

    1) APA requirements. Section 557 sets forth statutory requirements for hearing examiners.

        a) When a hearing is required. Subsection (b) of section 557 provides that when a trial-type hearing is required to be held, the examiner must render an initial decision unless the agency or statute requires that he certify the record to the agency for decision.

        b) Recommended decision. Even when the examiner is to certify the record to the agency for a decision, he is first to give a "recommended decision."

        c) Rulemaking. In rulemaking situations, where a hearing is required, the agency can omit the recommended decision where it finds that timely execution of its functions requires such omission. [5 U.S.C. §557(b)(2)]

        d) Findings and conclusions. All decisions by the agency are part of the record; they must include a statement of findings, conclusions, and the reasons therefor. Prior to a recommended or initial decision, or a decision on agency review of the examiner's decision, the parties are entitled to a reasonable opportunity to submit proposed findings and conclusions (or exceptions to the decision made) and supporting reasons therefor. The record must show the ruling on each such finding or conclusion. [5 U.S.C. §557(c)]

 e) **Notice.** In adjudicatory-type hearings, notice of the hearing giving adequate indication of the issues must be given.

 f) **Appeal.** On appeal from or review of the initial decision, the agency has all of the powers that it would have in making the initial decision. [5 U.S.C. §557(b)]

2) Constitutional requirements.

 a) **Introduction.** Prior to the enactment of the APA, the Supreme Court gave some indication of the constitutional requirements for hearing examiners to render initial decisions.

 b) **No decision required.** In *NLRB v. Mackay Radio & Telegraph Co.*, 304 U.S. 333 (1938), a complaint was issued that stated the issues. After the examiner took the evidence, the agency took over the case without having an opinion or decision from the examiner. This procedure was upheld by the Court.

 c) **Conclusion.** As long as there is a narrowing of issues so that parties have a fair opportunity to respond, it makes little difference at what point this occurs. Thus, there is no constitutional need for the examiner to render a decision. Of course, today, with the APA, the question of whether the examiner must first render a decision is largely a statutory one.

b. The obligations of notice and hearing.

1) Responsibility to hear the evidence--Morgan v. United States (Morgan I), 298 U.S. 468 (1936).

Morgan v.
United States
(Morgan I)

 a) **Facts.** This case involves a rulemaking situation concerning maximum rates for livestock brokers in the Kansas City Stockyards. The Department of Agriculture was required by statute to hold a hearing. The important fact here is that the Secretary of Agriculture did not conduct the hearing, the hearing officer gave no decision, and the Secretary made the decision without familiarity with all of the evidence in the case, but in reliance on the opinions and conclusions of other employees in the Department. Morgan and others (Ps) appeal on grounds of improper agency procedure.

 b) **Issue.** Has the Secretary followed the required decisionmaking procedure set forth in the governing statute?

 c) **Held.** No. Demurrer sustained.

  (1) There has been a violation of the statute that gives a right to a hearing.

(2)   Evidence can be taken by an examiner and the evidence can be sifted and analyzed by subordinate employees. But the person making the decision must consider the evidence and the arguments that are made.

d)   **Comment.** This decision made it impossible for agency heads to be decisionmakers except at the end of a decisionmaking process; *i.e.,* to play a review role.

(1)   Therefore, responsibility for making initial decisions was pushed down to the hearing examiners.

(2)   In many cases, intermediate review boards were set up which were composed of key agency employees.

(3)   And, in some cases, the agency heads were split up into divisions, so that they could handle more cases.

Morgan v.
United States
(Morgan II)

2)   **Inadequate hearing procedures--Morgan v. United States (Morgan II),** 304 U.S. 1 (1938).

a)   **Facts.** *See* preceding case. Notice was given that rates were being investigated. There was a long hearing, with thousands of pages of evidence, but the Department never requested the examiner to produce a report. Instead, the Secretary allowed a brief oral argument and then decided the case (with some reference to the transcripts). He was assisted by his staff, who searched the record and prepared findings.

b)   **Issue.** Did the Secretary's procedure violate Morgan's (P's) due process rights?

c)   **Held.** Yes.

(1)   The procedure violated the right to due process; thus, the hearing was defective. There was no notice of the issues to be decided and no indication of the government's position. All the brokers knew was that there was an inquiry going on concerning commission rates, and this is insufficient

d)   **Comment.** The speculation concerning the case was that it stood for the proposition that the examiner need not give a report as long as at some point before decision, the parties were given adequate notice of the issues involved and an opportunity to present their arguments.

3)   **Modification of the *Morgan* rule.** *Morgan v. United States (Morgan IV),* 313 U.S. 409 (1941), is the fourth *Morgan* case. The issue concerned the validity of a rate order promulgated by the Secretary to supplement the one that had initiated all of the litigation in the first place. The Court sustained the order. The Court held that it is improper to question the decisionmaker (in this case the Secretary) in an agency decision to determine how he had made the decision and what he had considered in the decisionmaking process. The effect of this *Morgan* case was to substantially undermine *Morgan I.*

4)   **Exceptions to *Morgan IV*.**

a) **General rule.** Although the general rule now is that it is impossible to question the decisionmaker about how he came to the decision, there are some exceptions to this rule.

b) **Where the decision seems irregular.** There have been cases where external circumstances lend credence to the view that the decision-making process has not been what it should be. In these cases, the courts have gone around the *Morgan IV* rule and looked into the way the decision was made.

   (1) **Illustration.** For example, in *S.D. Warren Co. v. NLRB*, 342 F.2d 814 (1st Cir. 1965), several documents important to the case disappeared from the agency file prior to a decision. The documents had been removed for copying. The issue was whether the members of the Board had had a chance to see the copies. If so, then they had a full record to review. If not, then the full record was not available, and a basis for reversal existed. The court held that upon receipt of affidavits by Board members that they had received the copies, the appeal would be dismissed.

c. **The impact of multiple roles.**

1) **Multiplicity of functions.** Merely because an agency performs multiple functions does not mean that it is biased in performing a later function (even though the later function depends on the findings of an earlier function).

   a) **Due process concerns.** While limiting their activity primarily to the area of adjudication, agencies adjudicate, legislate, and perform executive functions. While these functions can be impermissibly combined so as to violate parties' constitutional rights, the mere fact that agencies perform all three functions and other functions necessary to accomplish them does not constitute a per se violation of a party's rights.

   b) **State licensing board--Withrow v. Larkin,** 421 U.S. 35 (1975).

Withrow
v. Larkin

   (1) **Facts.** Larkin (P), a licensed Michigan physician, performed abortions at a Milwaukee office at a time when such actions were criminal. The state medical examining board ("Board") informed P that it would conduct an investigatory hearing into P's conduct, at which P's and his attorney's participation would be limited to explaining evidence that had been presented. Subsequently, the Board formally charged P with certain professional violations and set a date for a contested hearing. P then persuaded a federal district court to restrain the Board from conducting the hearing until P could bring and complete an action against the Board on the grounds that the statute was unconstitutional in its assignment of investigating and adjudicating roles to the same tribunal. The Board held further investigatory hearings, found "probable cause" to believe that P had criminally violated state law, and referred the matter to the Milwaukee District Attorney for prosecution. Later, the three-judge district court ruled that P had shown a high likelihood of success in his constitutional claim and preliminarily enjoined the Board from conducting a hearing on the formal charges against P. The Board appeals to the United States Supreme Court.

(2) **Issue.** Is a statute unconstitutional which delegates to a state medical examining board the authority to investigate, prosecute, and judge the professional conduct of a state-licensed physician?

(3) **Held.** No. Judgment reversed and remanded.

(a) State administrators are assumed to be persons of conscience and intellectual discipline, capable of judging a particular controversy fairly on the basis of its own circumstances. The combination of investigative and adjudicatory functions does not, without more, constitute a due process violation.

(b) The presumption is that the Board was unbiased and did not engage in prejudgment. P has not overcome that presumption with any evidence or law he presented. It is very typical for members of administrative agencies to receive results of investigations; approve the filing of charges, formal complaints, or enforcement proceedings; and then participate in the ensuing hearings. Judges repeatedly issue arrest warrants based on probable cause, preside at preliminary hearings to decide whether enough evidence exists to hold a defendant for hearing, and then preside at the actual trial. Likewise, the risk of bias or prejudgment in this administrative sequence of functions had not been considered to be intolerably high or to raise a sufficiently great possibility that the adjudicators would be so psychologically wedded to their complaints that they would consciously or subconsciously avoid the appearance of having erred or changed position.

(4) **Comment.** This case involves an action to revoke a medical license. While the Board could recommend criminal prosecution to state authorities, the Board itself could not criminally prosecute and was limited to actions regarding the license.

c) **The rule of necessity.** The rule of necessity holds that where there is only one tribunal that has the power to hear and decide the case, even if it is biased it must be allowed to proceed under the "rule of necessity." [Brinkley v. Hassig, 83 F.2d 351 (10th Cir. 1936)] However, where this occurs, the reviewing court will take the bias into consideration and the review will be more stringent than normal.

Gibson v. Berryhill

d) **Pecuniary interest as bias--Gibson v. Berryhill,** 411 U.S. 564 (1973).

(1) **Facts.** Employees of Lee Optical (Ps) challenged the fairness of the Alabama Board of Optometry (D) on grounds that it was impermissibly biased. It was alleged that D could not fairly adjudicate claims that the practice of optometry by corporate employees was no longer permissible under Alabama law. If D concluded that Ps' operations were unlawful, the members of D (who were optometrists, not employees of corporations) would fall heir to Ps' business.

(2) Issue. Are the members of the Board so biased by prejudgment and pecuniary interests that they cannot conduct hearings on the issue of revocation of Ps' licenses?

(3) Held. Yes.

    (a) A pecuniary stake in the dispute by the decisionmaker need not be a direct one. Here, the indirect financial gain arising from putting one's competitors out of business was deemed sufficient to warrant disqualification.

    (b) The Board was comprised of individuals who would likely benefit from the license revocation of their competitors.

d. Obstacles to integrity arising from contacts with others.

1) "On-the-record" proceedings. In formal rulemaking and adjudication, communications between the agency and interested parties are prohibited, unless all parties are provided with adequate notice thereof and an opportunity to participate therein. Any ex parte communications must be summarized promptly by agency decisionmakers participating in them, and these summaries must be placed in the record. [5 U.S.C. §557(d)]

    a) Illustration--Professional Air Traffic Controllers Organization v. FLRA, 685 F.2d 547 (D.C. Cir. 1982).

        (1) Facts. Professional Air Traffic Controllers Organization (P) called a strike in 1981. The FAA applied to the Federal Labor Relations Authority (D) for revocation of P's certification under the Civil Service Reform Act. Allegations of ex parte communications with D's members led to an investigation by a specially appointed ALJ. It revealed that Department of Transportation Secretary Drew Lewis and the president of the American Federation of Teachers had communicated with D's members.

        (2) Issue. May interested persons freely attempt to influence the decisionmaker outside the formal proceedings?

        (3) Held. No. (Here it was harmless error.)

            (a) 5 U.S.C. section 557(d) prohibits ex parte communications between decisionmakers and an "interested person." This term is to be construed liberally.

            (b) 5 U.S.C. section 551(4) defines an ex parte communication to include "an oral or written communication not on the public record to which reasonable prior notice to all parties is not given," but does not include requests for status reports.

            (c) 5 U.S.C. section 557(d) prohibits communications "relevant to the merits of the proceeding."

Professional
Air Traffic
Controllers
Organization
v. FLRA

(d) Disclosure of ex parte communications is important both to avoid the appearance of impropriety and to insure fair decision-making (so that an opposing party can respond effectively).

(e) Undisclosed and improper ex parte communications render the agency decision voidable, not void.

(f) In assessing whether the agency's decision should be reversed or remanded, the issue is whether its decisional process was "irrevocably tainted so as to make the ultimate judgment of the agency unfair, either to an innocent party or to the public interest that the agency was obliged to protect." In determining whether this has occurred, the court weighs several factors: (i) "the gravity of the ex parte communications;" (ii) "whether the contacts may have influenced the agency's ultimate decision;" (iii) "whether the party making the improper contacts benefitted from the agency's ultimate decision;" (iv) "whether the contents of the communications were known to opposing parties, who therefore had no opportunity to respond;" and (v) "whether vacation of the agency's decision and remand for new proceedings would serve a useful purpose."

(g) It is not acceptable for any member of the public, an interested person, or a party to a proceeding to attempt to influence the decision of a decisionmaker outside the proceedings. When a decisionmaker is so approached, he should promptly terminate the conversation.

(h) Here, the communications were improper, but harmless error.

b) **Purposes of the ex parte prohibition.**

(1) **Basis.** The prohibition against ex parte communications enhances the likelihood that the agency decision will have an adequate basis in fact.

(2) **Accuracy.** The rule also insures that opposing parties will be able to challenge the accuracy of the assertions.

(3) **Judicial review.** On appeal, the courts can better evaluate the reasonableness of the agency's decision.

2) **Participation of the staff in decisionmaking.**

a) **APA provision.** Section 554(d) provides that a hearing examiner may not consult with a "person or party on a fact in issue, unless on notice and opportunity for all parties to participate. . . ." There is an exception for "the agency or a member or members of the body comprising the agency."

b) **Constitutional limitations.**

(1) **General rule.** There is no due process violation when the heads of an agency consult with members of the staff who have not actively taken part in the prosecution or investigation of the case.

    (a) This was the situation in the first *Morgan* case, where the Secretary relied on staff attorneys and others for advice and counsel.

    (b) Compare with this result, however, the view in *Mazza v. Cavicchia*, 15 N.J. 498 (1954), which indicated that everything considered by the person making the decision (including the hearing examiner's report) had to be made part of the record. This is a broader view of due process than that which prevails generally.

(2) **Exception to the general rule.** If the ex parte contact involves contact with personnel who have been active in the prosecution or investigation of the case, due process questions can arise.

    (a) **Statutory limitations.** The APA has some provisions that touch on this matter, at least as far as hearing examiners are concerned.

        1] **APA.** Section 554(d) provides that the hearing examiner may not be "responsible to or subject to the supervision or direction of an employee or agent engaged in the performance of an investigative or prosecuting function for an agency." Also, "an employee or agent engaged in the performance of investigative or prosecuting functions for an agency in a case may not, in that or a factually related case, participate or advise in the decision, recommended decision, or agency review pursuant to section 557 of this title, except as witness or counsel in public proceedings."

        2] **Exceptions.** There are some exceptions to this later part. It does not apply to (i) applications for initial licenses; (ii) proceedings involving the validity or application of rates, facilities, or practices of public utilities or carriers; or (iii) the agency or a member or members of the body comprising the agency.

(3) **Application--American Telephone & Telegraph Co.,** 60 FCC 1 (1976).

American Telephone & Telegraph Co.

    (a) **Facts.** The FCC considered for a long time a revision of rates for certain commercial services provided by American Telephone & Telegraph Company ("AT&T"). A judicial order mandated that the FCC resolve the issues presented within the next few months. At the rate hearings, the FCC's Common Carrier Bureau adduced evidence through its own witnesses, cross-examined witnesses, and took positions on the highly controverted issues in the case. At the close of the hearings, the Bureau filed a recommended decision with the FCC. AT&T responded with its own exceptions to the recommended decision and supporting briefs to their exceptions. AT&T requested an order from the FCC prohibiting members of the Bureau from further participation in the decision.

    (b) **Issue.** Do fairness and due process require a federal agency engaged in rulemaking proceedings to prohibit agency personnel who represented the agency in the proceedings from further ex parte participation in the decision?

(c) **Held.** No. Request denied.

1] Fairness and due process do not require a federal agency engaged in rulemaking proceedings to prohibit from further participation in the decision agency personnel who represented the agency in the proceedings.

2] The rate revision hearings were, according to prior holdings by the Commission and the courts, rulemaking proceedings, and neither the Communications Act, the APA, nor the Due Process Clause of the United States Constitution require separation of the Bureau from the decisionmaking process. While such further participation may be, as AT&T contends, "ill-advised"—indeed, the FCC recently passed an order that provides for the prospective and not retroactive separation of trial staff in restricted rulemaking proceedings involving common carrier matters—there is no legal mandate here for such separation, and no injustice will result because AT&T will have adequate voice for their positions in their exceptions and support briefs and because the Bureau is required in any further participation to give impartial expert advice. Lastly, the ultimate decision is to be made by the Commission on the evidence in the record, according to the principles of law and equity.

(d) **Separate statement** (Chairman Wiley). While not a matter of mandatory procedural due process, absent our current time constraints the better approach would be to grant the relief requested. However, since the court of appeals has mandated that time is of the essence here, we cannot afford the time loss entailed in turning the matter over to an entirely new staff but must consider the Bureau's recommended decision with the assistance of all available staff resources.

(e) **Dissent** (Commissioner Robinson). While neither the Communications Act, the APA, nor the Due Process Clause mandate the Bureau's separation from further participation, the Commission has acted unfairly in failing to separate not the entire Bureau but, as requested, the Bureau personnel who actively participated in the prosecution of the case through the time of the preparation of the recommended decision of the Bureau. The majority's unwillingness to separate itself from the prosecutorial personnel underscores the concern complained of—that the Commission will depend more on the Bureau's advice than on the arguments and facts on the official record.

(f) **Comment.** Agencies and courts are unwilling to reverse decisions and necessitate the expense and wasted time of a second proceeding where error, if it occurred, was not prejudicial and not likely to change the outcome of a second hearing even if removed.

Portland Audubon Society v. The Endangered Species Committee

(4) **Ex parte communications--Portland Audubon Society v. The Endangered Species Committee,** 984 F.2d 1534 (9th Cir. 1993).

(a) **Facts.** Under the Endangered Species Act, a seven-member committee must vote to grant exemptions to the Act. Here, the Endangered Species Committee (D) allowed exemptions in 13 of 44 sites, allowing timber sales in areas protecting the northern spotted owl. According to the Portland

Audubon Society (P), the decision to allow the exemptions was "the product of improper ex parte contacts" (*i.e.,* pressure from the Executive Branch).

(b) Issue. Are D's proceedings subject to the ex parte communications ban, and do the communications from the Executive Branch fall within this branch?

(c) Held. Yes.

    1] The communications in this case were barred. Under 5 U.S.C. section 557(d)(1), "ex parte communications relevant to the merits of an agency proceeding between 'any member of the body comprising the agency' or any agency employee who 'is or may reasonably be expected to be involved in the decisional process'" are prohibited. The government argues that the President was not covered by the ban, as he was an "interested person" in every deliberation, giving him a great amount of influence. Based on legislative history, the Act "explicitly vests discretion to make exception decisions in the Committee," without the aid of the President. The government also argues that by banning executive communications, it would equal congressional influence on the Committee. We disagree. Congress's objectives are greater than any impact on executive functions. Congress clearly intended to establish an independent body with the Act.

3) "Political influence" and "pressure."

a) Introduction. In this section, the problem of external influences on the decisionmaker in the course of his deliberations is considered. In addition to such criminal practices as bribery, the decisional process can be influenced by political pressure, personal associations, communications from influential people, etc.

b) Improper influence.

    (1) An example. In the case *In re Applications of WKAT*, 29 FCC 221 (1958), four parties competed for an award of a television station license. WKAT approached an FCC Commissioner through three Senators and personal friends. Another used the Commissioner's lawyer, who had the Commission in financial hock. A third got an ex-Congressman to have friends introduce a bill in Congress that would prevent the first two applicants from receiving the license. Ultimately, a judgment that all three be disqualified was upheld. [WKAT, Inc. v. FCC, 296 F.2d 375 (D.C. Cir. 1961)] The Commissioner resigned shortly thereafter.

    (2) Proper influence.

        (a) Executive Branch. The Constitution provides that the President is to execute the laws. How much influence should the Executive Branch have?

(b) Legislative Branch. Congress has traditionally kept a close watch on the administrative branch through a review of its decisions. Also, many Congressmen regularly communicate with the agencies, believing that it is part of their job as representatives. How far can this go and still be proper?

(3) Congressional interference--Pillsbury Co. v. FTC, 354 F.2d 952 (5th Cir. 1966).

(a) Facts. The FTC had reversed a trial examiner's decision to dismiss the complaint against Pillsbury Company for violations of the merger part of the antitrust laws. The FTC remanded for further proceedings. While hearings were still going on, FTC Commissioners were subjected to severe questioning and criticism for their views in the case in a congressional hearing before the Subcommittee on Antitrust and Monopoly. Members of this subcommittee questioned the FTC Commissioners and expressed disapproval of the FTC decision (holding, rather than finding a per se violation, that proof of lessened competition had to be shown). The FTC Chairman disqualified himself, but other Commissioners took part.

(b) Issue. Is a congressional committee's intrusion into the adjudicatory process of a case pending before a federal administrative agency a denial of due process to the regulatee whose case is under consideration?

(c) Held. Yes. Decision reversed and remanded.

1] Due process has been violated. Congressional meddling has gone too far, giving rise to the appearance of partiality.

2] If the questioning had been on generalized issues of policy, there would have been no problem. Here, there was reference to a particular case, an explicit view was expressed, and Commissioners were made to publicly defend their position while their own hearings were still going on.

3] New Commissioners had joined the FTC, so an impartial agency existed on remand.

c) The revolving door problem--LaSalle National Bank v. County of Lake, 703 F.2d 252 (7th Cir. 1983).

(1) Facts. Lake County, Illinois (D) is the former employer of an attorney now practicing law with a large law firm. D moved to disqualify the attorney's law firm because of D's former relationship with the attorney. The district court granted the motion, finding that the past association gave rise to an appearance of impropriety and holding that both the attorney and the entire law firm (Ps) must be disqualified. Ps appeal.

(2) Issue. Should the disqualification of an attorney due to a previous relationship be extended to an entire law firm?

(3) Held. Yes. Judgment affirmed.

(a)   Unless the presumption of shared knowledge is effectively rebutted by establishing that the infected attorney was properly screened or insulated from all participation in and information about a case, the attorney's law firm will be disqualified based on his prior employment.

(b)   If past employment in government results in the disqualification of future employers from representing some of their long-term clients, it seems clearly possible that government attorneys will be regarded as "Typhoid Marys." Many talented lawyers, in turn, may be unwilling to spend a period of time in government service, if that service makes them unattractive or risky for large law firms to hire. In recognition of this problem, several courts have begun to approve the use of screening as a means to avoid disqualification of an entire law firm by "infection." The screening arrangements that courts and commentators have approved contain certain common characteristics: (i) the attorney is denied access to relevant files, (ii) the attorney receives no share in profits or fees derived from the representation in question, (iii) the discussion of the suit is prohibited in the attorney's presence and no members of the firm are permitted to show him any documents relating to the case, (iv) both the disqualified attorney and others in his firm affirm these facts under oath, and (v) the screening arrangement is set up at the time when the potentially disqualifying event occurred.

B. INFORMAL RULEMAKING

1.   **Informal Agency Decision.** Courts have reached divergent views on whether ex parte communications are prohibited where informal rulemaking procedures are employed. The APA appears explicitly to prohibit ex parte communications only in formal "on-the-record" proceedings. But some courts also prohibit ex parte communications in informal rulemaking where the decision involves conflicting private claims to a valuable privilege.

    a.   **Conflicting private claims--Sangamon Valley Television Corp. v. United States,** 269 F.2d 221 (D.C. Cir. 1959).

Sangamon Valley Television Corp. v. United States

        1)   **Facts.** The FCC conducted informal rulemaking proceedings in which it decided to move the location of a VHF station from Springfield, Illinois, to St. Louis, Missouri. Several parties engaged in ex parte communications with Commissioners.

        2)   **Issue.** Are ex parte communications allowed in informal rulemaking?

3) Held. No.

    a) Although the agency's decision arose in an informal rulemaking context, it nevertheless involved the "resolution of conflicting private claims to a valuable privilege." Hence, notions of fundamental fairness require that such decisions be made in the open.

Home Box Office, Inc. v. FCC

b. Ex parte communications forbidden--Home Box Office, Inc. v. FCC, 567 F.2d 9 (D.C. Cir. 1977), *cert. denied,* 434 U.S. 829 (1977).

    1) Facts. After widespread ex parte communications, the FCC (D), in informal rulemaking, adopted regulations limiting the type of programming to be offered by cable television services. Home Box Office, Inc. and others (Ps) sought review on the grounds that D had engaged in ex parte communications.

    2) Issue. May an agency promulgating rules in informal rulemaking properly engage in ex parte communications?

    3) Held. No. FCC decision reversed.

        a) The notion that there may be one record for the public and for purposes of judicial review and another for the FCC and those who are informed is intolerable.

        b) The courts must compare the agency's conclusions against the record before the decisionmaker when he made his decision, in order to discern whether that decision was arbitrary and capricious.

        c) Even if the agency informs the court of the basis of its action, where it fails to introduce it into the record prior to a final decision, it has been denied the benefits of adversarial analysis thereof.

        d) Secrecy is inconsistent "with fundamental notions of fairness implicit in due process and with the ideal of reasoned decisionmaking on the merits."

        e) Ex parte communications received prior to the publication of notice of proposed rulemaking in the Federal Register need not be put into the public record, unless they form the basis for the agency decision.

        f) But once such notice has been published, those involved in the decisional process should refuse to discuss the rulemaking with interested persons. If ex parte communications are nevertheless received, a written summary of them should be placed in the record so that interested persons may comment thereon.

Action for Children's Television v. FCC

c. Ex parte communications permitted--Action for Children's Television v. FCC, 564 F.2d 458 (D.C. Cir. 1977).

    1) Facts. In informal rulemaking procedures, the FCC (D) declined to adopt the rules governing children's TV programming advertising that were proposed by Action for Children's Television (P). Prior to its decision, D had engaged in ex parte communications with representatives of the National Association of Broadcasters.

2) **Issue.** Do D's ex parte communications invalidate the proceeding?

3) **Held.** No. FCC decision upheld.

    a) In informal rulemaking, an agency may go beyond the record, drawing "upon its own expertise in interpreting the facts or upon broader policy considerations not present in the record."

    b) The prior cases on ex parte communications in informal rulemaking can be distinguished on the grounds that they involved "conflicting private claims to a valuable privilege," while the rules involved here encompass policies of general applicability.

d. **Closed mind?--C & W Fish Co. v. Fox,** 931 F.2d 1556 (D.C. Cir. 1991).

    C & W Fish Co. v. Fox

1) **Facts.** In 1990, the National Oceanic and Atmospheric Administration ("NOAA"), under the Department of Commerce ("DOC"), banned the use of drift nets in a fishery. Under the Magnuson Act, the DOC was given the authority to create fish conservation programs, with the states' interests represented through eight regional councils. In 1989, two councils attempted to ban the use of gillnet fishing. A rule was adopted that regulated, but did not prohibit, this type of fishing. In 1990, a new proposal was submitted but rejected. Fox (D), a new NOAA assistant administrator, revived the proposal. Before joining NOAA, D had been a strong opponent of gillnet fishing. C & W Fish Company and others (Ps) sought review of the ban. The district court granted D summary judgment. Ps appeal.

2) **Issue.** Did D have an "unalterably closed mind" when he made the decision to ban gillnet fishing, thus violating Ps' due process rights?

3) **Held.** No. Judgment affirmed.

    a) There was no "clear and convincing evidence of a closed-minded decision."

    b) It "would eviscerate the proper evolution of policymaking . . . to disqualify every administrator who has opinions on the correct course of his agency's future actions."

e. **Agency advising decisionmaker--United Steelworkers of America, AFL-CIO-CLC v. Marshall,** 647 F.2d 1189 (D.C. Cir. 1980), *cert. denied*, 453 U.S. 913 (1981).

    United Steelworkers of America, AFL-CIO-CLC v. Marshall

1) **Facts.** The Occupational Safety and Health Administration ("OSHA") issued new rules designed to protect American workers from exposure to airborne lead in the workplace. In these consolidated appeals, United Steelworkers of America (P), representing both labor union and industry interests, challenge virtually every aspect of the new lead standard and the massive rulemaking from which it emerged. The unions claimed that

OSHA had failed to carry out its statutory duty to insure that no employee would suffer material impairment of health. The industry parties charged OSHA with almost every procedural sin of which an agency can be guilty in informal rulemaking, attacked some of the most important substantive provisions of the standard as exceeding OSHA's statutory authority, and asserted that the agency had failed to present substantial evidence to support the factual bases of the standard. The procedural attack was aimed at OSHA staff attorneys who, it was argued, acted essentially as advocates for a stringent lead standard by consulting with and persuading the Assistant Secretary as she drew her conclusions from the record.

2) **Issue.** Does the APA bar a staff advocate from advising the decisionmaker in setting a final rule?

3) **Held.** No. Judgment affirmed.

   a) Nothing in the APA bars a staff advocate from advising the decisionmaker in setting a final rule. In establishing the special hybrid procedures in the OSH Act, Congress never intended to impose the separation-of-functions requirement it imposes in adjudications. Rulemaking is essentially an institutional, not an individual, process, and it is not vulnerable to communication from within an agency in the same sense as it is to communication from without. In an enormously complex proceeding like an OSHA standard setting, it may simply be unrealistic to expect an official facing a massive record to isolate herself from the people with whom she worked in generating the record.

   b) In a proceeding to create a general rule it makes little sense to speak of an agency employee advocating for one side over another. However contentious the proceeding, the concept of advocacy does not apply easily where the agency is not determining the specific rights of a specific party, and where the proposed rule undergoes detailed change in its journey toward a final rule. The standard's attorney may have been an advocate for some new lead standard, and probably even a stringent one, but not necessarily for one specific standard supported by one specific party.

4) **Dissent** (MacKinnon, J.). Fundamental requirements of fairness and due process in administrative law compel that these outside consultants to whom the agency delegates its obligation to evaluate the evidence must be unbiased and neutral in their evaluation of the record. No court should condone allowing paid consultants to legally change their hats from expert witnesses, subject to cross-examination during the hearings, to agency staff hired after the close of hearings to evaluate the credibility of their own testimony and that of others.

Sierra Club v. Costle

f. **Computer-generated economic model--Sierra Club v. Costle,** 657 F.2d 298 (D.C. Cir. 1981).

   1) **Facts.** In June 1979, the EPA issued revised new source performance standards ("NSPS") to govern the extent to which new coal-fired power stations must control their atmospheric emissions of sulfur dioxide and particulates. The standards resulted from a lengthy, prominent, and heated

rulemaking proceeding conducted under the hybrid rulemaking procedures of the Clean Air Act, a proceeding on which considerable political pressure had been brought to bear. The standards were promptly challenged from all sides. Among the issues the agency had to resolve in conducting the rulemaking was how to predict the impact of various possible standards on utility planning and, consequently, on overall reduction in sulfur dioxide pollution. To make this analysis—which ultimately resulted in adoption of a variable standard for required scrubbing (removing sulfur dioxide from the emissions of a plant)—the EPA developed a computer program to assess the impacts of various standards on a number of complex factors, including the following: total air emissions, new plant investment, consumer costs, energy production and consumption, fuel choice (coal, oil, gas, etc.), and the regional impacts on coal production and transportation. The program and the assumptions on which it was based were reviewed within the government by a working group of representatives from several agencies (the EPA, Department of Energy, Council of Economic Advisors, and Council on Wage and Price Stability), subjected to public comments, and revised; the results were published and publicly discussed. Subsequently, the model was used to evaluate alternative standards. On review, the Sierra Club (P) asserted that the econometric model employed by the EPA was so speculative and otherwise unreliable that the modeling results are not substantial evidence.

2) **Issues.**

a)   Are oral post-comment communications allowed under the Clean Air Act?

b)   Must all oral post-comment communications be included in the rulemaking docket?

c)   Did the input of a legislator amount to undue interference with the agency such that the adopted rule should be invalidated?

3) **Held.** a) Yes. b) No. c) No. Decision affirmed.

a)   The Clean Air Act does not expressly deal with the problem of post-comment period communications between the EPA and outsiders. Nor does the Act prohibit oral communications concerning a proposed rule. The reason for the nontreatment of these issues may be a recognition by Congress that agencies, when conducting rulemaking as opposed to adjudicatory functions, must be free to interact informally with persons outside the agency. Interaction on an informal basis with the public, the affected industry, and other interested parties serves to encourage support for agency actions, establish a good working relationship between the agency and these parties, and provide the agency with necessary information. The allowance of oral communications applies to the post-comment period as well as during the comment period.

b)   Not all oral post-comment communications need be included in the rulemaking docket. The Act requires only that information relied on by the EPA, in whole or in part, in promulgating its rule must be placed in the docket. Furthermore, the Act vests the EPA with sole discretion to determine what information was relied upon and what therefore must be docketed.

(1)   As to the May 1 meeting during which Senate staff personnel
       were briefed on the content of the proposed rule, this was
       merely for purposes of explanation of the rule to the staff. Such
       a briefing is not the type of communication required to be
       docketed under the Act.

(2)   As to the April 30 meeting during which the President and the
       White House staff were briefed and made comments concerning
       the proposed rule, this was nothing more than an instance of the
       President exercising control and supervision over executive
       policymaking. There is nothing in the Act that forbids such
       meetings or that requires that they be docketed, unless of course
       the agency intends to base its rule in whole or in part on infor-
       mation elicited at such a meeting.

c)   The rule set forth in *D.C. Federation of Civic Associations v. Volpe*,
      459 F.2d 1231 (D.C. Cir. 1971), *cert. denied*, 405 U.S. 1030 (1972),
      is applicable to instances of alleged congressional pressure on agency
      rulemaking. The two-part *D.C. Federation* test asks: (i) is the
      content of the pressure designed to force the agency to decide the
      issue based upon factors not deemed relevant by Congress in the
      applicable statute, and (ii) was the agency decision affected by those
      extraneous considerations? In this case, Senator Byrd's input has not
      run afoul of the *D.C. Federation* test. While the Senator did express
      the strong views of his constituency as well as himself, there is no
      evidence that he exerted "extraneous" pressure on the EPA. The
      Senator was merely fulfilling his duty as a representative of the
      people in expressing his and their views; he did nothing improper.

IX. JUDICIAL CONTROL OF ADMINISTRATIVE ACTION

A. INTRODUCTION

1. **Final Step of Control.** The road to judicial review begins with the breakdown of informal negotiations for a settlement of a dispute, continues through some form of more formal administrative proceedings, and finally reaches the courts.

2. **Restricted Control of Judicial Review.** The control of administrative actions through the courts is restricted due to the nature and limitations of judicial review. This restriction is caused by the following factors:

   a. **Discretion granted to the agency.** Normally, the legislature has granted certain power or discretion to the administrative agency. The court can find administrative action unconstitutional, or the court can find that the agency has acted outside the scope of its delegated power. Normally, however, the court cannot decide the case de novo; it is restricted to a determination of whether the agency has exceeded the discretion granted to it.

   b. **Other factors.**

      1) Court process is expensive.

      2) Delay.

      3) Adverse publicity.

      4) Administrative actions can control the economics of the situation so as to make judicial review meaningless (*e.g.,* as where an administrative agency can issue injunctions, stop orders, etc.).

      5) On judicial reversal and remand, the agency often can correct the "error" and still reach the same result.

3. **Benefits of Judicial Review.** Despite its limitations, judicial review is still an important control device. Review is a deterrence to arbitrary agency action. The agency must articulate its reasons and provide a record. There must also be substantial evidence to support the decision.

B. METHODS OF OBTAINING JUDICIAL REVIEW

1. **Special Statutory Review.**

   a. **Definition.** Specific statutory review is authorized when a statute specifically states that orders or other actions by an agency are reviewable by the courts.

   b. **Reviewing court.** Normally, the court is an appellate court (such as the circuit court of appeals), although there are instances in which the federal district courts are given this function.

c. **Enforcement of administrative orders.** On other occasions, an agency must go to court in order to enforce its orders. The NLRB is in this situation. When this is the case, the reviewing court will normally review the correctness of the agency's decision.

2. **General Statutory Review.** The legislature may enact general statutes providing for judicial review of administrative actions (as opposed to a specific statute providing for review of specific agency actions). The obvious example of this is the APA.

3. **Nonstatutory Review.**

a. **Introduction.** Whenever there is not a specific statutory or general statutory basis for review, resort must be to common law remedies.

b. **Injunctions and declaratory judgments.**

1) **Introduction.** These are theoretically separate remedies. In practice, however, they are normally sought together.

2) **Injunction.** An injunction seeks to have the court enjoin an agency from taking some action.

3) **Declaratory judgment.** A declaratory judgment asks the court to find that an action proposed by an agency would be illegal.

4) **Differences.** There are differences in the two remedies. For example, in an injunction the party must show that unless an injunction is issued, she will suffer irreparable injury. This requirement does not apply to declaratory judgments.

5) **Jurisdictional requirements.** Jurisdiction in a federal court is based on a section of the United States Code.

a) Under 28 U.S.C. section 1331, jurisdiction is provided where the question arises under the Constitution, laws, or treaties of the United States.

b) Under 28 U.S.C. section 1337, jurisdiction is given to the district courts where the cause of action arises under any Act of Congress regulating commerce.

c) Under 28 U.S.C. section 1343, jurisdiction is conferred in cases involving the deprivation of constitutional rights by state officials.

6) **Discretion.** Both injunctions and declaratory judgments rest within the power of the courts to grant or deny, according to their discretion (that is, in these requests the courts are largely depending on their own view of the equities on each side in reaching a decision).

c. **The prerogative writs.** The writs are an inheritance from the English courts. They are often surrounded with very technical requirements.

1) **Mandamus.** This common law writ is available in most states. In the federal courts, it is set forth in section 1361, which provides that the district courts have jurisdiction in mandamus actions to compel officers or employees of the United States (including agency employees) to perform a "ministerial" duty owed to the plaintiff.

   a) **Discretionary actions.** Mandamus does not lie to force performance of a duty that is "discretionary" with the officer or employee.

   b) **Basis of decisions.** However they may be characterized (*e.g.,* "discretionary," "ministerial," etc.), the basis of the decisions is a balancing of the equities involved on each side and a decision in the "discretion" of the court.

2) **Certiorari.** Certiorari is a writ by which a superior tribunal calls upon a lower one to certify the record on which the lower tribunal made its decision. The purpose is to review the record to determine the legality of the decision. Many states permit such a writ in connection with judicial review of administrative actions. The Supreme Court, however, has held that this writ is not available to the federal courts in reviewing administrative agency decisions.

3) **Habeas corpus.** A writ of habeas corpus may be used to test the legality of interference with an individual's bodily liberty.

4) **Quo warranto.** Where it exists, quo warranto is a civil action to test the right of some person to hold office. Normally, it does not lie to test the legality of actions taken by public officials.

C. STANDING TO INVOKE JUDICIAL REVIEW

1. **Introduction.** The standing issue concerns the question of whether the plaintiff should be able to obtain judicial review. The doctrine of standing has both constitutional and nonconstitutional bases.

   a. **Constitutional basis.** The constitutional basis arises out of the "case or controversy" requirement. This means that the plaintiff must present a concrete case for decision and be in a sufficiently adverse posture so as to pursue resolution of the controversy in a vigorous manner.

   b. **Nonconstitutional basis.** Traditionally, the courts have also required that the plaintiff be more closely connected with and personally affected by the case than the purely constitutional interest would require.

   c. **Administrative Procedure Act.** The APA confers standing upon a "person suffering legal wrong . . . or adversely affected or aggrieved by agency action within the meaning of a relevant statute." [5 U.S.C. §702]

Allen v.
Wright

d. **The contemporary doctrinal framework--Allen v. Wright, 468 U.S. 737 (1984).**

1) **Facts.** The Internal Revenue Code prohibited tax-exempt status for schools that practiced racial discrimination. In a class action suit, Wright and others (Ps) (parents of African-American students) sued on the ground that the IRS was insufficient in identifying these racially-segregated schools, thus allowing tax-exempt status to such schools. The district court dismissed for lack of standing, and the court of appeals reversed. The Supreme Court granted certiorari.

2) **Issue.** Did Ps have standing to bring this suit?

3) **Held.** No. Judgment reversed.

a) Ps charged that the actions of the IRS harmed them in two ways: (i) by allowing for financial assistance to segregated schools, and (ii) by "foster[ing] and encourag[ing] the organization, operation, and expansion of institutions providing racially segregated educational opportunities." We find there was no direct injury; "[t]he first fails . . . because it does not constitute judicially cognizable injury [and t]he second fails because the alleged injury is not fairly traceable to the assertedly unlawful conduct of the IRS." As to the first, the government only recognizes claims by those "who are personally denied equal treatment" under the law. As to the second, the causal link between the IRS actions and the alleged injury is tenuous.

2. **What Sort of Interests Count?**

Associated
Industries
of New York
State, Inc.
v. Ickes

a. **"Injury in fact"--Associated Industries of New York State, Inc. v. Ickes,** 134 F.2d 694 (2d Cir. 1943), *vacated as moot*, 320 U.S. 707 (1943).

1) **Facts.** Associated Industries of New York State, Inc. (P) was an organization of firms, many of which were substantial consumers of coal. The Commission set minimum prices under the Coal Act of 1937. Section 6(b) of the Act authorized "any person aggrieved by an order issued by the Commission" to seek judicial review in the court of appeals. P petitioned for review; the Commission moved to dismiss.

2) **Issue.** Did P have standing?

3) **Held.** Yes. Motion denied.

a) Under Article III, section 2 of the United States Constitution, there is no justiciable controversy unless a plaintiff shows that conduct will invade a private, legally-protected interest that existed at common law or was created by statute.

b) Under standards developed by the courts, P would have no standing here (no standing exists for a party threatened with financial loss from increased competition).

c)   However, the statute granting standing to "persons aggrieved" has expanded the category of those who have standing. This definition covers those threatened with financial loss from increased competition, and it covers P here.

4)   **Comment.** The courts interpreted these statutory provisions to give standing to certain groups in order to protect the "public interest."

b.   **Private causes of action.**

1)   **Against an agency.** The early rule was that if the plaintiff would have a cause of action against a private party, the plaintiff had standing to complain of the same action by the administrative agency.

2)   **By an organization.** In *Joint Anti-Fascist Refugee Committee v. McGrath*, 341 U.S. 123 (1951), the plaintiff, a charitable organization, had been listed by the Attorney General as a Communist organization. If a private party had taken a similar action (which interfered with the plaintiff's ability to raise funds), there would have been a cause of action (defamation). Hence, the plaintiff had standing to seek review of the Attorney General's action.

c.   **Competition from the government.** The traditional rule was that no party had standing to object to competition from the government. The rationale was that there would be no cause of action by the plaintiff against a private party for such competition.

d.   **The judicial development of an interest representation model of administrative law.** Traditionally, only those directly affected by agency action were deemed eligible to participate in the agency's proceeding and to secure judicial review thereof. The focus during this period was on the judiciary's limitation of the coercive power of government. More recently, the rights of public-interest individuals or groups have been expanded to include standing to participate in and appeal agency decisions. This interest representation model seeks to insure the equitable exercise of power by administrative agencies by requiring that a wider spectrum of interests are represented in agency proceedings.

e.   **The rationale of expanded standing to obtain judicial review.** Modern courts have been very generous in allowing a wide spectrum of interests to be represented before administrative agencies, including those suffering technological interference, economic injury, consumer injury, and aesthetic or ecological injury. The issue of standing to intervene is related to the question of standing to appeal adverse agency action. In either case, one who suffers an adverse effect is ordinarily deemed to have standing.

f.   **The *Data Processing* test.**

1)   **Justiciability.** Article III of the United States Constitution limits judicial power to the resolution of cases and controversies. This is the source of the standing requirement. One who seeks judicial review must allege that he has suffered some actual or threatened injury as a result of the illegal conduct of the defendant, that the injury is fairly traceable to the defendant's actions, and that it is likely to be remedied by a favorable decision. These requirements tend to assure that an actual case or controversy exists,

and that the court will not be adjudicating some abstract issue. The dispute must be presented in an adversary context and in a form capable of judicial resolution.

Association of Data Processing Service Organizations, Inc. v. Camp

2) **Principal case--Association of Data Processing Service Organizations, Inc. v. Camp,** 397 U.S. 150 (1970).

   a) **Facts.** The Association of Data Processing Service Organizations, Inc. (P), which sells data process services, objects to the Comptroller of the Currency's (D's) determination that banks should be allowed to market such services.

   b) **Issue.** Does P have standing?

   c) **Held.** Yes. Judgment reversed and remanded.

      (1) The essential requirements of standing are (i) the parties must demonstrate actual injury and (ii) P's interest must fall within the zone of interests protected by the statute or constitutional provision in question.

      (2) The legal interest test, pursuant to which an individual is denied standing unless the right invaded is a legal one (*e.g.,* arising out of contract, property, tort, or statute), goes to the merits of the controversy, not to the issue of standing.

      (3) Here, P clearly suffered economic injury as a result of the government's action.

      (4) The interests protected may be aesthetic, conservational, recreational, economic, or spiritual. One who suffers financial injury may be an appropriate person to vindicate the public interest. This is called the "zone of interests" test.

      (5) Here, there is no evidence that Congress intended to preclude judicial review.

   d) **Dissent** (Brennan, J.). Only injury in fact is relevant to a determination of standing. The second criterion (*i.e.,* the zone of interests test) comes close to the purportedly discredited legal interest test and goes to the merits rather than the issue of standing. The Court must be careful to segregate issues of standing, reviewability, and the merits.

Barlow v. Collins

3) *Data Processing* **applied--Barlow v. Collins,** 397 U.S. 159 (1970).

   a) **Facts.** Tenant farmers (Ps) are eligible for payments under the Upland Cotton Program enacted as part of the Food and Agriculture Act of 1965. Initially, payments under the Act could not be assigned as security for all or part of the rent on a farm. The Secretary then required tenants to buy all supplies, seed, etc., from the government at high prices and at exorbitant interest rates.

   b) **Issue.** Do Ps have standing?

c) Held. Yes.

(1) The reasoning under these facts is exactly the same as in *Data Processing, supra*. Article III is satisfied. Tenant farmers are within the zone of interests protected by the Act, since one of the purposes of the Act is to protect tenant farmers. And, since the Act does not provide for judicial review, nonreviewability should not be inferred.

d) Concurrence and dissent (Brennan, White, JJ.). Under *Data Processing*, the Court must make two inquiries to determine whether a party has standing. The first is whether the party has alleged that the action he challenges caused him injury in fact. The second is "whether the interest sought to be protected by the complainant is arguably within the zone of interests to be protected or regulated" by the law in question. In my view, the Court should only make the first inquiry; in making the second inquiry, the Court comes close "to perpetuating the discredited requirement that conditioned standing on a showing by the plaintiff that the challenged governmental action invaded one of his legally protected interests."

4) The definition of "injury in fact."

a) No standing for environmental injury--Sierra Club v. Morton, 405 U.S. 727 (1972).

Sierra Club v. Morton

(1) **Facts.** The Sierra Club (P) brought an action to appeal the decision of the United States Forest Service (D) to authorize construction of a $35 million ski resort in the Mineral King Valley by Walt Disney Enterprises, Inc.

(2) **Issue.** Does P have standing to allege injury to aesthetic interests?

(3) **Held.** No. Judgment reversed.

(a) The injury alleged was aesthetic and ecological. This may constitute an injury in fact sufficient to satisfy the requirements of 5 U.S.C. section 702; however, the injury must be one directly affecting an individual.

(b) P failed to allege that it or its members would suffer adverse effects by the development, or that they presently use Mineral King for any purpose. The requirement that an individual must allege that he himself is injured is imposed to insure that those who advocate a position before the courts will have a direct stake in its outcome. A mere interest in a problem does not satisfy the APA requirement that one must be "adversely affected" or "aggrieved."

(4) **Dissent** (Douglas, J.). Individuals or groups should have standing to bring an action on behalf of inanimate objects threatened by development.

(5) **Comment.** Would a party be likely to file a court action to appeal an agency decision unless it had a strong motivation to advocate forcefully against it?

b) **Compare—standing for environmental injury--United States v. SCRAP,** 412 U.S. 669 (1973).

(1) **Facts.** An environmental group, SCRAP (P), challenged the failure of the ICC (D) to prepare an environmental impact statement before allowing the rail industry to enjoy a general rate increase. P contended that the increase would discourage production of recyclable commodities (since they would incur freight charges in both directions), and that this would encourage more litter and pollution. P was comprised of five law students who alleged they enjoyed the parks, forests, and trails of Washington, D.C., which would become less desirable with the increase of pollution caused by the rate increase.

(2) **Issue.** Does P have standing?

(3) **Held.** Yes. (Relief was denied on other grounds.)

(a) The environmental injury suffered by P clearly falls within the zone of interests protected by the National Environmental Policy Act.

(b) The five law students proved that they would suffer harm in their use of recreational facilities in the Washington, D.C. area. "A plaintiff must allege that he has, or will, in fact be perceptibly harmed by the challenged agency action, not that he could imagine circumstances in which he could be" harmed. Here, P "alleged a specific and perceptible harm that distinguishes them from other citizens who had not used the natural resources claimed to be affected." Thus, P has "a direct stake in the outcome of the litigation, rather than a mere interest in the problem."

(c) In *Data Processing, supra*, we held that 5 U.S.C. section 10 conferred standing to challenge agency action on those who could show that the action caused them an "injury in fact" where that injury is within the zone of interests protected by the statute that the agency purportedly violated. Injury in fact is not limited to economic harm and may consist of injury to environmental well-being.

(d) An injury is no less an injury because it is shared by many. Otherwise, the most injurious governmental actions could be challenged by no one. Thus, even though the injury complained of here could conceivably affect everyone who breathes air in this country, P has standing.

(4) **Dissent** (White, J.). The threshold requisites for standing are not met here, because there is no injury in fact. The injuries alleged are too remote and no more substantial than injuries alleged in taxpayer cases where standing is denied.

c) **Direct harm--Lujan v. Defenders of Wildlife,** 504 U.S. 555 (1992).

(1) **Facts.** The Endangered Species Act ("ESA") of 1973 split the authority for defending endangered species between the Secretary of Labor and the Secretary of the Interior. All federal agencies must consult with one of these secretaries to insure that their actions do not threaten endangered species. Both secretaries ultimately decided to restrict the scope of their oversight to projects in the United States and its high seas. Several environmental groups (Ps) sued, attempting to force the secretaries to also include international projects. On remand, the district court denied the government's (D's) motion for summary judgment that argued that Ps lacked standing. The court of appeals affirmed. D appeals.

(2) **Issue.** Because the harm does not directly affect Ps, do they have standing to challenge the decision of the secretaries?

(3) **Held.** No. Judgment reversed.

   (a) There are three requirements for standing: there must be injury in fact (injury must be concrete and particularized), the defendant's conduct must be the cause of the injury, and the federal courts must be able to redress the harm. The plaintiff bears the burden of showing standing; the evidence necessary to show standing is more extensive where the injury does not harm the plaintiff directly, but affects some third party. Ps argue that their injury was the potential loss of species abroad. When parties who have traveled abroad in the past to view endangered species wish to make return trips at some point, such indefinite future plans cannot be the basis of "immediate harm." Ps' arguments go "beyond the limit . . . to say that anyone who observes or works with an endangered species, anywhere in the world, is appreciably harmed by a single project affecting some portion of that species with which he has no more specific connection."

   (b) As to the court of appeals finding of standing because Ps had suffered a "procedural injury" as they were authorized to bring a "citizen-suit" under the ESA on their own behalf to halt any agency from violating the Act, we also reverse. Allowing such a generalized grievance would "permit the Congress to convert the undifferentiated public interest in executive officers' compliance with the law into an 'individual right' vindicable in the courts [and thus] permit Congress to transfer from the President to the courts" his executory functions.

g. **Taxpayer standing.** Two criteria must be satisfied before taxpayers are deemed to have standing.

   1) **Taxing and Spending Clause.** The taxpayer must be objecting to an exercise of power under the Taxing and Spending Clause of the United States Constitution.

   2) **Constitutional limitation.** There must be a nexus between such taxpayer status and the constitutional provision allegedly being violated. The challenged expenditure must exceed specific constitutional limitations on that power. [Flast v. Cohen, 392 U.S. 83 (1968)]

3) **Application.** In *Valley Forge Christian College v. Americans United for Separation of Church and State, Inc.*, 454 U.S. 464 (1982), taxpayer standing under *Flast v. Cohen, supra,* was denied to an individual who objected on First Amendment grounds to the decision of HEW to transfer a United States military hospital to a church related college. The Court held that the transfer did not constitute an exercise of the Article I, section eight congressional spending power, but was merely an administrative exercise of the Article IV, section three power to administer and dispose of government property.

Control Data Corp. v. Baldrige

4) **Zone of interests revisited--Control Data Corp. v. Baldrige,** 655 F.2d 283 (D.C. Cir. 1981), *cert. denied*, 454 U.S. 881 (1981).

a) **Facts.** The Secretary of Commerce (D) promulgated standards establishing specifications to which automatic data processing ("ADP") equipment had to conform in order to be eligible for government purchase. Manufacturers and suppliers of ADP systems and equipment (Ps) brought suit in the district court, seeking a judgment declaring the specifications to be invalid and enjoining D from enforcing the specifications. Ps argued that because the specifications were similar to those of IBM, to which Ps' equipment did not presently conform, Ps would be required to expend large amounts of time and money in order to compete for government ADP contracts, that IBM would thus occupy a highly favored position vis-a-vis Ps, and that because Ps' equipment provided the only major alternative to IBM's equipment, enforcement of the specifications would hinder competition. Ps also urged that Congress desired to promote competition in order to achieve economic and efficient government procurement. The district court held that Ps lacked standing to challenge the specifications and dismissed the action. Ps appeal.

b) **Issue.** Did the Commerce Department injure an interest of Ps that was arguably within the zone of interests to be protected or regulated by the statute in question?

c) **Held.** No. Judgment affirmed.

(1) It is generally recognized that in applying the zone of interests test, a court must discern whether the interest asserted by a party in the particular instance is one intended by Congress to be protected or regulated by the statute under which suit is brought. The relevant statute in this case is the Brooks Act, passed in 1965 as an amendment to the Federal Property and Administrative Services Act of 1949. Both statutes express congressional interest in economic and efficient procurement of property, and in both Congress recognized the maximization of competition as an important means to its objective. This interest in competition is not, however, congruent with the interest in competition asserted by appellants. Only one end was sought—lower government ADP costs. Competition was not, therefore, valued for itself, but for the benefits it could bring the government.

(2) Although confusing and perhaps inconsistent, the law dictates the continued role of the zone of interests tests as a prudential limitation. We must therefore apply the test in appropriate circumstances and in a manner calculated to serve its intended purpose of allowing courts

to define those instances when they believe the exercise of their power at the instigation of a particular party is not congruent with the mandate of the Legislative Branch in a particular subject area. Because these circumstances involve the government's prerogative to dictate the specifications of those products it will purchase, our application must fully reflect our awareness of the test's importance as a limitation on the role of the courts in resolving public disputes.

5) **Clarification of standing test--Clarke v. Securities Industry Association,** 479 U.S. 388 (1987).

a) **Facts.** The Comptroller of the Currency permitted Security Pacific National Bank to open offices that sold "discount brokerage services" to the public. The McFadden Act limits the establishment of national bank "branches" to in-state branches allowed by states, defined under the statute as "any branch place of business . . . at which deposits are received, or checks paid, or money lent." The Comptroller determined that the discount brokerage services offices were not "branches" under the McFadden Act, and the Securities Industry Association (P) sued the Comptroller for misapplying the relevant portion of the Act. The Comptroller defended his action on the merits and alleged that P did not have standing, as it "did not fall within the zone of interests of the McFadden Act."

b) **Issue.** Did P, an association of securities dealers, have proper standing for judicial review in challenging the decision of the Comptroller to permit national banks to open discount brokerage offices, despite the provisions of the McFadden Act?

c) **Held.** Yes.

(1) We rely in part on the "zone of interests" test used in *Data Processing, supra*, to determine whether the challenging party is properly included in the class of potential plaintiffs. The zone of interests test looks at whether the interest sought to be protected by the plaintiff is arguably within the zone of interests to be protected or regulated by the statute or constitutional guarantee in question to determine whether the plaintiff has standing.

(2) However, we clarify the *Data Processing* test by distinguishing cases in which the plaintiff is not the subject of the legislative action. The plaintiff will not have standing if his interest is "so marginally related to or inconsistent with the purposes implicit in the statute" that Congress would not have intended to permit the suit. Based on our holding in *Block v. Community Nutrition Institute, infra*, the zone of interests question is not dispositive, and the question of standing ultimately turns on congressional intent.

(3) Congressional intent in passing the McFadden Act included the desire to limit national banks' ability to branch without regard to state law, prevent national banks from obtaining monopoly control over credit and money, and forestall the dangers of unlimited banking. Thus, congressional intent does not preclude a securities dealers association from judicial review.

(4)   There is sufficient evidence that P is part of the class that Congress intended to "be relied upon to challenge agency disregard of the law."

Air Courier
Conference
of America
v. American
Postal Work-
ers Union,
AFL-CIO

6)   Zone of interest--Air Courier Conference of America v. American Postal Workers Union, AFL-CIO, 498 U.S. 517 (1991).

a)   **Facts.** The Private Express Statutes ("PES") codified the Postal Service's postal monopoly. The purpose of the PES is to prevent private competitors from offering service on low-cost routes, which would leave the Postal Service only the high-cost routes. The PES allows the Postal Service to suspend restrictions on any mail route "where the public interest requires suspension." The Postal Service suspended restrictions for "extremely urgent letters," which allowed private courier services to provide overnight delivery of letters. Relying on that suspension, members of the Air Courier Conference of America (D) used private courier systems to deposit letters sent to foreign addresses directly with foreign postal systems, a practice called "international remailing." The Postal Service issued a final rule permitting such international remailing. The American Postal Workers Union (P) challenged the rule in federal court, claiming the rulemaking record was inadequate to support the finding that the rule was in the public interest. The district court granted summary judgment for D. The court of appeals vacated on the ground that the Postal Service relied on too narrow an interpretation of the "public interest." The Supreme Court granted certiorari.

b)   **Issue.** Where an agency is authorized to suspend statutory restrictions on private companies that prevent them from competing with the government if the suspension is in the public interest, are agency employees whose jobs are adversely affected by the suspension within the zone of interests encompassed by the statutory restrictions?

c)   **Held.** No. Judgment reversed.

(1)   To establish standing, the plaintiff must show that it has suffered a legal wrong because of the challenged agency action, or is adversely affected or aggrieved by the agency action within the meaning of a relevant statute. Then it must show that its interest is within the zone of interests sought to be protected through the statute.

(2)   The district court found that P satisfied the injury in fact requirement because the increased competition could adversely affect P's members' employment opportunities, and this finding was not appealed.

(3)   The court of appeals found that P satisfied the zone of interests requirement because the revenue protective purposes of the PES relate to P's interest in preventing the reduction of employment opportunities. But the language of the PES does not demonstrate congressional intent that postal workers were to be within the zone of interests protected by the PES. Congress was concerned with the receipt of necessary revenue for the Postal Service to perform its duties, not with opportunities for postal workers. The objectives of the grant of monopoly are to achieve national integration and to insure that all areas of the country are served equally.

(4) P notes that the Postal Reorganization Act ("PRA") contains a labor-management relations statute as well as the PES. Since the PES is the "linchpin" of the Postal Service, P claims employment opportunities are within the zone of interests covered by the PES. But the relevant statute in this case is the PES, because it is the one P alleges was violated, not the PRA, with all of its various provisions. None of the PES provisions have any integral relationship with the PRA's labor-management provisions. If the zone of interests test could extend to every provision in the PRA, it would lose virtually all meaning.

(5) P lacked standing to challenge D's order, and the courts should not have reached the merits of P's claim.

3. The Problem of Causation: The Requirements of Traceability and Redressability.

a. **Injury speculative--Simon v. Eastern Kentucky Welfare Rights Organization,** 426 U.S. 26 (1976).

Simon v. Eastern Kentucky Welfare Rights Organization

1) **Facts.** Several indigent individuals and organizations (Ps) challenged a decision of the IRS (D) to redefine charitable hospitals qualifying for tax deductible status so as to no longer require that they make medical services available to those who cannot pay for them. Ps alleged specific instances of deprivation of medical services from such hospitals.

2) **Issue.** Do Ps have standing to challenge D's redefinition of charitable hospitals?

3) **Held.** No. Judgment reversed.

a) Standing is a part of the cases or controversies requirement of Article III. An individual must have a personal interest in the controversy to have Article III standing.

b) Here, no hospital is a defendant. The Article III "case or controversy" limitation requires redress only for an "injury that fairly can be traced to the challenged action of the defendant and not to injury that results from the independent action of some third party not before the court." It is speculative whether denial of indigent services can be fairly traced to D's actions.

c) It is equally speculative whether these indigents would be provided with medical services if they were given the judicial relief they here seek.

b. **Causal connection shown--Duke Power Co. v. Carolina Environmental Study Group, Inc.,** 438 U.S. 59 (1978).

Duke Power Co. v. Carolina Environmental Study Group, Inc.

1) **Facts.** Environmental organizations and their members (Ps) attacked the constitutionality of the Price-Anderson Act, which places a ceiling

on liability for a nuclear plant accident of $560 million. Ps argue that but for the limit on liability, no plant would be built by Duke Power Company (D), from which they allegedly suffer immediate injury of increased radiation, thermal pollution in their streams and lakes, and exposure to potentially devastating risk.

   2) **Issue.** Do Ps have standing to object to the constitutionality of the Price-Anderson Act?

   3) **Held.** Yes (The Act's constitutionality was sustained.)

   a) Prior cases have established the standing requirements that Ps must suffer a "distinct and palpable injury" and that there must be a "fairly traceable causal connection" between the injury and D's conduct.

   b) The environmental and aesthetic effects of thermal pollution of the involved lakes constitutes injury in fact, as does the emission of radiation.

   c) The injury must be fairly traceable to D's action. Conversely, the court's remedial powers must be able to provide relief from the injury. The lower court concluded that these nuclear plants would likely not be built without the Price-Anderson Act.

   d) The nexus requirement for taxpayer suits is not required here. All that need be shown to prove that an Article III "case and controversy" exists is "injury in fact and a substantial likelihood that the judicial relief requested will prevent or redress the claimed injury."

   4) **Dissent** (Stevens, J.). "The string of contingencies that supposedly holds this case together is too delicate for use."

4. **Municipal Zoning.** In *Warth v. Seldin*, 422 U.S. 490 (1975), the United States Supreme Court held that the plaintiffs had failed to achieve standing to challenge a city's zoning ordinances as discriminatory, because they failed to demonstrate any specific harm to them. Taxpayers and low-income residents of other cities had failed to allege that they had sought housing in the municipality. In contrast, in *Village of Arlington Heights v. Metropolitan Housing Development Corp.*, 429 U.S. 252 (1977), on similar facts, the Court held that a developer who had contracted to build low-income housing in the municipality and a low-income individual who had expressed an interest in living there had standing to challenge the ordinance as discriminatory.

D. **REVIEWABILITY: AGENCY ACTIONS SUBJECT TO JUDICIAL SCRUTINY**

1. **Ripeness.** When a person seeks discretionary relief from the judiciary for an agency action, the courts may resist review until the controversy is "ripe." This avoids premature adjudication of disputes which have not

reached sufficient concreteness to warrant judicial interference and avoids disruption of agency decisionmaking until the impact thereof has run its course.

a. **Liberalization of ripeness.** The modern trend has been to relax the ripeness prohibition of discretionary judicial review. Where a party is faced with an agency decision having immediate adverse effects and the consequences of noncompliance are severe, courts have been willing to open the doors to judicial review.

b. **Fitness and hardship test--Abbott Laboratories v. Gardner,** 387 U.S. 136 (1967).

Abbott Labo-
ratories
v. Gardner

1) **Facts.** The Commissioner of Food and Drugs (D) promulgated regulations requiring drug manufacturers to include generic names on the labels of their prescription drugs and in their advertising literature. Thirty-seven drug manufacturers and their national associations (Ps) objected on grounds that the Commissioner had exceeded his authority. The district court granted the declaratory and injunctive relief sought, but the court of appeals concluded that pre-enforcement review was unauthorized and that no "case or controversy" existed.

2) **Issue.** Is this regulation ripe for review even though no enforcement thereof had commenced?

3) **Held.** Yes. Judgment reversed and remanded.

a) Injunctive and declaratory remedies are discretionary, and courts have been reluctant to apply them, unless the controversy is ripe for judicial review.

b) The ripeness doctrine prevents the courts from engaging in premature adjudication over abstract disagreements and protects the agencies from judicial interference until the agency decision has been rendered and its impact has been felt by the parties in a concrete way.

c) Two questions are asked to determine whether an issue is ripe: (i) fitness of the issues for judicial resolution, and (ii) hardship on the parties of withholding review.

d) Here, the issues presented are strictly legal: whether the agency regulations were ultra vires. The regulations are a "final agency action" within the meaning of 5 U.S.C. section 704.

e) The impact of the regulations upon Ps is sufficiently direct and immediate as to render the issue appropriate for judicial review. They place Ps on the horns of a dilemma. Either Ps must immediately comply and re-label all their stock of drugs and advertising material, at great expense, or they must run the risk of severe criminal and civil penalties.

f) "Where the legal issue presented is fit for judicial resolution, and where a regulation requires an immediate and significant change in the plaintiffs' conduct of their affairs with serious penalties attached to noncompliance, access to the courts . . . must be permitted."

Toilet Goods Association, Inc. v. Gardner

c. Premature review--Toilet Goods Association, Inc. v. Gardner, 387 U.S. 158 (1967).

1) Facts. The Commissioner of Food and Drugs (D) promulgated a regulation calling for immediate suspension of certification service if a company refused to permit FDA employees free access to all manufacturing facilities, processes, and formulae involved in the manufacture of color additives and intermediates from which color additives are derived. Toilet Goods Association, Inc. (P), an organization of cosmetic manufacturers, and 39 individual manufacturers and distributors sought declaratory and injunctive relief on the ground that the regulation was not authorized by the statute. The district court held that the issue was justiciable, but the court of appeals reversed. The Supreme Court granted certiorari.

2) Issue. Is the issue of whether the regulation promulgated by D is authorized by statute appropriate for judicial resolution?

3) Held. No. Judgment affirmed.

a) The test of ripeness, as we have noted, depends not only on how adequately a court can deal with the legal issue presented, but also on the degree and nature of the regulation's present effect on those seeking relief. Judicial appraisal is likely to stand on a much surer footing in the context of a specific application of this regulation than could be the case in the framework of the generalized challenge made here. This is not a situation in which primary conduct is affected (*e.g.*, when contracts must be negotiated, ingredients tested or substituted, or special records compiled). This regulation merely states that D may authorize inspectors to examine certain processes or formulae; no advance action is required of cosmetics manufacturers.

b) It is true that the administrative hearing will deal with the factual basis of the suspension, from which petitioners infer that D will not entertain and consider a challenge to his statutory authority to promulgate the regulation. Whether or not this assumption is correct, given the fact that only minimal, if any, adverse consequences will face petitioners if they challenge the regulation in this manner, we think it wiser to require them to exhaust this administrative process through which the factual basis of the inspection order will certainly be aired and where more light may be thrown on D's statutory and practical justifications for the regulation. Judicial review will then be available, and a court at that juncture will be in a better position to deal with the question of statutory authority.

d. Self-executing regulations. In *Gardner v. Toilet Goods Association, Inc.*, 387 U.S. 167 (1967), a pre-enforcement challenge to the *Toilet Goods* "additives rule," the Court held that the issues were ripe under *Abbott Laboratories, supra*, decided on the same day. Because the regulations were "self-executing" and thus have an "immediate and substantial impact upon the respondents" and because the respondents were forced to make the unfair choice between compliance with regulations it disagreed with and following the regulations, judicial consideration was timely.

2. Statutory Preclusion of Judicial Review.

    a. Statutory limitations. A basic question on reviewability is whether Congress intended that the matter in question be reviewable by the courts.

        1) Preclusion of judicial review. APA section 701(a) provides that its provisions apply (and review is allowed) except when statutes preclude judicial review.

        2) Agency discretion. Section 701 also provides that review may be limited where agency action is committed to agency discretion by law.

    b. Preclusion of review.

        1) Presumption of reviewability. In many cases, the Supreme Court has stated that there is a presumption favoring reviewability and that only on a showing of clear and convincing evidence of a contrary legislative intent will judicial review be limited. Two situations arise in determining whether such a legislative intent is present.

            a) Implied preclusion. Some cases have inferred judicial review where the statute has remained silent.

            b) Preclusion by statute. Preclusion statutes are ordinarily narrowly construed.

        2) Preclusion implied--Switchmen's Union v. National Mediation Board, 320 U.S. 297 (1943).

Switchmen's Union v. National Mediation Board

            a) Facts. The Switchmen's Union (P) objected to a decision of the National Mediation Board (D) which designated all yardmen as participants in an election for union representation.

            b) Issue. Do the courts have jurisdiction to review a National Mediation Board action?

            c) Held. No. Decision affirmed.

                (1) Where there is no explicit statutory provision authorizing judicial review, the type of problem involved and the history of the statute are germane in assessing whether review, nevertheless, is available.

                (2) Congress recognized that D would be addressing an explosive problem. Had it wanted judicial review, the legislature most surely would have made that clear.

                (3) Other provisions in the statute explicitly provide for judicial review. This suggests that none was intended here.

3) **Current law on judicial review.** *Abbott Laboratories v. Gardner, supra,* concluded that "[j]udicial review of a final agency action by an aggrieved party will not be cut off, unless there is a persuasive reason to believe that such was the purpose of Congress." Hence, there is a presumption that review exists, and the APA's judicial review provisions are read liberally.

a) **Congressional silence.** Where personal rights are created by statute, silence as to judicial review is not to be construed as a denial of judicial relief, particularly where the matter is of a type typically resolved in the courts.

b) **Ultra vires.** Where the legislature confers jurisdiction upon an agency, the agency's power is circumscribed by the parameters of the statutory authority. Courts may properly review agency behavior to the extent necessary to protect an individual interest against agency excesses.

Leedom
v. Kyne

c) **Review permitted--Leedom v. Kyne,** 358 U.S. 184 (1958).

(1) **Facts.** The NLRB included both professional and nonprofessional employees in the bargaining unit. The professional employees sought an injunction in district court on the basis that the NLRA required specifically that where professional employees were involved, they could only be included in a bargaining unit where the majority of such professional employees had voted for inclusion.

(2) **Issue.** Is the NLRB's inclusion of professional and nonprofessional employees in the same bargaining unit reviewable?

(3) **Held.** Yes. Judgment affirmed.

(a) The NLRB has acted in excess of its delegated powers. Courts may enforce the specific provisions of the NLRA. An injunction is granted.

c. **The presumption of reviewability.** Even where the legislature has not explicitly provided for judicial review (which it usually does), the absence of statutory authority for review has only occasionally been interpreted by the courts as constituting preclusion.

Block v.
Community
Nutrition
Institute

1) **Implied preclusion of reviewability--Block v. Community Nutrition Institute,** 467 U.S. 340 (1984).

a) **Facts.** The Agricultural Marketing Agreement Act of 1937 authorizes the Secretary of Agriculture (D), after due notice of and opportunity for a hearing, to issue milk market orders establishing minimum prices that processors of dairy products (handlers) must pay to producers (dairy farmers) for their milk. Pursuant to this authority, D issued some 45 milk market orders covering different regions of the country. The orders designated raw milk that is processed and bottled for fluid consumption as Class I milk. Raw milk that is used to produce milk products such as butter, cheese, or dry milk powder is termed Class II milk. The orders require handlers to pay a higher price for Class I products than for Class II products; all payments are made to a regional pool from which distributions are made to dairy farmers based on how much milk they have produced, regardless of its class. The orders require handlers to pay the lower minimum Class II price for "reconstituted milk," which is milk manufactured by mixing milk powder with water. The orders assume that handlers must make a compensatory payment to the regional pool equal to the difference between Class I and Class II milk product prices.

Three individual consumers of fluid dairy products, a handler regulated by the market orders, and a nonprofit organization (Ps) brought suit in federal district court, contending that by raising handlers' costs the compensatory payment requirement makes reconstituted fluid milk uneconomical for handlers to process. The district court held that the consumers and the nonprofit organization did not have standing and, in addition, that the Act precluded such persons from obtaining judicial review; the milk handler's action was dismissed because of failure to exhaust administrative remedies. The circuit court of appeals agreed that the handler and the nonprofit organization had been properly dismissed but held that the consumers had standing. The court also rejected the contention that the statute impliedly precluded consumers from challenging milk market orders, because the statutory structure and purposes of the Act did not reveal the type of clear and convincing evidence of congressional intent needed to overcome the presumption in favor of judicial review.

b)   **Issue.** Did Congress intend that judicial review of market orders issued under the Act ordinarily be confined to suits brought by handlers in accordance with 7 U.S.C. section 608c(15)?

c)   **Held.** Yes. Judgment reversed.

(1)   Section 608c(15) requires handlers first to exhaust the administrative remedies made available by D. After these formal administrative remedies have been exhausted, handlers may obtain judicial review of D's ruling in any federal district court in which they are inhabitants or have their principal place of business. The structure of this Act indicates that Congress intended only producers and handlers, and not consumers, to insure that the statutory objectives would be realized.

(2)   Whether and to what extent a particular statute precludes judicial review is determined not only from its express language, but also from the structure of the statutory scheme, its objectives, its legislative history, and the nature of the administrative action involved.

2)   **Statutory preclusion of reviewability--Bowen v. Michigan Academy of Family Physicians**, 476 U.S. 667 (1986).

a)   **Facts.** The Secretary of Health and Human Services (D) issued a regulation granting higher reimbursement levels from Medicare to family physicians who were "board certified" than to those who were not board certified. The Michigan Academy of Family Physicians (P) brought suit to challenge the regulation, arguing that distinguishing between board-certified and non-board-certified physicians violates the Fifth Amendment and the Medicare Act. The lower courts held for P on the Medicare Act ground and did not reach the Fifth Amendment ground. D appeals, arguing that the Medicare Act precludes judicial review of the agency action.

b) **Issue.** Does the Medicare Act preclude judicial review of D's regulation?

c) **Held.** No. Judgment affirmed.

(1) There has long been a presumption that Congress intends to permit judicial review of agency actions. In *Abbott Laboratories, supra,* we stated that "only upon a showing of 'clear and convincing evidence' of a contrary legislative intent should the courts restrict access to judicial review."

(2) Of course, Congress can limit or preclude judicial review. For matters involving the amount of benefits to be paid under Part B of the Act, Congress clearly intended to bar judicial review, instead delegating the task to carriers. We find that for those matters Congress did not delegate to carriers, Congress did not impliedly intend to bar judicial review.

3) **Express provisions limiting or restricting review.** Normally, where Congress has been specific about limiting or restricting review, the court will preclude such review.

a) **Vital interests.** But in situations where "vital" interests have been at stake, the Court has found various ways to grant review. For example, despite a statutory provision precluding review, the Court held that deportation orders were subject to some review in habeas corpus proceedings (review was limited to whether there were findings to support the administrative decision and whether the procedures used were fair). [Lloyd Sabaudo Societa v. Elting, 287 U.S. 329 (1932)]

b) **Less vital issues.** In cases where review is of statutorily-created economic benefits, courts normally uphold legislative restrictions on review. But where the Court wants to protect an interest, it finds a way to review. For example, Congress first provided that there would be no review of the Administrator's actions in veteran's administration benefit cases. The Court found an exception. Congress then amended the statute to provide that "courts have no jurisdiction." The Court still found an exception. Congress amended to "make it perfectly clear" that there was no review of noncontractual benefits provided veterans. In *Johnson v. Robison*, 415 U.S. 361 (1974), the Court held that the statute did not prevent a class action suit by conscientious objectors challenging the Act provisions which granted educational benefits to veterans, but excluded conscientious objectors who provided alternative service. The distinction made was that here, the plaintiff was not challenging the Administrator's decision, but the constitutionality of the statute.

c) **Restriction of review.** Rather than preclude review altogether, Congress may simply limit or restrict the access to the courts to specific situations, or it may limit the manner in which review may be obtained (as, for example, requiring that review only be granted after certain administrative actions have been completed).

d) **Constitutional issue.** Obviously, there is a constitutional issue here. Can review constitutionally be prohibited? It does not appear that the Court has really addressed itself directly to this issue in any of its decisions.

d. **"Committed to agency discretion."**

1) **Administrative Procedure Act.** The APA allows judicial review, except to the extent statutes preclude review, or the agency's determination is committed to its discretion by law. [5 U.S.C. §701] Preclusion of review is limited to those situations where agency action is reasonable rather than arbitrary. Thus, although an agency action may be committed to its discretion by law, review is permitted where the agency abuses its discretion. [5 U.S.C. §706(2)(A)]

2) **Action committed to agency discretion.** The APA has been construed to mean that agency decisionmaking may be precluded if committed to its discretion by law only if the exercise of discretion is reasonable. Stated differently, the courts may properly reverse agency action for abuse of discretion. The exception for action committed to agency discretion has been described as rather narrow and exists in those rare circumstances where the "statutes are drawn in such broad terms that in a given case there is no law to apply." [*See* Citizens to Preserve Overton Park, Inc. v. Volpe, *supra*]

3) **Presumption.** There appears to be a strong presumption in favor of judicial review.

4) **Exception.** As stated above, one of the situations where review is restricted occurs where "agency action is committed to agency discretion" by law. [APA §701(a)(2)] Note, however, that section 706(2)(A) provides that a court may "hold unlawful and set aside agency actions, findings, and conclusions found to be . . . arbitrary, capricious, an abuse of discretion, or otherwise not in accordance with law." These two provisions seem to conflict.

5) **Employee termination--Webster v. Doe,** 486 U.S. 592 (1988).

Webster
v. Doe

    a) **Facts.** The director of the Central Intelligence Agency ("CIA") terminated John Doe (P) from employment with the CIA because the plaintiff was homosexual. The CIA informed P that his homosexuality posed a threat to national security. Section 102(c) of the National Security Act ("NSA") provides that "[T]he Director of Central Intelligence may, in his discretion, terminate the employment of any officer or employee . . . whenever he shall deem such termination necessary or advisable in the interests of the United States." P challenged his termination on the grounds that the decision was arbitrary and capricious and violated his constitutional rights.

    b) **Issue.** Did the CIA director's dismissal of an employee based on sexual orientation exceed the statutory authority of the NSA and constitute an abuse of discretion subject to judicial review?

c) **Held.** No. Judicial review of the dismissal under the APA is precluded. Case remanded to address P's constitutional claims.

    (1) The director's discretion is unreviewable because it was "committed to agency discretion by law" under the provisions of NSA section 102(c).

        (a) The director may terminate employees whenever he "deems" it necessary, reflecting statutory deference to the director and precluding the application of judicial review.

        (b) The structure of the NSA and the CIA suggests that termination decisions were committed to agency discretion, since the effectiveness of the agencies and the ultimate goal of national security depends on a reliable and trustworthy work force. The director must have complete termination discretion to insure the integrity of the agency's employees.

    (2) However, the NSA does not preclude adjudication of constitutional claims arising out of the actions of CIA officials. The case is remanded for consideration of these claims.

e. **Prosecutorial discretion.** Ordinarily, the discretion of a prosecutor whether to initiate an enforcement action has been shielded from judicial review.

f. **The constitutionality of preclusion.** Article III, section 1 of the United States Constitution provides that judicial power may be vested in the Supreme Court and in such inferior courts as Congress may establish. Since it may, but need not, establish lower courts, might it not also limit their jurisdiction? If so, would such limitation of judicial review powers circumscribe an individual's due process protections? Probably not, if there is another court (*e.g.,* a state court) to review the government's deprivation of a liberty or property interest. But if there were no judicial forum for review, the issue might turn on the importance of the right of which the individual was being deprived and the government's interest in preclusion of review. The courts have not yet squarely addressed the issue.

E. THE TIMING OF JUDICIAL INTERVENTION

Ticor Title
Insurance
Co. v. FTC

1. **When Judicial Review Is Timely--Ticor Title Insurance Co. v. FTC,** 814 F.2d 731 (D.C. Cir. 1987).

    a. **Facts.** Section 5(b) of the Federal Trade Commission Act authorizes the FTC (D) "to initiate and prosecute complaints against persons suspected of engaging in unfair methods of competition, or unfair or deceptive trade practices." D initiated a complaint against Ticor Title Insurance Company and other title insurance companies (Ps) for illegally restraining competition. In response, Ps filed this suit, seeking a declaratory judgment that section 5(b) is unconstitutional, and to enjoin the FTC from continuing its prosecution. Ps' constitutional argument is that Article II of the Constitution prohibits federal agencies such as D who are not under the direct control of the President from exercising the law enforcement powers section 5(b) confers. The district court dismissed the action on the ground that the action is not ripe.

b. **Issue.** May Ps' action be adjudicated in the federal courts?

c. **Held.** No. Judgment affirmed. Three separate opinions were handed down by the court.

    1) Judge Edwards concluded that Ps must exhaust all nonconstitutional defenses in the course of D's action against them before bringing this constitutional challenge in federal court.

        a) The doctrines of ripeness and exhaustion are complementary, designed to prevent untimely judicial interference. However, while the ripeness doctrine is concerned with "the competence of the courts to resolve disputes without further administrative refinement of the issues," the exhaustion doctrine is concerned with the individual party's position, *i.e.*, whether the party is attempting to bypass the administrative process of the agency or rather has been diligently protecting his interests.

        b) The general rule is that exhaustion of the administrative process is a prerequisite to judicial review. There are two exceptions to this rule: (i) where "the agency's assertion of jurisdiction 'would violate a clear right of a petitioner by disregarding a specific and unambiguous statutory, regulatory, or constitutional directive';" or (ii) where postponing judicial review would cause irreparable injury to the plaintiff. In the present case, neither of these exceptions apply.

    2) Judge Williams concluded that the action is barred on the jurisdictional ground that the agency action is not "final."

        a) The principle of finality is distinct from the doctrines of exhaustion and finality. Finality looks to whether an agency has concluded a particular action, while exhaustion looks to what steps litigants must follow in seeking a remedy. And while finality looks to whether a court has the power to consider an agency action, ripeness looks to whether issues are fit for judicial review. Put another way, finality relates to jurisdiction, while exhaustion and ripeness are more prudential.

        b) Administrative decisions are final when they "impose an obligation, deny a right, or fix some legal relationship as a consummation of the administrative process." A court may only review a non-final administrative decision when the litigant asserts a "clear right" to review, such as an obvious violation of his statutory rights, or where there is a structural flaw that violates the litigant's rights. In this case, Ps asserted "right" is not clear, and there is no evidence of a "structural flaw." Ps are not entitled to review of D's non-final administrative action.

3) Judge Green concluded that the issue in this action is not ripe for review.

    a) Under *Abbott Laboratories, supra,* in determining whether an administrative challenge is ripe for review the courts must "evaluate both the fitness of the issues for judicial decision and the hardship to the parties of withholding court consideration." The issues raised by Ps meet the fitness prong of the test. However, Ps cannot succeed on the second prong, as they allege cost of litigation as the primary hardship they might suffer and, under *SOCAL, infra,* cost is insufficient to constitute irreparable injury.

    b) Unlike my colleagues, I believe that ripeness is the only bar to judicial review of Ps' challenges. Ps allege that D lacks constitutional authority to prosecute. Because D cannot and will not determine that it lacks authority to prosecute Ps, further exhaustion of administrative proceedings is futile, and D's assertion of its prosecutorial authority is final.

2. Exhaustion of Administrative Remedies.

    a. **Definition.** No one is entitled to judicial relief until the prescribed administrative remedy has been exhausted. Stated differently, a party may ordinarily not seek judicial review of administrative agency action until he has first utilized all of his appellate opportunities within the agency.

    b. **Rationale.**

        1) **Avoidance of premature adjudication.** Like a trial court, the agency has been established to apply the statute in the first instance. It is usually desirable to allow the agency the first opportunity to develop the facts and apply the law.

        2) **Efficiency.** It is ordinarily more efficient to allow the agency to proceed without interruption than to allow judicial review at the various intermediate steps.

        3) **Judicial review.** Judicial review is enhanced by allowing the agency to develop a factual record and to apply its expertise. The judiciary can more efficiently employ its resources by reviewing the agency record than by compiling its own independent findings of fact.

        4) **Judicial efficiency.** A party who is forced to exhaust his administrative remedies may choose not to appeal an adverse judgment. Judicial interference in the administrative process would also weaken the agencies by encouraging parties to ignore those procedures.

    c. **Jurisdictional challenges.** Parties who have objected to agency action on grounds that the action is ultra vires have had little success in the federal courts in securing review of the jurisdictional question prior to the administrative action. They have had greater success in state courts.

d. Court injunction inappropriate--Myers v. Bethlehem Shipbuilding Corp., 303 U.S. 41 (1938).

Myers v. Bethlehem Shipbuilding Corp.

  1) Facts. Bethlehem Shipbuilding Corporation (P) filed an injunction action in federal court against Myers (D), who was regional director of the NLRB, to prohibit the agency from pursuing a complaint alleging unfair labor practices under the NLRA. P contended that the NLRB had no jurisdiction because its operations at the facility involved, at Fore River, Massachusetts, were not in interstate commerce. Hence, P argued that the question was beyond the agency's jurisdiction and that agency proceedings would be unnecessarily costly to P and deleterious to its harmonious labor-management relations. The appellate court held that the district court had the power to grant such an injunction. D appeals.

  2) Issue. May a federal court properly enjoin agency proceedings at an early stage where it is alleged that the agency lacks subject matter jurisdiction?

  3) Held. No. Judgment reversed.

    a) The NLRB has jurisdiction to "prevent any person from engaging in any unfair practice affecting [interstate] commerce," and Congress has insisted that such power be exclusive.

    b) Even where a party alleges that the agency has no jurisdiction over the controversy, "no one is entitled to judicial relief for a supposed or threatened injury until the prescribed administrative remedy has been exhausted."

    c) The NLRB will decide initially whether it has jurisdiction. If the agency erroneously concludes that it does, the error can be rectified on review.

3. Exceptions to the General Rule.

  a. Unconstitutional procedures. A plaintiff may claim that the procedures to be employed by the agency are unconstitutional. If there is a factual question as to what the agency's procedures are, this claim will not permit P to avoid the administrative procedures. Note that a claim that the statute under which the agency proceeds is unconstitutional will not allow P to avoid the agency procedure (this should be decided in the first instance by the agency).

  b. Unauthorized agency action. A plaintiff may claim that the action taken by an agency is not authorized by the governing statute.

  c. Exhaustion not required. In *McCarthy v. Madigan*, 503 U.S. 140 (1992), McCarthy had filed an action pursuant to *Bivens, infra*, requesting monetary damages for an alleged violation of his Eighth Amendment rights, claiming that prison officials were deliberately indifferent to a medical condition he had. His case was dismissed by the district court, which held that he had not exhausted his administrative procedures and thus, could not get judicial review. The appellate court affirmed. The Supreme Court reversed. The Court first examined the principles underlying the requirement of exhaustion of administrative procedures—"protecting administrative agency authority and promoting judicial efficiency." However, the Court held that it had discretion not to require exhaustion in three broad areas: (i) if using the administrative process would cause "undue prejudice to a subsequent assertion of a court action" by the party seeking relief; (ii) if the agency could not give adequate relief; or (iii) if the agency has already predetermined the issue. The Court held that McCarthy's interests outweighed the administrative and judicial benefits in this case for two main reasons. First, the agency was unable to award the type of damages McCarthy sought. Second, the procedure in this specific case did not seem within the scope of the agency's activities, as the "Bureau's alleged failure to render medical care implicates only tangentially its authority to carry out the control and management of the federal prisons."

d. No statutory requirement. In *Darby v. Cisneros*, 509 U.S. 137 (1993), Darby, a real estate developer, had followed a financing plan developed by another developer which allowed him to avoid certain HUD restrictions in mortgaging properties. A bad market forced Darby to go into default on his mortgages, forcing HUD to assume the payments. The principle issue was whether federal courts could force a plaintiff to exhaust administrative remedies before getting judicial review under the APA. In this case, Darby had failed to request review of HUD's decision regarding his case before filing for judicial review. According-ing to the Court, under section 704 of the APA, an appeal to a "superior agency authority" is not necessary for judicial review unless expressly set forth by the statute. The HUD statute does not require such appeal.

FTC v. Standard Oil Co. of California (SOCAL)

e. Interlocutory review--FTC v. Standard Oil Co. of California (SOCAL), 449 U.S. 232 (1980).

   1) Facts. The FTC (D) averred that it had reason to believe that Standard Oil Company of California (P) was violating the law and instituted a complaint. P appeals on grounds that the cost and disruption of defending itself constituted irreparable harm.

   2) Issue. Is the FTC complaint reviewable?

   3) Held. No. Judgment reversed.

   a) 5 U.S.C. section 704 provides for review of a "final agency action," or matters otherwise "directly reviewable." The FTC complaint was neither.

   b) The complaint carries no legal force until the proceedings it inaugurates are concluded.

   c) Judicial review would interfere with the proper function of the agency and pose a burden on the judiciary.

   d) The burden of defending this action is "part of the social burden of living under government." It is not sufficient injury as to make the action ripe for purposes of judicial review.

f. Review under the Administrative Procedure Act--Pepsico, Inc. v. FTC, 472 F.2d 179 (2d Cir. 1972), *cert. denied,* 414 U.S. 876 (1973).

1) **Facts.** The FTC (D) sued Pepsico, Inc. (P), alleging unfair competition (by restricting bottlers from selling outside their designated territories). P moved to dismiss on the ground that its bottlers were indispensable parties who had not been joined. D denied the motion. P sued in district court to enjoin D from proceeding without the joinder.

2) **Issue.** Where the administrative agency is clearly proceeding in a manner that cannot result in a valid order, may P take the case to a federal court for an injunction?

3) **Held.** Yes. Injunction granted.

   a) The Federal Trade Commission Act limits judicial review to courts of appeals in limited situations. But APA section 704 provides that "agency action made reviewable by statute and final agency action for which there is no other adequate remedy in a court are subject to judicial review."

   b) There is confusion about the meaning of this section, but the court finds "final agency action for which there is no other adequate remedy in a court" if an agency refuses to dismiss a proceeding that is plainly beyond its jurisdiction as a matter of law or is being conducted in a manner that cannot result in a valid order (which was the case here).

g. State law. As a general rule, the state courts have not applied the "exhaustion rule" as stringently as the federal courts have.

h. Agency disruption--National Automatic Laundry & Cleaning Council v. Shultz, 443 F.2d 689 (D.C. Cir. 1971).

1) **Facts.** The National Automatic Laundry and Cleaning Council (P) wrote the Federal Wage and Hour Administrator (D), asking for an interpretation as to whether the Fair Labor Standards Act applied to employees of coin-operated laundries. D responded in the affirmative by letter.

2) **Issue.** Is D's letter-interpretation of this statute reviewable?

3) **Held.** Yes.

   a) The question is whether the problems created by pre-enforcement review outweigh the hardship upon P, so that review should be deferred.

   b) This ruling by the head of the agency is entitled to deference by the parties to whom it refers and by the courts. Therefore, finality and ripeness exist.

   c) Disruption of the affairs of the agency can be avoided with an affidavit by the agency head that policy is still being developed and requires further refinement.

F. ACTIONS FOR DAMAGES AS A FORM OF REVIEW

1. **Tort Actions Against Administrative Officials.**

   a. **Common law.** The common law rule was that government officials were liable for torts committed in the course of performance of their duties. Often liability was more stringent than negligence.

      1) **Exception—judges.** An exception to the common law rule concerned judges. Recognizing the difficulty of carrying out judicial duties if judges had to be worried about tort actions, they were given immunity except when they acted in matters over which they clearly knew they had no subject matter jurisdiction.

   b. **Change in the law; beginning of immunity.** Finally, with the growing importance of government, it was recognized that the same arguments that supported judicial immunity were applicable to other government officials.

Barr v. Matteo

2. **Libel Action--Barr v. Matteo,** 360 U.S. 564 (1959).

   a. **Facts.** Barr (D) fired Matteo and Madigan (Ps) from their positions in the office of Housing Expeditor. Ps complained that the press release that accompanied their termination was libelous. The trial court held for Ps. D appeals.

   b. **Issue.** Is D immune from a libel action on grounds of sovereign immunity?

   c. **Held.** Yes. Judgment reversed.

      1) After weighing Ps' interest in being protected from oppressive or malicious action by the government against the public's interest in shielding governmental officials from undue harassment, we find in favor of D.

      2) We recognize an analogy between D's immunity and the common law privilege held by judges as well as the constitutional protection afforded legislators.

      3) Government officials should be free to perform their official duties without fear of litigation.

      4) Although prior precedent had established an immunity privilege for cabinet officers, we believe that the shield should not be limited to agency heads.

3. **Limitations.**

   a. **Acts outside duties.** A court can, of course, find that an official's acts are not within the scope of his powers or duties.

   b. **Constitutional limitations.** In *Bivens v. Six Unknown Federal Narcotics Agents*, 403 U.S. 388 (1971), the plaintiff had been the victim of a brutal and illegal search of his home and an arrest without probable cause. The Court held that violation of Fourth Amendment rights could lead to an action against federal officials for damages.

1) **Remand.** On remand, the circuit court held that federal officials could successfully defend by proving that they had acted in "good faith" and with "reasonable belief" that their actions were proper.

2) **Immunity for constitutional violations.** Note that in dictum in *Bivens*, the Supreme Court indicated that some federal officials might still be immune even from constitutional violations (such as judges, presumably).

4. **Federal Executive Action--Butz v. Economou,** 438 U.S. 478 (1978).

a. **Facts.** The Department of Agriculture ("DOA") brought an administrative proceeding to revoke or suspend the registration of Arthur Economou & Company (P), a registered futures merchant which was controlled by Arthur Economou (P) and which traded on the Commodity Exchange, because the company allegedly willfully failed to maintain the minimum financial requirements prescribed by the DOA. A hearing was held without the issuance of a customary warning letter to the company. The DOA trial examiner upheld the charge, and the DOA Judicial Officer affirmed. Pending an appeal of the result to the Second Circuit, P and two of his companies sued the DOA, the Commodity Exchange Authority ("CEA"), the Secretary and Assistant Secretary of Agriculture, the Judicial Officer and Chief Hearing Examiner, the DOA attorney who had prosecuted the enforcement proceeding, auditors who had investigated or testified against the company, and several CEA officials, seeking $32 million in damages for alleged constitutional violations, such as deprivations of the First Amendment right to free expression and the Fifth Amendment right to notice. P also alleged common law torts of abuse of process, malicious prosecution, invasion of privacy, negligence, and trespass. The district court dismissed the complaints against the DOA and CEA on the basis of sovereign immunity; the complaints against the individuals were dismissed on the basis of absolute immunity of a federal government employee acting within the scope of his authority in performing a discretionary duty. The Second Circuit affirmed as to the DOA and CEA, but reversed as to the individuals on the basis that they had only qualified immunity of good faith and reasonable grounds. The Court granted certiorari.

b. **Issues.**

1) When federal agency regulatees sue agency personnel for violations of constitutional rights, do nonadjudicatory personnel have only qualified immunity?

2) Do adjudicatory personnel have absolute immunity?

c. **Held.** 1) Yes. 2) Yes. Judgment vacated and remanded.

1) When federal agency regulatees sue agency personnel for violation of constitutional rights, nonadjudicatory personnel have only qualified

immunity of good faith and reasonable grounds. Adjudicatory personnel have absolute immunity.

2) We have held in several past cases that state officers sued under section 1983 of the Civil Rights Act for violations of constitutional rights are protected by qualified immunity because of (i) the injustice, particularly in the absence of bad faith, of subjecting to liability an officer who is required, by the legal obligation of his position, to exercise discretion; and (ii) the danger that the threat of no immunity would deter his willingness to execute his office with the decisiveness and the judgment required for the public good. No logical reasons or policy considerations exist to justify holding to a different standard of immunity nonadjudicatory federal agency personnel and officers accused of violations of constitutional rights. We therefore hold that, in a suit for damages arising from unconstitutional action, federal executive officials exercising discretion are entitled only to the qualified immunity of good faith and reasonable grounds, subject to those exceptional situations where it is demonstrated that absolute immunity is essential for the conduct of the public business.

3) However, our decisions recognize that there are some officials whose special functions require a full exemption from liability. Those recognized by our former decisions as entitled to absolute immunity are judges, prosecutors, jurors, witnesses, and advocates, all being a necessary part of the adjudicatory process. The policies and reasons for this exception apply equally to administrative agencies. Thus, the Judicial Officer, the Chief Hearing Examiner, and the DOA attorney are all entitled to absolute immunity in this case, for their participation in the adjudicatory process.

Harlow v.
Fitzgerald

5. **Qualified Immunity Defined--Harlow v. Fitzgerald,** 457 U.S. 800 (1982).

a. **Facts.** Fitzgerald (P), a federal Defense Department employee, sued President Nixon and several others including presidential aide Harlow (Ds) for damages resulting from his discharge. P claimed he was discharged in retaliation for his testimony before Congress regarding defense finances, in violation of his constitutional and statutory rights. In *Nixon v. Fitzgerald*, 457 U.S. 731 (1982), the Court held that the President enjoyed absolute immunity. In this case, the Court considered whether other government officials enjoy absolute immunity.

b. **Issue.** Do government officials performing discretionary functions enjoy absolute immunity?

c. **Held.** No.

1) Generally, government officials are shielded from civil liability when they perform discretionary functions insofar as their conduct "does not violate clearly established statutory or constitutional rights of which a reasonable person would have known."

2) Qualified immunity, or "good faith" immunity, is an affirmative defense that has to be pleaded by the government official.

3) It would defeat qualified immunity if an official "knew or reasonably should have known that the action he took within his sphere of official responsibility would violate the constitutional rights of the [plaintiff], or if he took action with the malicious intention to cause a deprivation of constitutional rights or other injury. . . ." [Wood v. Strickland, 420 U.S. 308 (1975)]

4) The objective reasonableness of an official's conduct is measured by reference to clearly established law. On summary judgment, the court may determine not only the applicable law, but whether the applicable law was clearly established when the challenged action occurred. If the law was clearly established, the official ordinarily should not be able to invoke the immunity defense, because a "reasonably competent public official should know the law governing his conduct." However, the defense should be sustained if the official claims extraordinary circumstances and can prove that he "neither knew nor should have known of the relevant legal standard."

6. **State Officials and Constitutional Violations.** The Civil Rights Act (42 U.S.C. section 1983) provides a basis for liability against state officials for constitutional violations: "Every person who, under color of any statute, ordinance, regulation, custom or usage, of any State . . . subjects, or causes to be subjected, any . . . person . . . to the deprivation of any rights, privileges or immunities secured by the Constitution and laws, shall be liable to the party in an action at law, suit in equity, or other proper proceeding for redress."

7. **Federal Tort Claims Act of 1946.** The Federal Tort Claims Act provides for specific waiver of the defense of sovereign immunity for certain circumstances or agencies, specified torts, and discretionary acts by government employees. Although the statute provides that "[t]he United States shall be liable, respecting . . . tort claims, in the same manner and to the same extent as a private individual under like circumstances," the United States Supreme Court has refused to construe such language to embrace contemporary common law doctrines such as strict tort liability. [*See* Laird v. Nelms, 406 U.S. 797 (1972)]

8. **Administrative Procedure Act.** The problems created by these cases appear to have been partially resolved by 1976 amendments to the APA, which provide that an action against the United States "seeking relief other than money damages . . . shall not be dismissed on the ground that it is against the United States. . . . [I]f no special statutory review proceeding is applicable, the action for judicial review may be brought against the United States." [5 U.S.C. §§702, 703]

9. **Erosion of the Immunity Doctrine.** Sovereign immunity has been eroded significantly by judicial decisions in a growing number of states that treat government officials as they would any private tortfeasor.

10. **Damage Actions Against Government Entities.**

    a. **The states.**

       1) **Old rule.** The law for many years was that the government could not be held liable for torts committed by its employees.

a) **Corporate functions.** There was one exception. If the government was conducting a "corporate" or "proprietary" function, then it could be held liable for its tortious acts in the conduct of such functions. For example, the state might run an amusement park.

b) **Uncertain boundaries.** No clear lines of distinction ever developed in what was "proprietary" and what was not. Courts granted recovery where they wanted to.

2) **The modern trend.** The modern trend in the states is toward permitting the government to be sued for its tortious acts.

a) **Judicial decisions.** In some states, this has come about through court decisions.

b) **Comprehensive statutes.** Other states have passed comprehensive statutes covering tort liability.

c) **Individual statutes.** In other states, liability is determined under each statute passed.

b. **The federal government.**

1) **Federal Tort Claims Act.**

a) **The statute.** In 1946, the Federal Tort Claims Act was passed. This Act provides that the federal government is liable for personal injury or property damage caused by the negligent or wrongful acts of its employees acting within the scope of their employment, to the same extent that it would be liable if it were a private party.

b) **Exceptions to liability.** There are many exceptions to federal government tort liability.

(1) **Intentional torts.** The Act provides that the government shall not be liable for certain intentional torts, such as defamation, misrepresentation, etc. However, in 1974, the government became liable for many other intentional torts, such as assault, battery, false imprisonment, false arrest, abuse of process, trespass, etc.

(2) **Strict liability.** The Act has been held not to apply to strict liability torts. For example, in the absence of negligence, the government could not be held liable for ultra-hazardous activity (such as blasting).

(3) **Discretionary acts.** The largest exception is for "discretionary acts or omissions," even where such discretion is abused.

c. **Application of "discretionary acts" exception.**

Berkovitz v.
United States

1) **Discretionary function exception--Berkovitz v. United States, 486 U.S. 531 (1988).**

a) **Facts.** Berkovitz (P), a two-month-old, took a polio vaccine licensed by the federal government and soon afterward contracted polio. His parents filed suit under the Federal Tort Claims Act ("FTCA"). The government moved to dismiss on the ground that the agency's licensing actions fell within the discretionary function of the FTCA. The district court denied the motion, and the court of appeals reversed. P appeals.

b) **Issue.** Does the discretionary function exception to the FTCA bar suits based on the licensing by the government of a polio vaccine?

c) **Held.** No. Judgment reversed and remanded.

(1) The discretionary function exception examines whether a government's employee's action was "a matter of choice" for the employee. The exception does not apply if the employee has a mandated function. Here, if "the [Bureau of Biologics] policy did not allow the official who took the challenged action to release a noncomplying lot on the basis of policy considerations, the discretionary function exception does not bar the claim." It could be shown in court that there was no exercise of policy discretion.

2) **Discretionary function upheld--United States v. Gaubert,** 499 U.S. 315 (1991).

United States
v. Gaubert

a) **Facts.** Gaubert (P) was the chairman of the Independent American Savings Association ("IASA"), a federally insured savings and loan. Officials at the Federal Home Loan Bank Board ("FHLBB"), a federal institution, wanted to have the IASA merge with a failing Texas thrift, but were concerned about P's financial dealings and had him removed from the IASA management. P also had to post a $25 million interest in real property. The FHLBB officials then provided advice to facilitate the merger, but never instituted formal action against the IASA. Subsequently, the FHLBB threatened to close the IASA unless its directors resigned. They did so, and new management and directors took over. The FHLBB and its Dallas correspondent closely advised management in a variety of important matters. Shortly after they took over, the new directors announced that the IASA had a substantial negative net worth.

P filed an administrative tort claim with the federal agencies involved seeking $75 million for the lost value of his shares and $25 million for the property he lost under the guarantee he provided. P's claim was denied and he filed suit under the FTCA. The district court dismissed the suit on the ground that all of the challenged actions of the regulators fell within the discretionary function exception of the FTCA. The court of appeals affirmed in part but reversed in part on the ground that the regulators went beyond making policy-oriented decisions, which are immune under the FTCA, and provided operational actions by participating in the IASA's management decisions. The Supreme Court granted certiorari.

b) **Issue.** Are an agency's actions including participating in management of a regulated business exempt from liability under the FTCA "discretionary function" exception?

c) **Held.** Yes. Judgment reversed.

(1) The discretionary function exception protects the government against liability for actions of government employees who perform a discretionary function on the part of a federal agency, whether or not the discretion involved is abused. Where the challenged conduct involves an element of judgment, the conduct is protected only if the judgment is of the kind the discretionary function exception was designed to shield.

(2) If a regulation mandates particular conduct and the employee obeys the direction, the government is protected because the action furthered the policies that led to the promulgation of the regulation. If a regulation allows the employee discretion, the existence of the regulation creates a strong presumption that a discretionary act authorized by the regulation involves consideration of the same policies that led to the promulgation of the regulations.

(3) A discretionary act involves choice or judgment, but it is not limited to policymaking or planning functions. Day-to-day management involves choice or judgment, and can also be based on policy. There is no reason to hold that management or operational activities are outside the scope of the discretionary function exception. Since P basically alleged negligence by federal officials in their participation in the IASA's management, his claim is barred by the discretionary function exception to the FTCA.

Owen v. City of Independence

d. Section 1983--Owen v. City of Independence, 445 U.S. 622 (1980).

1) **Facts.** This case involves a claim brought under section 1983 of title 42 of the United States Code (which states, in essence, that anyone who causes the deprivation of another's rights is liable to that party). Owen (P) was the police commissioner in the City of Independence (D) until he was fired over a dispute regarding administrative policy in the police department. P sued for an alleged violation of his due process rights. The court of appeals held that D had a qualified immunity under 42 U.S.C. section 1983. P appeals.

2) **Issue.** Is D entitled to immunity from a section 1983 claim?

3) **Held.** No. Judgment reversed.

(a) Section 1983 does not explicitly allow for any immunities; however, if the immunity existed at the time of the adoption of the section, and immunity is compatible with the Civil Rights Act, it will be allowed. In this case, there is no precedent or historical support for a municipal immunity like the one claimed by D. Municipal corporations are generally granted two types of immunities: (i) immunity for governmental function (non-proprietary), and (ii) immunity from challenges to municipal corporations' discretionary authority. Neither of these apply in this case.

(b) Because the Civil Rights Act was instituted to allow for redress of injuries caused by a "misuse of power," allowing for immunity by a municipal corporation in this case would turn this rationale on its head, rendering most victims of city harms "remediless."

(c) Another purpose of section 1983 is to act as a deterrent against future harms; by not allowing an immunity, the municipal officials will be forced to act more carefully in the future.

(d) Finally, the decision to disallow immunity is congruent with the modern trend in torts, which seeks to spread costs; here, costs are spread to the victim, the municipal officer, and the public, via the municipal corporation.

TABLE OF CASES

(Page numbers of briefed cases in bold)

Notes

Notes

Notes

Notes

Publications Catalog

Features:
Gilbert Law Summaries
Legalines
Gilbert Interactive Software
CaseBriefs Interactive Software
Law School Legends Audio Tapes
Employment Guides
& Much More!

Prices Subject To Change Without Notice

Gilbert Law Summaries are the best selling outlines in the country, and have set the standard for excellence since they were first introduced more than twenty-five years ago. It's Gilbert's unique combination of features that makes it the one study aid you'll turn to for all your study needs!

Administrative Law
By Professor Michael R. Asimow, U.C.L.A.

Separation of Powers and Controls Over Agencies; (including Delegation of Power) Constitutional Right to Hearing (including Liberty and Property Interests Protected by Due Process, and Rulemaking-Adjudication Distinction); Adjudication Under Administrative Procedure Act (APA); Formal Adjudication (including Notice, Discovery, Burden of Proof, Finders of Facts and Reasons); Adjudicatory Decision Makers (including Administrative Law Judges (ALJs), Bias, Improper Influences, Ex Parte Communications, Familiarity with Record, Res Judicata); Rulemaking Procedures (including Notice, Public Participation, Publication, Impartiality of Rulemakers, Rulemaking Record); Obtaining Information (including Subpoena Power, Privilege

Against Self-incrimination, Freedom of Information Act, Government in Sunshine Act, Attorneys' Fees); Scope of Judicial Review; Reviewability of Agency Decisions (including Mandamus, Injunction, Sovereign Immunity, Federal Tort Claims Act); Standing to Seek Judicial Review and Timing.
ISBN: 0-15-900000-9 Pages: 300 $19.95

Agency and Partnership
By Professor Richard J. Conviser, Chicago Kent

Agency: Rights and Liabilities Between Principal and Agent (including Agent's Fiduciary Duty, Principal's Right to Indemnification); Contractual Rights Between Principal (or Agent) and Third Persons (including Creation of Agency Relationship, Authority of Agent, Scope of Authority, Termination of Authority, Ratification,

Liability on Agents, Contracts); Tort Liability (including Respondeat Superior, Master-Servant Relationship, Scope of Employment). Partnership: Property Rights of Partner; Formation of Partnership; Relations Between Partners (including Fiduciary Duty); Authority of Partner to Bind Partnership; Dissolution and Winding up of Partnership; Limited Partnerships.
ISBN: 0-15-900001-7 Pages: 142 $16.95

Antitrust
By Professor Thomas M. Jorde, U.C. Berkeley, Mark A. Lemley, University of Texas, and Professor Robert H. Mnookin, Harvard University

Common Law Restraints of Trade; Federal Antitrust Laws (including Sherman Act, Clayton Act, Federal Trade Commission Act, Interstate Commerce Requirement, Antitrust Remedies);

Monopolization (including Relevant Market, Purposeful Act Requirement, Attempts and Conspiracy to Monopolize); Collaboration Among Competitors (including Horizontal Restraints, Rule of Reason vs. Per Se Violations, Price Fixing, Division of Markets, Group Boycotts); Vertical Restraints (including Tying Arrangements); Mergers and Acquisitions (including Horizontal Mergers, Brown Shoe Analysis, Vertical Mergers, Conglomerate Mergers); Price Discrimination — Robinson-Patman Act; Unfair Methods of Competition; Patent Laws and Their Antitrust Implications; Exemptions From Antitrust Laws (including Motor, Rail, and Interstate Water Carriers, Bank Mergers, Labor Unions, Professional Baseball).
ISBN: 0-15-900328-8   Pages: 193 $16.95

All titles available at your law school bookstore
or call to order: 1-800-787-8717

Bankruptcy

By Professor Ned W. Waxman, College of William and Mary

Participants in the Bankruptcy Case; Jurisdiction and Procedure; Commencement and Administration of the Case (including Eligibility, Voluntary Case, Involuntary Case, Meeting of Creditors, Debtor's Duties); Officers of the Estate (including Trustee, Examiner, United States Trustee); Bankruptcy Estate; Creditor's Right of Setoff; Trustee's Avoiding Powers; Claims of Creditors (including Priority Claims and Tax Claims); Debtor's Exemptions; Nondischargeable Debts; Effects of Discharge; Reaffirmation Agreements; Administrative Powers (including Automatic Stay, Use, Sale, or Lease of Property); Chapter 7- Liquidation; Chapter 11- Reorganization; Chapter 13-Individual With Regular Income; Chapter 12- Family Farmer With Regular Annual Income.

ISBN: 0-15-900164-1   Pages: 356 $19.95

Basic Accounting for Lawyers

By Professor David H. Barber

Basic Accounting Principles; Definitions of Accounting Terms; Balance Sheet; Income Statement; Statement of Changes in Financial Position; Consolidated Financial Statements; Accumulation of Financial Data; Financial Statement Analysis.

ISBN: 0-15-900004-1   Pages: 136 $16.95

Business Law

By Professor Robert D. Upp, Los Angeles City College

Torts and Crimes in Business; Law of Contracts (including Contract Formation, Consideration, Statute of Frauds, Contract Remedies, Third Parties); Sales (including Transfer of Title and Risk of Loss, Performance and Remedies, Products Liability, Personal Property Security Interest); Property (including Personal Property, Bailments, Real Property, Landlord and Tenant); Agency; Business Organizations (including Partnerships, Corporations); Commercial Paper; Government Regulation of Business (including Taxation, Antitrust, Environmental Protection, and Bankruptcy).

ISBN: 0-15-900005-X   Pages: 295 $16.95

California Bar Performance Test Skills

By Professor Peter J. Honigsberg, University of San Francisco

Hints to Improve Writing; How to Approach the Performance Test; Legal Analysis Documents (including Writing a Memorandum of Law, Writing a Client Letter, Writing Briefs); Fact Gathering and Fact Analysis Documents; Tactical and Ethical Considerations; Sample Interrogatories, Performance Tests, and Memoranda.

ISBN: 0-15-900152-8   Pages: 216 $17.95

Civil Procedure

By Professor Thomas D. Rowe, Jr., Duke University, and Professor Richard L. Marcus, U.C. Hastings

Territorial (personal) Jurisdiction, including Venue and Forum Non Conveniens; Subject Matter Jurisdiction, covering Diversity Jurisdiction, Federal Question Jurisdiction; Erie Doctrine and Federal Common Law; Pleadings including Counterclaims, Cross-Claims, Supplemental Pleadings; Parties, including Joinder and Class Actions; Discovery, including Devices, Scope, Sanctions and Discovery Conference; Summary Judgment; Pretrial Conference and Settlements; Trial, including Right to Jury Trial, Motions, Jury Instruction and Arguments, and Post-Verdict Motions; Appeals; Claim Preclusion (Res Judicata) and Issue Preclusion (Collateral Estoppel).

ISBN: 0-15-900272-9   Pages: 447 $19.95

Commercial Paper and Payment Law

By Professor Douglas J. Whaley, Ohio State University

Types of Commercial Paper; Negotiability; Negotiation; Holders in Due Course; Claims and Defenses on Negotiable Instruments (including Real Defenses and Personal Defenses); Liability of the Parties (including Merger Rule, Suits on the Instrument, Warranty Suits, Conversion); Bank Deposits and Collections; Forgery or Alteration of Negotiable Instruments; Electronic Banking.

ISBN: 0-15-900009-2   Pages: 222 $17.95

Community Property

By Professor William A. Reppy, Jr., Duke University

Classifying Property as Community or Separate; Management and Control of Property; Liability for Debts; Division of Property at Divorce; Devolution of Property at Death; Relationships Short of Valid Marriage; Conflict of Laws Problems; Constitutional Law Issues (including Equal Protection Standards, Due Process Issues).

ISBN: 0-15-900235-4   Pages: 188 $17.95

Conflict of Laws

By Dean Herma Hill Kay, U.C. Berkeley

Domicile; Jurisdiction (including Notice and Opportunity to be Heard, Minimum Contacts, Types of Jurisdiction); Choice of Law (including Vested Rights Approach, Most Significant Relationship Approach, Governmental Interest Analysis); Choice of Law in Specific Substantive Areas; Traditional Defenses Against Application of Foreign Law; Constitutional Limitations and Overriding Federal Law (including Due Process Clause, Full Faith and Credit Clause, Conflict Between State and Federal Law); Recognition and Enforcement of Foreign Judgments.

ISBN: 0-15-900011-4   Pages: 260 $18.95

Constitutional Law

By Professor Jesse H. Choper, U.C. Berkeley

Powers of Federal Government (including Judicial Power, Powers of Congress, Presidential Power, Foreign Affairs Power); Intergovernmental Immunities, Separation of Powers; Regulation of Foreign Commerce; Regulation of Interstate Commerce; Taxation of Interstate and Foreign Commerce; Due Process, Equal Protection; "State Action" Requirements; Freedoms of Speech, Press, and Association; Freedom of Religion.

ISBN: 0-15-900265-6   Pages: 335 $19.95

Contracts

By Professor Melvin A. Eisenberg, U.C. Berkeley

Consideration (including Promissory Estoppel, Moral or Past Consideration); Mutual Assent; Defenses (including Mistake, Fraud, Duress, Unconscionability, Statute of Frauds, Illegality); Third-Party Beneficiaries; Assignment of Rights and Delegation of Duties; Conditions; Substantial Performance; Material vs. Minor Breach; Anticipatory Breach; Impossibility; Discharge; Remedies (including Damages, Specific Performance, Liquidated Damages).

ISBN: 0-15-900014-9   Pages: 326 $19.95

Corporations

By Professor Jesse H. Choper, U.C. Berkeley, and Professor Melvin A. Eisenberg, U.C. Berkeley

Formalities; "De Jure" vs. "De Facto"; Promoters; Corporate Powers; Ultra Vires Transactions; Powers, Duties, and Liabilities of Officers and Directors; Allocation of Power Between Directors and Shareholders; Conflicts of Interest in Corporate Transactions; Close Corporations; Insider Trading; Rule 10b-5 and Section 16(b); Shareholders' Voting Rights; Shareholders' Right to Inspect Records; Shareholders' Suits; Capitalization (including Classes of Shares, Preemptive Rights, Consideration for Shares); Dividends; Redemption of Shares; Fundamental Changes in Corporate Structure; Applicable Conflict of Laws Principles.

ISBN: 0-15-900342-3   Pages: 308 $19.95

Criminal Law

By Professor George E. Dix, University of Texas

Elements of Crimes (including Actus Reus, Mens Rea, Causation); Vicarious Liability; Complicity in Crime; Criminal Liability of Corporations; Defenses (including Insanity, Diminished Capacity, Intoxication, Ignorance, Self-Defense); Inchoate Crimes; Homicide; Other Crimes Against the Person; Crimes Against Habitation (including Burglary, Arson); Crimes Against Property; Offenses Against Government; Offenses Against Administration of Justice.

ISBN: 0-15-900217-6   Pages: 271 $18.95

Criminal Procedure

By Professor Paul Marcus, College of William and Mary, and Professor Charles H. Whitebread, U.S.C.

Exclusionary Rule; Arrests and Other Detentions; Search and Seizure; Privilege Against Self-Incrimination; Confessions; Preliminary Hearing; Bail; Indictment; Speedy Trial; Competency to Stand Trial; Government's Obligation to Disclose Information; Right to Jury Trial; Right to Counsel; Right to Confront Witnesses; Burden of Proof; Insanity; Entrapment; Guilty Pleas; Sentencing; Death Penalty; Ex Post Facto Issues; Appeal; Habeas Corpus; Juvenile Offenders; Prisoners' Rights; Double Jeopardy.

ISBN: 0-15-900347-4   Pages: 271 $18.95

Dictionary of Legal Terms

Gilbert Staff

Contains Over 3,500 Legal Terms and Phrases; Law School Shorthand; Common Abbreviations; Latin and French Legal Terms; Periodical Abbreviations; Governmental Abbreviations.

ISBN: 0-15-900018-1   Pages: 163 $14.95

Estate and Gift Tax

By Professor John H. McCord, University of Illinois

Gross Estate Allowable Deductions Under Estate Tax (including Expenses, Indebtedness, and Taxes, Deductions for Losses, Charitable Deduction, Marital Deduction); Taxable Gifts; Deductions; Valuation; Computation of Tax; Returns and Payment of Tax; Tax on Generation-Skipping Transfers.

ISBN: 0-15-900019-X   Pages: 283 $18.95

Evidence

By Professor Jon R. Waltz, Northwestern University, and Roger C. Park, University of Minnesota

Direct Evidence; Circumstantial Evidence; Rulings on Admissibility; Relevancy; Materiality; Character Evidence; Hearsay and the Hearsay Exceptions; Privileges; Competency to Testify; Opinion Evidence and Expert Witnesses; Direct Examination; Cross-Examination; Impeachment; Real, Demonstrative, and Scientific Evidence; Judicial Notice; Burdens of Proof; Parol Evidence Rule.

ISBN: 0-15-900020-3   Pages: 359 $19.95

Federal Courts

By Professor William A. Fletcher, U.C. Berkeley

Article III Courts; "Case or Controversy" Requirement; Justiciability; Advisory Opinions; Political Questions; Ripeness; Mootness; Standing; Congressional Power Over Federal Court Jurisdiction; Supreme Court Jurisdiction; District Court Subject Matter Jurisdiction (including Federal Question Jurisdiction, Diversity Jurisdiction); Pendent and Ancillary Jurisdiction; Removal Jurisdiction; Venue; Forum Non Conveniens; Law Applied in the Federal Courts (including Erie Doctrine); Federal Law in the State Courts; Abstention; Habeas Corpus for State Prisoners; Federal Injunctions Against State Court Proceedings; Eleventh Amendment.

ISBN: 0-15-900232-X   Pages: 310 $19.95

Future Interests & Perpetuities

By Professor Jesse Dukeminier, U.C.L.A.

Reversions; Possibilities of Reverter; Rights of Entry; Remainders; Executory Interest; Rules Restricting Remainders and Executory Interest; Rights of Owners of Future Interests; Construction of Instruments; Powers of Appointment; Rule Against Perpetuities (including Reforms of the Rule).

ISBN: 0-15-900218-4   Pages: 219 $17.95

Income Tax I - Individual

By Professor Michael R. Asimow, U.C.L.A.

Gross Income; Exclusions; Income Splitting by Gifts, Personal Service Income, Income Earned by Children, Income of Husbands and Wives, Below-Market Interest on Loans, Taxation of Trusts; Business and Investment Deductions; Personal Deductions; Tax Rates; Credits; Computation of Basis, Gain, or Loss; Realization; Nonrecognition of Gain or Loss; Capital Gains and Losses; Alternative Minimum Tax; Tax Accounting Problems.

ISBN: 0-15-900266-4   Pages: 312 $19.95

Income Tax II - Partnerships, Corporations, Trusts

By Professor Michael R. Asimow, U.C.L.A.

Taxation of Partnerships (including Current Partnership Income, Contributions of Property to Partnership, Sale of Partnership Interest, Distributions, Liquidations); Corporate Taxation (including Corporate Distributions, Sales of Stock and Assets, Reorganizations); S Corporations; Federal Income Taxation of Trusts.

ISBN: 0-15-900024-6   Pages: 237 $17.95

Labor Law

By Professor James C. Oldham, Georgetown University, and Robert J. Gelhaus

Statutory Foundations of Present Labor Law (including National Labor Relations Act, Taft-Hartley, Norris-LaGuardia Act, Landrum-Griffin Act); Organizing Campaigns, Selection of the Bargaining Representative; Collective Bargaining (including Negotiating the Agreement, Lockouts, Administering the Agreement, Arbitration); Strikes, Boycotts, and Picketing; Concerted Activity Protected Under the NLRA; Civil Rights Legislation; Grievance; Federal Regulation of Compulsory Union Membership Arrangements; State Regulation of Compulsory Membership Agreements; "Right to Work" Laws; Discipline of Union Members; Election of Union Officers; Corruption.

ISBN: 0-15-900340-7   Pages: 243 $17.95

Legal Ethics

By Professor Thomas D. Morgan, George Washington University

Regulating Admission to Practice Law; Preventing Unauthorized Practice of Law; Contract Between Client and Lawyer (including Lawyer's Duties Regarding Accepting Employment, Spheres of Authority of Lawyer and Client, Obligation of Client to Lawyer, Terminating the Lawyer-Client Relationship); Attorney-Client Privilege; Professional Duty of Confidentiality; Conflicts of Interest; Obligations to Third Persons and the Legal System (including Counseling Illegal or Fraudulent Conduct, Threats of Criminal Prosecution); Special Obligations in Litigation (including Limitations on Advancing Money to Client, Duty to Reject Certain Actions, Lawyer as Witness); Solicitation and Advertising; Specialization; Disciplinary Process; Malpractice; Special Responsibilities of Judges.

ISBN: 0-15-900026-2   Pages: 252 $18.95

Legal Research, Writing and Analysis

By Professor Peter J. Honigsberg, University of San Francisco

Court Systems; Precedent; Case Reporting System (including Regional and State Reporters, Headnotes and the West Key Number System, Citations and Case Finding); Statutes, Constitutions, and Legislative History; Secondary Sources (including Treatises, Law Reviews, Digests, Restatements); Administrative Agencies (including Regulations, Looseleaf Services); Shepard's Citations; Computers in Legal Research; Reading and Understanding a Case (including Briefing a Case); Using Legal Sourcebooks; Basic Guidelines for Legal Writing;

Organizing Your Research; Writing a Memorandum of Law; Writing a Brief; Writing an Opinion or Client Letter.

ISBN: 0-15-900305-9   Pages: 162 $16.95

Multistate Bar Examination

By Professor Richard J. Conviser, Chicago Kent

Structure of the Exam; Governing Law; Effective Use of Time; Scoring of the Exam; Jurisdictions Using the Exam; Subject Matter Outlines; Practice Tests, Answers, and Subject Matter Keys; Glossary of Legal Terms and Definitions; State Bar Examination Directory; Listing of Reference Materials for Multistate Subjects.

ISBN: 0-15-900030-0   Pages: 210 $17.95

Personal Property

Gilbert Staff

Acquisitions; Ownership Through Possession (including Wild Animals, Abandoned Chattels); Finders of Lost Property; Bailments; Possessory Liens; Pledges; Trover; Gift; Accession; Confusion (Commingling); Fixtures; Crops (Emblements); Adverse Possession; Prescriptive Rights (Acquiring Ownership of Easements or Profits by Adverse Use).

ISBN: 0-15-900031-9   Pages: 69 $12.95

Professional Responsibility

(see Legal Ethics)

Property

By Professor Jesse Dukeminier, U.C.L.A.

Possession (including Wild Animals, Bailments, Adverse Possession); Gifts and Sales of Personal Property; Freehold Possessory Estates; Future Interests (including Reversion, Possibility of Reverter, Right of Entry, Executory Interests, Rule Against Perpetuities); Tenancy in Common; Joint Tenancy; Tenancy by the Entirety; Condominiums; Cooperatives; Marital Property; Landlord and Tenant; Easements and Covenants; Nuisance; Rights in Airspace and Water; Right to Support; Zoning; Eminent Domain; Sale of Land (including Mortgage, Deed, Warranties of Title); Methods of Title Assurance (including Recording System, Title Registration, Title Insurance).

ISBN: 0-15-900032-7   Pages: 496 $21.95

Remedies

By Professor John A. Bauman, U.C.L.A., and Professor Kenneth H. York, Pepperdine University

Damages; Equitable Remedies (including Injunctions and Specific Performance); Restitution; Injuries to Tangible Property Interests; Injuries to Business and Commercial Interests (including Business Torts, Inducing Breach of Contract, Patent Infringement, Unfair Competition, Trade Defamation); Injuries to Personal Dignity and Related Interests (including Defamation, Privacy, Religious Status, Civil and Political Rights); Personal Injury and Death; Fraud; Duress, Undue Influence, and Unconscionable Conduct; Mistake; Breach of Contract; Unenforceable Contracts (including Statute of Frauds, Impossibility, Lack of Contractual Capacity, Illegality).

ISBN: 0-15-900325-3   Pages: 375 $20.95

Sale and Lease of Goods

By Professor Douglas J. Whaley, Ohio State University

UCC Article 2; Sales Contract (including Offer and Acceptance, Parol Evidence Rule, Statute of Frauds, Assignment and Delegation, Revision of Contract Terms); Types of Sales (including Cash Sale Transactions, Auctions, "Sale or Return" and "Sale on Approval" Transactions); Warranties (including Express and Implied Warranties, Privity, Disclaimer, Consumer Protection Statutes); Passage of Title; Performance of the Contract; Anticipatory Breach; Demand for Assurance of Performance; Unforeseen Circumstances; Risk of Loss; Remedies; Documents of Title; Lease of Goods; International Sale of Goods.

ISBN: 0-15-900219-2   Pages: 222 $17.95

Secured Transactions

By Professor Douglas J. Whaley, Ohio State University

Coverage of Article 9; Creation of a Security Interest (including Attachment, Security Agreement, Value, Debtor's Rights in the Collateral); Perfection; Filing; Priorities; Bankruptcy Proceedings and Article 9; Default Proceedings; Bulk Transfers.

ISBN: 0-15-900231-1   Pages: 213 $17.95

Securities Regulation

By Professor David H. Barber, and Professor Niels B. Schaumann, William Mitchell College of Law

Securities and Exchange Commission; Jurisdiction and Interstate Commerce; Securities Act of 1933 (including Persons and Property Interest Covered, Registration Statement, Exemptions From Registration Requirements, Liabilities); Securities Exchange Act of 1934 (including Rule 10b-5, Tender Offers and Repurchases of Stock, Regulation of Proxy Solicitations, Liability for Short-Swing Profits on Insider Transactions, S.E.C. Enforcement Actions); Regulation of the Securities Markets; Multi-national Transactions; State Regulation of Securities Transactions.

ISBN: 0-15-9000326-1   Pages: 415 $20.95

Torts

By Professor Marc A. Franklin, Stanford University

Intentional Torts; Negligence; Strict Liability; Products Liability; Nuisance; Survival of Tort Actions; Wrongful Death; Immunity; Release and Contribution; Indemnity; Workers' Compensation; No-Fault Auto Insurance; Defamation; Invasion of Privacy; Misrepresentation; Injurious Falsehood; Interference With Economic Relations; Unjustifiable Litigation.

ISBN: 0-15-900220-6   Pages: 439 $19.95

Trusts

By Professor Edward C. Halbach, Jr., U.C. Berkeley

Elements of a Trust; Trust Creation; Transfer of Beneficiary's Interest (including Spendthrift Trusts); Charitable Trusts (including Cy Pres Doctrine); Trustee's Responsibilities, Power, Duties, and Liabilities; Duties and Liabilities of

Beneficiaries; Accounting for Income and Principal; Power of Settlor to Modify or Revoke; Powers of Trustee Beneficiaries or Courts to Modify or Terminate; Termination of Trusts by Operation of Law; Resulting Trusts; Purchase Money Resulting Trusts; Constructive Trusts.

ISBN: 0-15-900039-4   Pages: 268 $18.95

Wills

By Professor Stanley M. Johanson, University of Texas

Intestate Succession; Simultaneous Death; Advancements; Disclaimer; Killer of Decedent; Elective Share Statutes; Pretermitted Child Statutes; Homestead; Formal Requisites of a Will; Revocation of Wills; Incorporation by Reference; Pour-Over Gift in Inter Vivos Trust; Joint Wills; Contracts Relating to Wills; Lapsed Gifts; Ademption; Exoneration of Liens; Will Contests; Probate and Estate Administration.

ISBN: 0-15-900040-8   Pages: 310 $19.95

LAW SCHOOL LEGENDS SERIES

America's Greatest Law Professors on Audio Cassette

Wouldn't it be great if all of your law professors were law school legends? You know — the kind of professors whose classes everyone fights to get into. The professors whose classes you'd take, no matter what subject they're teaching. The kind of professors who make a subject sing. You may never get an opportunity to take a class with a truly brilliant professor, but with the Law School Legends Series, you can now get all the benefits of the country's greatest law professors…on audio cassette!

Administrative Law
Professor To Be Announced
Call For Release Date
TOPICS COVERED (Subject to Change): Classification Of Agencies; Adjudicative And Investigative Action; Rule Making Power; Delegation Doctrine; Control By Executive; Appointment And Removal; Freedom Of Information Act; Rule Making Procedure; Adjudicative Procedure; Trial Type Hearings; Administrative Law Judge; Power To Stay Proceedings; Subpoena Power; Physical Inspection; Self Incrimination; Judicial Review Issues; Declaratory Judgment; Sovereign Immunity; Eleventh Amendment; Statutory Limitations; Standing; Exhaustion Of Administrative Remedies; Scope Of Judicial Review.
3 Audio Cassettes
ISBN 0-15-900189-7 $39.95

Agency & Partnership
Professor Richard J. Conviser
Chicago Kent College of Law
TOPICS COVERED: Agency: Creation; Rights And Duties Of Principal And Agent; Sub-Agents; Contract Liability–Actual Authority: Express And Implied; Apparent Authority; Ratification; Liabilities Of Parties; Tort Liability–Respondeat Superior; Frolic And Detour; Intentional Torts. *Partnership:* Nature Of Partnership; Formation; Partnership By Estoppel; In Partnership Property; Relations Between Partners To Third Parties; Authority Of Partners; Dissolution And Termination; Limited Partnerships.
3 Audio Cassettes
ISBN: 0-15-900351-2 $39.95

Antitrust Law
Professor To Be Announced
Call For Release Date
TOPICS COVERED (Subject to Change): How U.S. Antitrust Lawyers And Economists Think And Solve Problems: Antitrust Law's First Principle — Consumer Welfare Opposes Market Power; Methods Of Analysis — Rule Of Reason, Per Se, Quick Look; Sherman Act Section 1 — Civil And Criminal Conspiracies In Unreasonable Restraint Of Trade; Sherman Act Section 2 — Illegal Monopolization And Attempts To Monopolize; Robinson Patman Act Price Discrimination And Related Distribution Problems; Clayton Act Section Section 7 — Mergers And Joint

Ventures; Antitrust And Intellectual Property; U.S. Antitrust And International Competitive Relationships — Extraterritoriality, Comity, And Convergence; Exemptions And Regulated Industries; Enforcement By The Department Of Justice, Federal Trade Commission, National Association Of State Attorneys General, And By Private Litigation; Price And Non-Price Restraints.
2 Audio Cassettes
ISBN: 0-15-900341-5 $39.95

Bankruptcy
Professor Elizabeth Warren
Harvard Law School
TOPICS COVERED: The Debtor/Creditor Relationship; The Commencement, Conversion, Dismissal and Reopening Of Bankruptcy Proceedings; Property Included In The Bankruptcy Estate; Secured, Priority And Unsecured Claims; The Automatic Stay; Powers Of Avoidance; The Assumption And Rejection Of Executory Contracts; The Protection Of Exempt Property; The Bankruptcy Discharge; Chapter 13 Proceedings; Chapter 11 Proceedings; Bankruptcy Jurisdiction And Procedure.
4 Audio Cassettes
ISBN: 0-15-900273-7 $45.95

Civil Procedure
By Professor Richard D. Freer
Emory University Law School
TOPICS COVERED: Subject Matter Jurisdiction; Personal Jurisdiction; Long-Arm Statutes; Constitutional Limitations; In Rem And Quasi In Rem Jurisdiction; Service Of Process; Venue; Transfer; Forum Non Conveniens; Removal; Waiver; Governing Law; Pleadings; Joinder Of Claims; Permissive And Compulsory Joinder Of Parties; Counter-Claims And Cross-Claims; Ancillary Jurisdiction; Impleader; Class Actions; Discovery; Pretrial Adjudication; Summary Judgment; Trial; Post Trial Motions; Appeals; Res Judicata; Collateral Estoppel.
5 Audio Cassettes
ISBN: 0-15-900322-9 $59.95

Commercial Paper
By Professor Michael I. Spak
Chicago Kent College Of Law
TOPICS COVERED: Introduction; Types Of Negotiable Instruments; Elements Of Negotiability; Statute Of Limitations; Payment-In-

Full Checks; Negotiations Of The Instrument; Becoming A Holder-In-Due Course; Rights Of A Holder In Due Course; Real And Personal Defenses; Jus Teril; Effect Of Instrument On Underlying Obligations; Contracts Of Maker And Indorser; Suretyship; Liability Of Drawer And Drawee; Check Certification; Warranty Liability; Conversion Of Liability; Banks And Their Customers; Properly Payable Rule; Wrongful Dishonor; Stopping Payment; Death Of Customer; Bank Statement; Check Collection; Expedited Funds Availability; Forgery Of Drawer's Name; Alterations; Imposter Rule; Wire Transfers; Electronic Fund Transfers Act .
3 Audio Cassettes
ISBN: 0-15-900275-3 $39.95

Conflict Of Laws
Professor Richard J. Conviser
Chicago Kent College of Law
TOPICS COVERED: Domicile; Jurisdiction; In Personam, In Rem, Quasi In Rem; Court Competence; Forum Non Conveniens; Choice Of Law; Foreign Causes Of Action; Territorial Approach To Choice/Tort And Contract; "Escape Devices"; Most Significant Relationship; Governmental Interest Analysis; Recognition Of Judgments; Foreign Country Judgments; Domestic Judgments/Full Faith And Credit; Review Of Judgments; Modifiable Judgments; Defenses To Recognition And Enforcement; Federal/State (Erie) Problems; Constitutional Limits On Choice Of Law.
3 Audio Cassettes
ISBN: 0-15-900352-0 $39.95

Constitutional Law
By Professor John C. Jeffries, Jr.
University of Virginia School of Law
TOPICS COVERED: Introduction; Exam Tactics; Legislative Power; Supremacy; Commerce; State Regulation; Privileges And Immunities; Federal Court Jurisdiction; Separation Of Powers; Civil Liberties; Due Process; Equal Protection; Privacy; Race; Alienage; Gender; Speech And Association; Prior Restraints; Religion—Free Exercise; Establishment Clause.
5 Audio Cassettes
ISBN: 0-15-900319-9 $45.95

Contracts
By Professor Michael I. Spak
Chicago Kent College Of Law
TOPICS COVERED: Offer; Revocation; Acceptance; Consideration; Defenses To Formation; Third Party Beneficiaries; Assignment; Delegation; Conditions; Excuses; Anticipatory Repudiation; Discharge Of Duty; Modifications; Rescission; Accord & Satisfaction; Novation; Breach; Damages; Remedies; UCC Remedies; Parol Evidence Rule.
4 Audio Cassettes
ISBN: 0-15-900318-0 $45.95

Copyright Law
Professor Roger E. Schechter
George Washington University Law School
TOPICS COVERED: Constitution; Patents And Property Ownership Distinguished; Subject Matter Copyright; Duration And Renewal; Ownership And Transfer; Formalities; Introduction; Notice, Registration And Deposit; Infringement; Overview; Reproduction And Derivative Works; Public Distribution; Public Performance And Display; Exemptions; Fair Use; Photocopying; Remedies; Preemption Of State Law.
3 Audio Cassettes
ISBN: 0-15-900295-8 $39.95

Corporations
By Professor Therese H. Maynard
Loyola Marymount School of Law
TOPICS COVERED: Ultra Vires Act; Corporate Formation; Piercing The Corporate Veil; Corporate Financial Structure; Stocks; Bonds; Subscription Agreements; Watered Stock; Stock Transactions; Insider Trading; 16(b) & 10b-5 Violations; Promoters; Fiduciary Duties; Shareholder Rights; Meetings; Cumulative Voting; Voting Trusts; Close Corporations; Dividends; Preemptive Rights; Shareholder Derivative Suits; Directors; Duty Of Loyalty; Corporate Opportunity Doctrine; Officers; Amendments; Mergers; Dissolution.
4 Audio Cassettes
ISBN: 0-15-900320-2 $45.95

Criminal Law
By Professor Charles H. Whitebread
USC School of Law
TOPICS COVERED: Exam Tactics; Volitional Acts; Mental States; Specific Intent; Malice; General Intent; Strict Liability; Accomplice Liability; Inchoate Crimes; Impossibility; Defenses;

Insanity; Voluntary And Involuntary Intoxication; Infancy; Self-Defense; Defense Of A Dwelling; Duress; Necessity; Mistake Of Fact Or Law; Entrapment; Battery; Assault; Homicide; Common Law Murder; Voluntary And Involuntary Manslaughter; First Degree Murder; Felony Murder; Rape; Larceny; Embezzlement; False Pretenses; Robbery; Extortion; Burglary; Arson.
4 Audio Cassettes
ISBN: 0-15-900279-6 $39.95

Criminal Procedure
By Professor Charles H. Whitebread
USC School of Law
TOPICS COVERED: Incorporation Of The Bill Of Rights; Exclusionary Rule; Fruit Of The Poisonous Tree; Arrest; Search & Seizure; Exceptions To Warrant Requirement; Wire Tapping & Eavesdropping; Confessions (Miranda); Pretrial Identification; Bail; Preliminary Hearings; Grand Juries; Speedy Trial; Fair Trial; Jury Trials; Right To Counsel; Guilty Pleas; Sentencing; Death Penalty; Habeas Corpus; Double Jeopardy; Privilege Against Compelled Testimony.
3 Audio Cassettes
ISBN: 0-15-900281-8 $39.95

Evidence
By Professor Faust F. Rossi
Cornell Law School
TOPICS COVERED: Relevance; Insurance; Remedial Measures; Settlement Offers; Causation; State Of Mind; Rebuttal; Habit; Character Evidence; "MIMIC" Rule; Documentary Evidence; Authentication; Best Evidence Rule; Parol Evidence; Competency; Dead Man Statutes; Examination Of Witnesses; Present Recollection Revived; Past Recollection Recorded; Opinion Testimony; Lay And Expert Witness; Learned Treatises; Impeachment; Collateral Matters; Bias, Interest Or Motive; Rehabilitation; Privileges; Hearsay And Exceptions.
5 Audio Cassettes
ISBN: 0-15-900282-6 $45.95

Family Law
Professor To Be Announced
TOPICS COVERED (Subject to change): National Scope Of Family Law; Marital Relationship; Consequences Of Marriage; Formalities And Solemnization; Common Law Marriage; Impediments; Marriage And Conflict Of Laws; Non-Marital Relationship; Law Of Names; Void And Voidable Marriages; Marital Breakdown; Annulment And Defenses; Divorce — Fault And No-Fault; Separation; Jurisdiction For Divorce; Migratory Divorce; Full Faith And Credit; Temporary Orders; Economic Aspects Of Marital Breakdown; Property Division; Community Property Principles; Equitable Distribution; Marital And Separate Property; Types Of Property Interests; Equitable Reimbursement; Alimony; Modification And Termination Of Alimony; Child Support; Health Insurance; Enforcement Of Orders; Antenuptial And Postnuptial Agreements; Separation And Settlement Agreements; Custody Jurisdiction And Awards; Modification Of Custody; Visitation Rights; Termination Of Parental Rights; Adoption; Illegitimacy; Paternity Actions.
3 Audio Cassettes
ISBN: 0-15-900283-4 $39.95

Federal Courts
Professor To Be Announced
TOPICS COVERED (Subject to change): History Of The Federal Court System; "Court Or Controversy" And Justiciability; Congressional

Power Over Federal Court Jurisdiction; Supreme Court Jurisdiction; District Court Subject Matter Jurisdiction—Federal Question Jurisdiction, Diversity Jurisdiction And Admiralty Jurisdiction; Pendent And Ancillary Jurisdiction; Removal Jurisdiction; Venue; Forum Non Conveniens; Law Applied In The Federal Courts; Federal Law In The State Courts; Collateral Relations Between Federal And State Courts; The Eleventh Amendment And State Sovereign Immunity.
3 Audio Cassettes
ISBN: 0-15-900296-6 $39.95

Federal Income Tax
By Professor Cheryl D. Block
George Washington University Law School
TOPICS COVERED: Administrative Reviews; Tax Formula; Gross Income; Exclusions For Gifts; Inheritances; Personal Injuries; Tax Basis Rules; Divorce Tax Rules; Assignment Of Income; Business Deductions; Investment Deductions; Passive Loss And Interest Limitation Rules; Capital Gains & Losses; Section 1031, 1034, and 121 Deferred/Non Taxable Transactions.
4 Audio Cassettes
ISBN: 0-15-900284-2 $45.95

Future Interests
By Dean Catherine L. Carpenter
Southwestern University Law School
TOPICS COVERED: Rule Against Perpetuities; Class Gifts; Estates In Land; Rule In Shelley's Case; Future Interests In Transferor and Transferee; Life Estates; Defeasible Fees; Doctrine Of Worthier Title; Doctrine Of Merger; Fee Simple Estates; Restraints On Alienation; Power Of Appointment; Rules Of Construction.
2 Audio Cassettes
ISBN: 0-15-900285-0 $24.95

Law School ABC's
By Professor Jennifer S. Kamita
Loyola Marymount Law School, and
Professor Rodney O. Fong
Golden Gate University School of Law
TOPICS COVERED: Introduction; Casebooks; Hornbooks; Selecting Commercial Materials; Briefing; Review; ABC's Of A Lecture; Taking Notes; Lectures & Notes Examples; Study Groups; ABC's Of Outlining; Rules; Outlining Hypothetical; Outlining Assignment And Review; Introduction To Essay Writing; "IRAC"; Call Of The Question Exercise; Issue Spotting Exercise; IRAC Defining & Writing Exercise; Form Tips; ABC's Of Exam Writing; Exam Writing Hypothetical; Practice Exam And Review; Preparation Hints; Exam Diagnostics & Writing Problems.
4 Audio Cassettes
ISBN: 0-15-900286-9 $45.95

Law School Exam Writing
By Professor Charles H. Whitebread
USC School of Law
TOPICS COVERED: With "Law School Exam Writing," you'll learn the secrets of law school test taking. In this fascinating lecture, Professor Whitebread leads you step-by-step through his innovative system, so that you know exactly how to tackle your essay exams without making point draining mistakes. You'll learn how to read questions so you don't miss important issues; how to organize your answer; how to use limited exam time to your maximum advantage; and even how to study for exams.
1 Audio Cassette
ISBN: 0-15-900287-7 $19.95

Professional Responsibility
By Professor Erwin Chemerinsky
USC School of Law
TOPICS COVERED: Regulation of Attorneys; Bar Admission; Unauthorized Practice; Competency; Discipline; Judgment; Lawyer-Client Relationship; Representation; Withdrawal; Conflicts; Disqualification; Clients; Client Interests; Successive And Effective Representation; Integrity; Candor; Confidences; Secrets; Past And Future Crimes; Perjury; Communications; Witnesses; Jurors; The Court; The Press; Trial Tactics; Prosecutors; Market; Solicitation; Advertising; Law Firms; Fees; Client Property; Conduct; Political Activity.
3 Audio Cassettes
ISBN: 0-15-900288-5 $39.95

Real Property
By Professor Paula A. Franzese
Seton Hall Law School
TOPICS COVERED: Estates—Fee Simple; Fee Tail; Life Estate; Co-Tenancy—Joint Tenancy; Tenancy In Common; Tenancy By The Entirety; Landlord-Tenant Relationship; Liability For Condition Of Premises; Assignment & Sublease; Easements; Restrictive Covenants; Adverse Possession; Recording Acts; Conveyancing; Personal Property—Finders; Bailments; Gifts; Future Interests.
4 Audio Cassettes
ISBN: 0-15-900289-3 $45.95

Remedies
By Professor William A. Fletcher
University of California at Berkeley, Boalt Hall School of Law
TOPICS COVERED: Damages; Restitution; Equitable Remedies (including Constructive Trust, Equitable Lien, Injunction, and Specific Performance); Tracing; Rescission and Reformation; Specific topics include Injury and Destruction of Personal Property; Conversion; Injury to Real Property; Trespass; Ouster; Nuisance; Defamation; Trade Libel; Inducing Breach of Contract; Contracts to Purchase Personal Property; Contracts to Purchase Real Property (including Equitable Conversion); Construction Contracts; and Personal Service Contracts.
3 Audio Cassettes
ISBN: 0-15-900353-9 $45.95

Sales & Lease of Goods
By Professor Michael I. Spak
Chicago Kent College of Law
TOPICS COVERED: Goods; Contract Formation; Firm Offers; Statute Of Frauds; Modification; Parol Evidence; Code Methodology; Tender; Payment; Identification; Risk Of Loss; Warranties; Merchantability; Fitness; Disclaimers; Consumer Protection; Remedies; Anticipatory Repudiation; Third Party Rights.
3 Audio Cassettes
ISBN: 0-15-900291-5 $39.95

Secured Transactions
By Professor Michael I. Spak
Chicago Kent College of Law
TOPICS COVERED: Collateral; Inventory; Intangibles; Proceeds; Security Agreements; Attachment; After-Acquired Property; Perfection; Filing; Priorities; Purchase Money Security Interests; Fixtures; Rights Upon Default; Self-Help; Sale; Constitutional Issues.
3 Audio Cassettes
ISBN: 0-15-900292-3 $39.95

Torts
By Professor Richard J. Conviser
Chicago Kent College of Law
TOPICS COVERED: Essay Exam Techniques; Intentional Torts—Assault; Battery; False Imprisonment; Intentional Infliction Of Emotional Distress; Trespass To Land; Trespass To Chattels; Conversion; Defenses: Defamation—Libel; Slander; Defenses; First Amendment Concerns; Invasion Of Right Of Privacy; Misrepresentation; Negligence—Duty; Breach; Actual And Proximate Causation; Damages; Defenses; Strict Liability; Products Liability; Nuisance; General Tort Considerations.
4 Audio Cassettes
ISBN: 0-15-900185-4 $45.95

Wills & Trusts
By Professor Stanley M. Johanson
University of Texas School of Law
TOPICS COVERED: Attested Wills; Holographic Wills; Negligence; Revocation; Changes On Face Of Will; Lapsed Gifts; Negative Bequest Rule; Nonprobate Assets; Intestate Succession; Advancements; Elective Share; Will Contests; Capacity; Undue Influence; Creditors' Rights; Creation Of Trust; Revocable Trusts; Pourover Gifts; Charitable Trusts; Resulting Trusts; Constructive Trusts; Spendthrift Trusts; Self-Dealing; Prudent Investments; Trust Accounting; Termination; Powers Of Appointment.
4 Audio Cassettes
ISBN: 0-15-900294-X $45.95

All titles available at your law school bookstore
or call to order: 1-800-787-8717

Legalines

Legalines gives you authoritative, detailed case briefs of every major case in your casebook. You get a clear explanation of the facts, the issues, the court's holding and reasoning, and any significant concurrences or dissents. Even more importantly, you get an authoritative explanation of the significance of each case, and how it relates to other cases in your casebook. And with Legalines' detailed table of contents and table of cases, you can quickly find any case or concept you're looking for. But your professor expects you to know more than just the cases. That's why Legalines gives you more than just case briefs. You get summaries of the black letter law, as well. That's crucial, because some of the most important information in your casebooks isn't in the cases at all...it's the black letter principles you're expected to glean from those cases. Legalines is the only series that gives you both case briefs and black letter review. With Legalines, you get everything you need to know—whether it's in a case or not!

Administrative Law
Keyed to the Breyer Casebook
ISBN: 0-15-900169-2   206 pages $17.95

Administrative Law
Keyed to the Gellhorn Casebook
ISBN: 0-15-900170-6   268 pages $19.95

Administrative Law
Keyed to the Schwartz Casebook
ISBN: 0-15-900044-0   155 pages $17.95

Antitrust
Keyed to the Areeda Casebook
ISBN: 0-15-900046-7   209 pages $17.95

Antitrust
Keyed to the Handler Casebook
ISBN: 0-15-900045-9   174 pages $17.95

Civil Procedure
Keyed to the Cound Casebook
ISBN: 0-15-900314-8   316 pages $19.95

Civil Procedure
Keyed to the Field Casebook
ISBN: 0-15-900048-3   388 pages $21.95

Civil Procedure
Keyed to the Hazard Casebook
ISBN: 0-15-900324-5   253 pages $18.95

Civil Procedure
Keyed to the Rosenberg Casebook
ISBN: 0-15-900052-1   312 pages $19.95

Civil Procedure
Keyed to the Yeazell Casebook
ISBN: 0-15-900241-9   240 pages $18.95

Commercial Law
Keyed to the Farnsworth Casebook
ISBN: 0-15-900176-5   170 pages $17.95

Conflict of Laws
Keyed to the Cramton Casebook
ISBN: 0-15-900056-4   144 pages $16.95

Conflict of Laws
Keyed to the Reese (Rosenberg) Casebook
ISBN: 0-15-900057-2   279 pages $19.95

Constitutional Law
Keyed to the Brest Casebook
ISBN: 0-15-900059-9   235 pages $18.95

Constitutional Law
Keyed to the Cohen Casebook
ISBN: 0-15-900261-3   235 pages $18.95

Constitutional Law
Keyed to the Gunther Casebook
ISBN: 0-15-900060-2   395 pages $21.95

Constitutional Law
Keyed to the Lockhart Casebook
ISBN: 0-15-900242-7   348 pages $20.95

Constitutional Law
Keyed to the Rotunda Casebook
ISBN: 0-15-900315-6   281 pages $19.95

Constitutional Law
Keyed to the Stone Casebook
ISBN: 0-15-900236-2   296 pages $19.95

Contracts
Keyed to the Calamari Casebook
ISBN: 0-15-900065-3   256 pages $19.95

Contracts
Keyed to the Dawson Casebook
ISBN: 0-15-900268-0   188 pages $19.95

Contracts
Keyed to the Farnsworth Casebook
ISBN: 0-15-900067-X   219 pages $18.95

Contracts
Keyed to the Fuller Casebook
ISBN: 0-15-900069-6   206 pages $17.95

Contracts
Keyed to the Kessler Casebook
ISBN: 0-15-900070-X   340 pages $20.95

Contracts
Keyed to the Murphy Casebook
ISBN: 0-15-900072-6   272 pages $19.95

Corporations
Keyed to the Cary Casebook
ISBN: 0-15-900172-2   407 pages $21.95

Corporations
Keyed to the Choper Casebook
ISBN: 0-15-900173-0   270 pages $19.95

Corporations
Keyed to the Hamilton Casebook
ISBN: 0-15-900313-X   248 pages $19.95

Corporations
Keyed to the Vagts Casebook
ISBN: 0-15-900078-5   213 pages $17.95

Criminal Law
Keyed to the Boyce Casebook
ISBN: 0-15-900080-7   318 pages $19.95

Criminal Law
Keyed to the Dix Casebook
ISBN: 0-15-900081-5   113 pages $15.95

Criminal Law
Keyed to the Johnson Casebook
ISBN: 0-15-900082-3   169 pages $17.95

Criminal Law
Keyed to the Kadish Casebook
ISBN: 0-15-900083-1   209 pages $17.95

Criminal Law
Keyed to the La Fave Casebook
ISBN: 0-15-900084-X   202 pages $17.95

Criminal Procedure
Keyed to the Kamisar Casebook
ISBN: 0-15-900088-2   310 pages $19.95

Decedents' Estates & Trusts
Keyed to the Ritchie Casebook
ISBN: 0-15-900339-3   277 pages $19.95

Domestic Relations
Keyed to the Clark Casebook
ISBN: 0-15-900090-4   128 pages $16.95

Domestic Relations
Keyed to the Wadlington Casebook
ISBN: 0-15-900091-2   215 pages $18.95

Enterprise Organization
Keyed to the Conard Casebook
ISBN: 0-15-900092-0   316 pages $19.95

Estate & Gift Taxation
Keyed to the Surrey Casebook
ISBN: 0-15-900093-9   100 pages $15.95

Evidence
Keyed to the McCormick Casebook
ISBN: 0-15-900095-5   310 pages $19.95

Evidence
Keyed to the Sutton Casebook
ISBN: 0-15-900096-3   310 pages $19.95

Evidence
Keyed to the Waltz Casebook
ISBN: 0-15-900334-2   224 pages $17.95

Evidence
Keyed to the Weinstein Casebook
ISBN: 0-15-900097-1   241 pages $18.95

Family Law
Keyed to the Areen Casebook
ISBN: 0-15-900263-X   262 pages $19.95

Federal Courts
Keyed to the McCormick Casebook
ISBN: 0-15-900101-3   213 pages $17.95

Income Tax
Keyed to the Freeland Casebook
ISBN: 0-15-900222-2   154 pages $17.95

Income Tax
Keyed to the Klein Casebook
ISBN: 0-15-900302-4   174 pages $17.95

Labor Law
Keyed to the Cox Casebook
ISBN: 0-15-900107-2   211 pages $17.95

Labor Law
Keyed to the Merrifield Casebook
ISBN: 0-15-900108-1   202 pages $17.95

Partnership & Corporate Taxation
Keyed to the Surrey Casebook
ISBN: 0-15-900109-9   118 pages $15.95

Property
Keyed to the Browder Casebook
ISBN: 0-15-900110-2   315 pages $19.95

Property
Keyed to the Casner Casebook
ISBN: 0-15-900111-0   291 pages $19.95

Property
Keyed to the Cribbet Casebook
ISBN: 0-15-900112-9   328 pages $20.95

Property
Keyed to the Dukeminier Casebook
ISBN: 0-15-900264-8   186 pages $17.95

Real Property
Keyed to the Rabin Casebook
ISBN: 0-15-900114-5   208 pages $17.95

Remedies
Keyed to the Re Casebook
ISBN: 0-15-900116-1   333 pages $20.95

Remedies
Keyed to the York Casebook
ISBN: 0-15-900118-8   289 pages $19.95

Sales & Secured Transactions
Keyed to the Speidel Casebook
ISBN: 0-15-900166-8   320 pages $19.95

Securities Regulation
Keyed to the Jennings Casebook
ISBN: 0-15-900253-2   368 pages $20.95

Torts
Keyed to the Epstein Casebook
ISBN: 0-15-900120-X   245 pages $18.95

Torts
Keyed to the Franklin Casebook
ISBN: 0-15-900240-0   166 pages $17.95

Torts
Keyed to the Henderson Casebook
ISBN: 0-15-900123-4   209 pages $17.95

Torts
Keyed to the Keeton Casebook
ISBN: 0-15-900124-2   278 pages $19.95

Torts
Keyed to the Prosser Casebook
ISBN: 0-15-900301-6   365 pages $20.95

Wills, Trusts & Estates
Keyed to the Dukeminier Casebook
ISBN: 0-15-900127-7   192 pages $17.95

For more information visit our World Wide Web site at http://www.gilbertlaw.com or write for a free 32 page catalog:
Harcourt Brace Legal and Professional Publications, 176 West Adams, Ste. 2100, Chicago, Illinois 60603

Current & Upcoming Software Titles

Gilbert Law Summaries

Interactive Software For Windows

Gilbert's Interactive Software features the full text of a Gilbert Law Summaries outline. Each title is easy to customize, print, and take to class. You can access the Lexis and Westlaw systems through an icon on the tool bar (with a valid student I.D.), as well as CaseBriefs Interactive Software, and Gilbert's On-Screen Dictionary Of Legal Terms (sold separately).

Administrative Law 0-15-900205-2	Asimow $27.95
Civil Procedure 0-15-900206-0	Marcus, Rowe $27.95
Constitutional Law 0-15-900207-9	Choper $27.95

Contracts 0-15-900208-7	Eisenberg $27.95
Corporations 0-15-900209-5	Choper, Eisenberg $27.95
Criminal Law 0-15-900210-9	Dix $27.95
Criminal Procedure 0-15-900211-7	Marcus, Whitebread $27.95
Evidence 0-15-900212-5	Kaplan, Waltz $27.95
Income Tax 1 0-15-900213-3	Asimow $27.95
Property 0-15-900214-1	Dukeminier $27.95
Secured Transactions 0-15-900215-X	Whaley $27.95
Torts 0-15-900216-8	Franklin $27.95

CaseBriefs

Interactive Software For Windows

Each title is adaptable to *all* casebooks in a subject area. For example, the Civil Procedure CaseBriefs title is adaptable to Civil Procedure by Cound, Hazard, Yeazell, etc... Simply select the casebook you're using when installing the software, and the program will do the rest! CaseBriefs is easy to customize, print, and take to class. You can access the Lexis and Westlaw systems through an icon on the tool bar (with a valid student I.D.), as well as Gilbert Law Summaries Interactive Software, and Gilbert's On-Screen Dictionary Of Legal Terms (sold separately).

Administrative Law 0-15-900190-0	Adaptable To All Casebooks $27.95
Civil Procedure 0-15-900191-9	Adaptable To All Casebooks $27.95
Conflict Of Laws 0-15-900192-7	Adaptable To All Casebooks $27.95
Constitutional Law 0-15-900193-5	Adaptable To All Casebooks $27.95

Contracts 0-15-900194-3	Adaptable To All Casebooks $27.95
Corporations 0-15-900195-1	Adaptable To All Casebooks $27.95
Criminal Law 0-15-900196-X	Adaptable To All Casebooks $27.95
Criminal Procedure 0-15-900197-8	Adaptable To All Casebooks $27.95
Evidence 0-15-900198-6	Adaptable To All Casebooks $27.95
Family Law 0-15-900199-4	Adaptable To All Casebooks $27.95
Income Tax 0-15-900200-1	Adaptable To All Casebooks $27.95
Property 0-15-900201-X	Adaptable To All Casebooks $27.95
Remedies 0-15-900202-8	Adaptable To All Casebooks $27.95
Torts 0-15-900203-6	Adaptable To All Casebooks $27.95
Wills, Trusts & Estates 0-15-900204-4	Adaptable To All Casebooks $27.95

Gilbert's On Screen Dictionary Of Legal Terms:
Features over 3,500 legal terms and phrases, law school shorthand, common abbreviations, Latin and French legal terms, periodical abbreviations, and governmental abbreviations.

ISBN: 0-15-900-311-3   Macintosh $24.95
ISBN: 0-15-900-308-3   Windows $24.95

Legalines

Summary of Subjects Available

- Administrative Law
- Antitrust
- Civil Procedure
- Commercial Law
- Conflict of Laws
- Constitutional Law
- Contracts
- Corporations
- Criminal Law
- Criminal Procedure
- Decedents' Estates & Trusts
- Domestic Relations
- Enterprise Organization
- Estate & Gift Taxation
- Evidence
- Family Law
- Federal Courts
- Income Tax
- Labor Law
- Partnership & Corporate Taxation
- Property
- Real Property
- Remedies
- Sales & Secured Transactions
- Securities Regulation
- Torts
- Wills, Trusts & Estates

**All titles available at your law school bookstore
or call to order: 1-800-787-8717**

Current & Upcoming Titles

Gilbert's Pocket Size Law Dictionary
Gilbert

A dictionary is useless if you don't have it when you need it. If the only law dictionary you own is a thick, bulky one, you'll probably leave it at home most of the time — and if you need to know a definition while you're at school, you're out of luck!

With Gilbert's Pocket Size Law Dictionary, you'll have any definition you need, when you need it. Just pop Gilbert's dictionary into your pocket or purse, and you'll have over 3,500 legal terms and phrases at your fingertips. Gilbert's dictionary also includes a section on law school shorthand, common abbreviations, Latin and French legal terms, periodical abbreviations, and governmental abbreviations.

With Gilbert's Pocket Size Law Dictionary, you'll never be caught at a loss for words!

Available in your choice of 4 colors, $7.95 each:
- ■ Black   ISBN: 0-15-900255-9
- ■ Blue   ISBN: 0-15-900257-5
- ■ Burgundy   ISBN: 0-15-900256-7
- ■ Green   ISBN: 0-15-900258-3

Limited Edition: Simulated Alligator Skin Cover
- ■ Black   ISBN: 0-15-900316-4 $7.95

What Lawyers Earn: Getting Paid What You're Worth
NALP

"What Lawyers Earn" provides up-to-date salary information from lawyers in many different positions, all over the country. Whether you're negotiating your own salary — or you're just curious! — "What Lawyers Earn" tells you how much lawyers really make.
ISBN: 0-15-900183-8 $17.95

The 100 Best Law Firms To Work For In America
Kimm Alayne Walton, J.D.

An insider's guide to the 100 best places to practice law, with anecdotes and a wealth of useful hiring information. Also included are special sections on the top law firms for women and the best public interest legal employers.
ISBN: 0-15-900180-3 $19.95

The 1996-1997 National Directory Of Legal Employers
NALP

The National Association for Law Placement has joined forces with Harcourt Brace to bring you everything you need to know about 1,000 of the nation's top legal employers, fully indexed for quick reference.

It includes:
- Over 22,000 job openings.
- The names, addresses and phone numbers of hiring partners.
- Listings of firms by state, size, kind and practice area.
- What starting salaries are for full time, part time, and summer associates, plus a detailed description of firm benefits.
- The number of employees by gender and race, as well as the number of employees with disabilities.
- A detailed narrative of each firm, plus much more!

The National Directory Of Legal Employers has been published for the past twenty years, but until now has only been available to law school career services directors, and hiring partners at large law firms. Through a joint venture between NALP (The National Association For Law Placement) and Harcourt Brace, this highly regarded, exciting title is now available for students.
ISBN: 0-15-900179-X $49.95

Proceed With Caution: A Diary Of The First Year At One Of America's Largest, Most Prestigious Law Firms
William R. Keates

In "Proceed With Caution" the author chronicles the trials and tribulations of being a new associate in a widely coveted dream job. He offers insights that only someone who has lived through the experience can offer. The unique diary format makes Proceed With Caution a highly readable and enjoyable journey.
ISBN: 0-15-900181-1 $17.95

The Eight Secrets Of Top Exam Performance In Law School
Charles Whitebread

Wouldn't it be great to know exactly what your professor's looking for on your exam? To find out everything that's expected of you, so that you don't waste your time doing anything other than maximizing your grades?

In his easy-to-read, refreshing style, nationally-recognized exam expert Professor Charles Whitebread will teach you the eight secrets that will add precious points to every exam answer you write. You'll learn the three keys to handling any essay exam question, and how to add points to your score by making time work for you, not against you. You'll learn flawless issue spotting, and discover how to organize your answer for maximum possible points. You'll find out how the hidden traps in "IRAC" trip up most students… but not you! You'll learn the techniques for digging up the exam questions your professor will ask, before your exam. You'll put your newly-learned skills to the test with sample exam questions, and you can measure your performance against model answers. And there's even a special section that helps you master the skills necessary to crush any exam, not just a typical essay exam — unusual exams like open book, take home, multiple choice, short answer, and policy questions.

"The Eight Secrets of Top Exam Performance in Law School" gives you all the tools you need to maximize your grades — quickly and easily!
ISBN: 0-15-900323-7 $9.95

Guerrilla Tactics for Getting the Legal Job of Your Dreams
Kimm Alayne Walton, J.D.

Whether you're looking for a summer clerkship or your first permanent job after school, this revolutionary new book is the key to getting the job of your dreams!

"Guerrilla Tactics for Getting the Legal Job of Your Dreams" leads you step-by-step through everything you need to do to nail down that perfect job! You'll learn hundreds of simple-to-use strategies that will get you exactly where you want to go.

"Guerrilla Tactics" features the best strategies from the country's most innovative law school career advisors. The strategies in "Guerrilla Tactics" are so powerful that it even comes with a guarantee: Follow the advice in the book, and within one year of graduation you'll have the job of your dreams… or your money back!

Pick up a copy of "Guerrilla Tactics" today…and you'll be on your way to the job of your dreams!
ISBN: 0-15-900317-2 $24.95

Checkerboard Careers: How Surprisingly Successful Attorneys Got To The Top, And How You Can Too!
NALP

Fast paced and easy to read, "Checkerboard Careers" is an inspirational guide, packed with profiles and monologues of how successful attorneys got to the top and how you can, too.
ISBN: 0-15-900182-X $17.95

FREE! Gilbert Law Summaries 1st Year Survival Manual

Available from your BAR/BRI Bar Review Representative or write:

Gilbert Law Summaries
176 West Adams, Ste. 2100
Chicago, Illinois 60603

Also available on our World Wide Web site at
http://www.gilbertlaw.com

To Order Any Of The Items In This Publications Catalog, Call Or Write:
Harcourt Brace Legal and Professional Publications, 176 West Adams, Ste. 2100, Chicago, Illinois 60603

1-800-787-8717